Police Abuse in Contemporary Democracies

Michelle D. Bonner · Guillermina Seri
Mary Rose Kubal · Michael Kempa
Editors

Police Abuse
in Contemporary
Democracies

Editors
Michelle D. Bonner
University of Victoria
Victoria, BC, Canada

Mary Rose Kubal
St. Bonaventure University
St. Bonaventure, NY, USA

Guillermina Seri
Union College
Schenectady, NY, USA

Michael Kempa
University of Ottawa
Ottawa, ON, Canada

ISBN 978-3-319-72882-7   ISBN 978-3-319-72883-4   (eBook)
https://doi.org/10.1007/978-3-319-72883-4

Library of Congress Control Number: 2018933056

Cover image: © IndiaUniform/Getty Images
Cover design: Emma J. Hardy

Printed on acid-free paper

This Palgrave Macmillan imprint is published by the registered company Springer International Publishing AG part of Springer Nature
The registered company address is: Gewerbestrasse 11, 6330 Cham, Switzerland

ACKNOWLEDGEMENTS

This book is the result of many conversations, with many people, over many years. We would like to thank all those who contributed to these discussions, including the authors of the chapters in this volume and those who have attended or participated in our panels and workshops at the conferences of the International Political Science Association, Canadian Political Science Association, American Political Science Association, Western Political Science Association, and the Latin American Studies Association.

Some people have gone out of their way to help us with various aspects of the compilation and editing of the book. Thank-you especially to Reeta Tremblay, Amy Verdun, as well as Michelle Bonner's research assistant, Marta Kleiman, who took on many of the detailed tasks involved in copyediting. Thank-you also to the anonymous reviewers for their supportive and thoughtful comments and to the editors at Palgrave Macmillan, Anca Pusca and her editorial assistant Katelyn Zingg.

Funding and support for this project came from the Social Sciences and Humanities Research Council, the Centre for Global Studies (University of Victoria), St. Bonaventure University (School of Arts & Sciences), The Faculty Resource Network (New York University), and the Briger Fund (Department of Political Science, Union College).

CONTENTS

1   Introduction   1
    Michelle D. Bonner, Michael Kempa, Mary Rose Kubal
    and Guillermina Seri

Part I   Citizenship

2   Police Abuse and the Racialized Boundaries
    of Citizenship in France   31
    Cathy Lisa Schneider

3   Police as State: Governing Citizenship Through Violence   55
    Guillermina Seri and Jinee Lokaneeta

4   Development of the Concept of "Political Profiling":
    Citizenship and Police Repression of Protest in Quebec   81
    Francis Dupuis-Déri

Part II   Accountability

5   Holding Police Abuse to Account: The Challenge
    of Institutional Legitimacy, a Chilean Case Study   113
    Michelle D. Bonner

6   Police Abuse and Democratic Accountability:
     Agonistic Surveillance of the Administrative State   135
     Rosa Squillacote and Leonard Feldman

7   Protest and Police Abuse: Racial Limits on Perceived
     Accountability   165
     Christian Davenport, Rose McDermott
     and David Armstrong

Part III   Socioeconomic (In)Equality

8   Supporting the "Elite" Transition in South Africa:
     Policing in a Violent, Neoliberal Democracy   195
     Marlea Clarke

9   Policing as Pacification: Postcolonial Legacies,
     Transnational Connections, and the Militarization
     of Urban Security in Democratic Brazil   221
     Markus-Michael Müller

Part IV   Conclusion

10   Conclusion: Rethinking Police Abuse
      in Contemporary Democracies   251
      Michelle D. Bonner

Appendix A   257

Appendix B   265

Appendix C   267

Index   269

EDITORS AND CONTRIBUTORS

About the Editors

Michelle D. Bonner is an Associate Professor of Political Science at the University of Victoria (Canada). She is the author of *Policing Protest in Argentina and Chile* (First Forum/Lynne Rienner, 2014) and *Sustaining Human Rights: Women and Argentine Human Rights Organizations* (Penn State, 2007), as well as many articles. Her book *Policing Protest in Argentina and Chile* was awarded the Canadian Political Science Association's 2015–2016 Comparative Politics Book Prize. She has been writing and publishing on issues pertaining to democracy and police violence for many years through the lens of protest policing, punitive populism, media, transitional justice, and discourse.

Guillermina Seri is an Associate Professor in the Department of Political Science at Union College, Schenectady, New York (USA), where she teaches courses in political theory and Latin American Politics. Seri is the author of *Seguridad: Crime, Police Power, and Democracy in Argentina* (Continuum, 2012; Bloomsbury, 2013), she has published book chapters and articles exploring the tensions between policing, citizenship rights, and democracy, and she is working on a book manuscript on the persistence of unlawful governance in democracies.

Mary Rose Kubal is an Associate Professor of Political Science at St. Bonaventure University (USA). She is currently finishing a book manuscript looking at the international diffusion of public security policy: *Importing Security? The Transnational Politics of Citizen Security Policy in Argentina and Chile.* Her chapter "Transnational Policy Networks and Public Security Policy in Argentina and Chile," was published in *Comparative Public Policy in Latin America* (University of Toronto Press, 2012). And she has a forthcoming article in the *Journal of Latin American Studies* (with Guillermina Seri) on democratic security in Argentina.

Michael Kempa is an Associate Professor in Criminology at the University of Ottawa (Canada). He holds a Ph.D. in Law from the Australian National University. His program of research draws upon Political Science, International Relations, and Sociological theory to address the ways in which states and non-state organizations variously conceive of and attempt to institutionalize "police power" in such domains as the economy, new forms of urban communal space, and international security.

Contributors

David Armstrong is an Associate Professor and Canada Research Chair in Political Methodology with appointments in the Department of Political Science and, by courtesy, in the Department of Statistics and Actuarial Sciences at Western University (Canada). He is the coauthor of *Analyzing Spatial Models of Choice and Judgment in R* (CRC Press, 2014) along with several articles that focus on measurement, published in outlets like the *American Journal of Political Science*, the *Journal of Peace Research and Electoral Studies.* His current research interests lie at the intersections of Machine/Statistical learning and hypothesis testing.

Marlea Clarke is an Associate Professor of Political Science at the University of Victoria (Canada), and a research associate with the Labour and Enterprise Policy Research Group at the University of Cape Town (South Africa). Her work focuses on democratic transitions in southern Africa, and employment and labour market restructuring from a comparative and feminist political economy perspective. In addition to journalist articles, she is coauthor of *Working Without Commitments* (with Wayne Lewchuk and Alice de Wolff) and coeditor (with Carolyn Bassett) of two special issues of the *Journal of Contemporary African Studies* on issues of democratization in Southern Africa.

Christian Davenport is a Professor of Political Science at the University of Michigan (USA) as well as a Faculty Associate at the Center for Political Studies and Research Professor at the Peace Research Institute Oslo. He is the author of six books, including: *How Social Movements Die: Repression and Demobilization* (2015, Cambridge University Press). His primary research interests include political conflict (e.g., human rights violations, genocide/politicide, torture, political surveillance, civil war, and social movements), measurement, racism, and popular culture.

Francis Dupuis-Déri is a Professor of Political Science at Université du Québecà Montréal (Canada), and a member of the Observatoire sur les profilages racial, social et politique (OSP) and of the Collectif de recherche interdisciplinaire sur la contestation (CRIC). He is the author of several books, including *À qui la rue?: Répression policière et mouvements sociaux* (2013, Who's Street? Police Repression and Social Movements) and *Who's Afraid of the Black Blocs?* (2013). He was one of the commissar of the Commission populaire sur la répression politique (CPRP, Popular Commission on Political Repression), and one of the authors of its report.

Leonard Feldman is an Associate Professor of Political Science at Hunter College and the Graduate Center, CUNY (USA). He is the author of *Citizens Without Shelter: Homelessness, Democracy, and Political Exclusion* (Cornell University Press, 2004), which examines the criminalization of homelessness using the resources of critical and democratic theory. He has published many articles on topics including police emergencies and emergency powers, the political and legal discourses of necessity, political criminology, and Locke's theory of executive prerogative and popular political judgment. From 2015 to 2020 he is the Associate Editor for Political Theory of *Polity*.

Jinee Lokaneeta is an Associate Professor in Political Science and International Relations at Drew University (USA). Her areas of interest include Law and Violence, Political Theory, and Interdisciplinary Legal Studies. In addition to numerous articles, she is the author of *Transnational Torture: Law, Violence, and State Power in the United States and India* (NYU Press, 2011). She is currently completing a book manuscript titled *The Truth Machines: Policing, Violence, and Scientific Interrogations in India* that theorizes the relationship between state power and legal violence by focusing on the intersection of law, science, and policing though a study of forensic techniques.

Rose McDermott is the David and Mariana Fisher University Professor of International Relations at Brown University (USA) and a Fellow in the American Academy of Arts and Sciences. She is the author of five books, coeditor of two, and author of over two hundred academic articles across a wide variety of disciplines encompassing topics such as experimentation, emotion and decision making, and the biological and genetic bases of political behavior. Her most recent books include: *Intelligence, Successes and Failure: The Human Factor* (Oxford University Press, 2017, with Uri Bar-Joseph) and *Evils of Polygyny* (Cornell University Press, 2018, with Kristen Monroe).

Markus-Michael Müller is an Assistant Professor of Political Science at the ZI Lateinamerika-Institut, Freie Universität Berlin (Germany). His work focuses on violence and security governance with a regional focus on the Americas. In addition to many articles, he is the author of *The Punitive City. Privatized Policing and Protection in Neoliberal Mexico* (2016, Zed Books), *Public Security in the Negotiated State. Policing in Latin America and Beyond* (2012, Palgrave Macmillan) and coeditor of *The Global Making of Policing. Postcolonial Perspectives* (2016, Routledge) as well *as Reconfiguring Intervention: Complexity, Resilience and the "Local Turn" in Counterinsurgent Warfare* (2017, Palgrave Macmillan).

Cathy Lisa Schneider is an Associate Professor in American University's School of International Service (USA), and holds a Ph.D. from Cornell University. She is the author of *Police Power and Race Riots: Urban Unrest in Paris and New York* (University of Pennsylvania Press, 2014, 2017 pbk) and *Shantytown Protest in Pinochet's Chile* (Temple University Press, 1995) and coeditor of *Collective Violence, Contentious Politics and Social Change: A Charles Tilly Reader* (Routledge, 2017).

Rosa Squillacote is a Ph.D. candidate in Political Science at the Graduate Center, City University of New York (USA), where she is studying American Politics and Political Theory. She holds a J.D. from UC Berkeley School of Law, where she worked on reentry employment policy, and drafted legislation signed into law making it easier for formerly incarcerated individuals to have misdemeanor convictions expunged from their records in California. Prior to returning to graduate school, she cofounded the Police Reform Organizing Project, an organization that seeks to end abusive NYPD practices such as Stop-and-Frisk and surveillance of Muslim communities.

LIST OF FIGURES

Fig. 3.1 Judicial independence in Argentina and India
          (*Source* CIRI Dataset, Cingranelli et al. 2014)   72
Fig. 3.2 Physical violence index for Argentina and India
          (*Source* Varieties of Democracy (V-Dem)
          [Coppedge et al. 2017])   75

List of Tables

Table 7.1	Protester, police, and observer identity combinations	175
Table 7.2	Race of respondents by experimental treatment	178
Table 7.3	Conditional distributions of responses	180
Table 7.4	Multinomial logistic regression results	182
Table 7.5	Difference in predicted probability between white and black observers	183
Table 7.6	Probability of protester blame	184
Table 7.7	Probability of police blame	185

CHAPTER 1

Introduction

Police Abuse in Contemporary Democracies

Michelle D. Bonner, Michael Kempa, Mary Rose Kubal and Guillermina Seri

On August 9, 2014, 18-year-old Michael Brown was fatally shot by a police officer in Ferguson, Missouri. He was suspected of petty theft but was unarmed. A subsequent trial found the officer's actions to be justified as self-defense. Despite the institutions of democracy working as they are designed, large protests (themselves met with a significant police response, including repression, and arrests) registered profound public disagreement with the outcome. For many protesters this was one example, among numerous others, of police abuse aimed at African Americans that undermines their inclusion in American democracy.

M. D. Bonner (✉)
University of Victoria, Victoria, BC, Canada

M. Kempa
University of Ottawa, Ottawa, ON, Canada

M. R. Kubal
St. Bonaventure University, St. Bonaventure, NY, USA

G. Seri
Union College, Schenectady, NY, USA

© The Author(s) 2018
M. D. Bonner et al. (eds.), *Police Abuse in Contemporary Democracies*,
https://doi.org/10.1007/978-3-319-72883-4_1

1

That is, what constitutes police abuse and its relationship with democracy was contested.

Such powerful disagreements are not unique to democracy in the United States. Abuse of police authority happens in all democracies. It can include arbitrary arrest, selective surveillance and crowd control, harassment, sexual assault, torture, killings, or even disappearances. In newer democracies, police abuse is likely to be considered by political scientists as a legacy of previous authoritarian regimes or civil war. Its persistence is understood to reflect weak democratic institutions (the primary focus of political scientists) and poorly functioning police institutions (a more common focus for criminologists).

Certainly, the field of political science counts with seminal contributions and a tradition of research scrutinizing the impact of police power on the government such as: the various governing roles of the police exposed by Michael Lipsky's study of "street-level bureaucrats" (Lipsky 1980), William Ker Muir, Jr.'s study of the police as "street-corner politicians" (Muir 1977), or Otwin Marenin's (1985) work on the police's "political economy of ruling" and its impact on democracy, not to mention Michel Foucault's (1977) thorough genealogy of police, or Mark Neocleous' (2000) research showing the role of police in *fabricating* modern social order. Yet, students of democratization and theorists alike have largely ignored this scholarship. Most political scientist research stubbornly keeps treating policing as law enforcement.

Along these lines, in established democracies, police abuse is often treated in political science and popular accounts as an aberration, an act that has little to no bearing on democracy and that is adequately addressed by existing or tweaked mechanisms of institutional accountability. This is in part the reason why police abuse has received more attention in newer than in established democracies and from criminologists rather than political scientists, gaps that concerning trends call to address.

As the introduction to a recent *Perspectives on Politics* volume on the politics of policing and incarceration admonished, "it is now clear that a truly general, comparative, and nonparochial political science must account for the fact that the topics of policing, police brutality, incarceration, and repression more generally are not limited to authoritarian regimes" (Isaac 2015, p. 610). Here we take this agenda a step further asking, is police abuse best understood as deviance that requires a technical institutional fix? or should its pervasiveness fundamentally alter our understanding of democracy? This book argues that police abuse challenges political scientists—especially—to rethink the concept of democracy in a manner that forefronts policing.

Rather than merely one of many bureaucratic bodies subordinated to democratic politics, police are the only institution with the legitimate right to use deadly violence against citizens. The boundaries of this violence are ideally defined by respect for human rights. However, in practice, these boundaries are found at the point of connection between police discretion, police ability to justify their actions, and state and society's willingness to accept such justifications. For example, as seen in the Michael Brown case, police powers include homicide, as long as the officer can justify the action as necessary for the fulfillment of police duties or for the safety of the officer(s) and that state officials and society accept the justification the officer provides as valid. Judges, courts, and oversight and governance bodies are often lenient toward the police, achieving little effective accountability (see Bonner, Chapter 5; Squillacote and Feldman, Chapter 6; Davenport et al., Chapter 7).

In many cases, established inequalities in a society determine if some forms of police abuse even need to be justified or are instead accepted as "normal" by the affected community, police, political leaders, or society at large. Poor or marginalized youth may experience police harassment and beatings as a regular part of their interactions with the police. Society at large, whose opinion is often filtered through the mass media, may accept such action on the part of the police as necessary due to these communities being perceived as "violent" or "criminal." Reciprocally, influential police reformers within government often advocate for targeting what they see as the most dangerous classes— typically those that threaten the stability of the political and economic order. In these cases, police abuse may not even be perceived as such. This is as true in established democracies such as France (e.g., in relation to Algerians) or the United States (e.g., in relation to African American communities), as it is in newer democracies such as Argentina or South Africa (e.g., in relation to youth living in economically poorer neighborhoods) (see Schneider, Chapter 2; Seri and Lokaneeta, Chapter 3; Squillacote and Feldman, Chapter 6; Davenport et al., Chapter 7; Clarke, Chapter 8).

Thus similar to "police repression" or "police violence," we define police abuse as police actions that may or may not be "illegal" but severely limit selective citizens' rights, receive minimal punishment (limited accountability), and may play a role in maintaining (or promoting) particular political and economic objectives. That is, we use the term "police abuse" in this book, not as a term to denote when police have overstepped the law, but rather in terms of how police actions may be perceived by those affected, or by those unfamiliar with or unaccepting of the justifications, or both. Other terms, such as "police excesses" or "unnecessary violence" suggest that the only problematic actions by police are those that exceed legal boundaries or cannot be justified according to dominant societal norms. As we have explained here, legal boundaries are often intentionally blurry and dominant social norms may discriminate against marginalized communities or be accepting of high levels of police violence.

The chapters that follow primarily concentrate on acts of police abuse that pertain to physical violence (e.g., beatings, torture, forced disappearance, and homicide), as well as the surveillance, arrest, or "stop and frisk" of people targeted based on class, race, political orientation, etc. We chose these because their dramatic nature highlights the tensions between policing and democracy. Of course, the types of police abuse examined in this volume are not exhaustive of all its forms. Police abuse can also include corruption, white-collar crime, political policing, spying, and gender-based violence, to name only a few important additional areas of inquiry. We aim for the themes explored in this book to be a useful starting point for debate and exploration on a wider range of police abuses and their relationship to democracy.

Though far from the drama of military coups, persistent police abuses of all forms can corrode a democratic regime and reinforce its internal borders—creating a neo-feudal type landscape of privileged spaces of democratic inclusion and surrounding badlands of democratic exclusion. This book contends that police abuse is a structural and conceptual dimension of extant democracies, not an exceptional occurrence or aberration, and by doing so draws our attention to the part it plays in the persistence of hybrid democracies, the uneven quality of democracy within nations, and in the overall decline of democracy (Puddington 2015). Policing is thus of great consequence for the quality of experience of democracy.

Of course, the degree of police abuse (both in form and quantity) varies over time, as well as between countries and citizens. The chapters that comprise this volume, which span ten countries and five continents, explore a number of causal factors for this variation including: racism, classism, political biases, political economy, and the relative (in)ability of liberal democratic institutions to act as a check on the impact of these factors on policing. That is, reducing police abuse is not limited to holding individual officers to account, but also addressing more systemic problems linked to the manner in which democracy is conceptualized.

We begin this chapter by presenting the place of police abuse in democracy and its overlooked importance to discussions on the recent decline of democracy. We then explore the implications of police abuse for democracy through three key dimensions that make the impact of policing apparent: citizenship, accountability, and socioeconomic (in) equality. Unlike assessments of "democratic policing" that start with the institutional structures of the police or the criminal justice system, our analysis draws attention to how the structure and concept of democracy itself shapes choices about policing. In turn, we consider the impacts for political science of centering policing in the study of democracy.

POLICE ABUSE, DEMOCRACY, AND THE DECLINE OF DEMOCRACY

In political science, liberal democracy defines the contours of the dominant literature. Liberal democracy is assumed to be a politically neutral set of institutions and the benchmark upon which new and established democracies are measured (Schmitter and Karl 1991, p. 77; Plattner 2015). With these conceptual assumptions, the "democratic policing" model has been promoted internationally as part of the liberal democratic package, and political theorists and comparativists have worked to improve the conceptual quality and robustness of these institutions. This, despite the fact that these very premises are contested, that there is no clarity about the meaning of "democratic policing," and that democratization is undergoing a crisis and seeming reversal in the so-called "donor" or "seigniorial" countries that export their ideals and actual practices.

The most recent, historical, "third wave" of democratization started with the end of the Salazar dictatorship in Portugal in 1974 and then expanded through Southern Europe, South America, Eastern Europe, South Asia, and Africa through the 1980s and the 1990s (Huntington 1996). Especially since the 1990s, this process led to conceptual and empirical comparative studies that sought to contribute to the project of establishing and consolidating democracy around the world. The expansion of elections, democratic principles, and institutions brought the largest number of electoral democracies ever into existence, which rose from around 40 in the mid-1970s to 69 in 1989 to a peak of 123 in 2005–2006. The extension of the democratic universe brought nuances and questions of how to distinguish between gradients among these regimes and improve the quality of democracy in countries around the world. To this day, the appropriate indicators of democracy remain contested, though the field is advancing with projects such as Varieties of Democracy (e.g., Munck 2009; Levitsky and Way 2015; Diamond 2015; Bermeo 2016; Coppedge et al. 2017).

Moving beyond Joseph Schumpeter's (1943) very minimal definition of democracy as competitive elections, many studies draw on Robert Dahl's (1971) concept of "polyarchy." Minimally, scholars note, democracies must: enforce the rule of law (including the protection of civil rights); hold regular, free, fair, and competitive elections; ensure those elected the power to control government policy (without the interference of unelected officials, e.g., military veto); and citizens the right to run for office, freedom of speech, freedom of association, and freedom of information (Schmitter and Karl 1991, pp. 81–82; Linz and Stepan 1996, pp. 3–7; Fukuyama 2015, p. 12). In turn, scholars developing a robust procedural definition of democracy bring together electoral politics with the design and implementation of policies coherent with the electorate's choices. These scholars note that the democratic rights needed to participate across the political process, thus defined, encompass access to electoral participation as much as a certain level of income, socioeconomic equality, and legal and political inclusion (Munck 2007, p. 32; Munck 2009; O'Donnell 1994).

Free, competitive elections are crucial, yet individual rights and freedoms are no less fundamental to the democratic enterprise (Møller and Skaaning 2013, p. 84). These rights and freedoms are ideally protected by the rule of law and form the basis for equal and inclusive citizenship. Generally emphasizing first-generation civil and political rights, scholars of democracy often assume that fine-tuned constitutions and courts, along with political commitment to and public trust in liberal democracy, are the means for improving their delivery. Empirical studies also indicate that democracies respect human rights more than nondemocratic regimes due to: the political costs of repression in democratic settings; the consistency between democratic values and individual freedoms; and, evidence gathered through comparative studies (Møller and Skaaning 2013, p. 87; Clark 2014, p. 396).

It was in this context of "third wave" democratization and democracy promotion that a number of scholars, experts, and practitioners contributed to the literature with studies and insight on how to democratize policing, especially in newly democratized or "transitional" societies. Since criminologists author many of these studies, it is not surprising to find that the problems and solutions of policing in democracy are most often located within the police institution itself (or closely related institutions).

For example, David H. Bayley (2006, pp. 19–20) argues that there are four fundamental features that characterize "democratic policing:" police must be accountable to the law (not to the government); police must protect human rights; police must be accountable to people outside their organization; and, police must give service priority to individual citizens and private groups (not government) (for similar lists see Jones et al. 1994, pp. 43–44; Hinton and Newburn 2009, pp. 4–5). Mark Ungar (2011), a political scientist, provides an equally technical definition, which links democratic policing to a particular approach to crime control called "problem-oriented policing." In this approach, police identify a "problem," collect data on it, design an appropriate response, and assess the response (Ungar 2011, p. 6). The various institutional changes proposed by these studies are then adopted into international police reform programs as a politically neutral technical fix that ideally, it is assumed, will further democracy through reducing crime and police violence, and in turn strengthen the rule of law.

Yet policing, and police abuse in particular, plays a more fundamental role in democracy than merely another weak institution that requires fixing. Different definitions of democracy hold different expectations for police and policing, which are understood by police and society at large, and often supersede the structures that define police institutions and their actions (Chan 1996; della Porta 1998; Sklansky 2008). Indeed democracy nests, and has always precariously nested, within particular forms of policing. For example, Athenian democracy, enjoyed by free male heads of households, coexisted with a form of citizen-based policing predicated upon the nondemocratic management of household members (wife, children, daughters, servants, slaves, chattle, and inanimate objects) by the householder (autonomous free male) (Hunter 1994; Dubber 2005). If contributing to prevent violence in the city, within the limits of household economics, the householder defined and executed policing powers within his household with little to no restrictions; he established that which was considered wrongdoing, the corresponding punishment, and its application (Dubber 2005). Over time, kings and later states (now represented by police institutions) assumed responsibility for these inherently discretionary policing powers.

Historically, policing stood at the center of the study of political economy and politics generally. Distinctively, the study of political economy brings back the central place that police had earlier in the study of government and that in modern political science was lost. The concept of "police" was at one stage synonymous with the field of study and policy of luminary political economists. The programs for peaceful and prosperous nation states that they inspired considered that policing *was* the blended science and art of "political oeconomy" (Dubber 2005). Under mercantilism, "acts of police" were understood as exercises of state power in pursuit of market growth, in turn conducive to the greatness of the kingdom. Police, it was believed, would expand the market and the tax base, which, in turn, would keep the sovereign strong and capable of maintaining order throughout the polity and staving off foreign invasion.

Yet, as the rise of liberal capitalism redirected markets away from serving the sovereign and focused on rewarding the industry of individual citizens, the concept of "police" became conceptually, and, later, institutionally divorced from market intervention. Mark Neocleous (1998), in his genealogies of early modern policing, identifies both streams of thinking in early and later career Adam Smith, as he shifted to his more fully developed program for liberal capitalist political economy in the *Wealth of Nations*. This shift gave rise to the classic liberal "night watchman" state—which protected the honest, industrious citizens, who deserved full admission to the rights of democracy, and the protection of their property from the depredation of criminals (Neocleous 1998).

In this context, it became possible to begin to think of "policing" as the professional enforcement of law and maintenance of disciplinary surveillance in public space by uniformed professionals. Both mercantilist and liberal capitalist notions of policing shared a preoccupation with the underclass: "feckless citizens" who either could not, or would not be persuaded to work for a wage and thus had to be controlled through surveillance and coercion. The movement and leisure activities of such groups have always been at the heart of the political economy of modern policing. Randall Williams (2003), for example, notes the harsh approach to paramilitary policing developed in Britain's "first colony" of Ireland, deemed necessary to impose order upon the working classes that Britain needed to maintain the pace of its own engines of production. In parallel, Daleiden (2006) emphasizes that policing in the south of the United States has its roots in limiting the flight of slaves to protect the antebellum economy.

Controlling the "dangerous classes" has been the flipside of policing in democracy judged necessary by notable political economists and policing reformers such as Patrick Colquhoun, Adam Smith, Jeremy Bentham, and John Stuart Mill in the eighteenth and nineteenth centuries, through to such "professional" policing reformers of the twentieth century as August Vollmer and O.W Wilson. As such, police abuse of authority and selective application of police power has been tolerated by classic, (neo)liberal, and critical political economists as an art of government to be perfected, in the first case, as the enforcement of the law supporting the market-driven order, in the second, and, as a problem to be eradicated by redefining a more just political economy, in the latter. Thus choices related to political economy play an important role in how policing and police abuse shape democratic citizenship and when mechanisms of accountability will be activated. In collaboration with various other forms of policing, including private guards, the modern state police have had a daily impact on citizens' lives (Clarke, Chapter 8; Müller, Chapter 9). To date, however, police powers remain discretional and vaguely defined. They hold a unique and complicated, yet underexplored, relationship with democracy.

At the same time that this rich and nuanced history of police and politics has been largely neglected in the political science literature on democracy, concerns that democratization has stalled and may be reversing have gained ground (Diamond 1997, 2015; Cooley 2015; Fukuyama 2015; Puddington 2015). Over the last decade, there has been a net loss both in the number of such regimes and in the quality of democracy. Scholars in comparative politics emphasize the weaknesses of liberal democracy in practice (e.g., Plattner 2015). Adjectives such as "delegative," "low-intensity," "illiberal," "semi-," "incomplete," etc., draw attention to liberal democratic deficits (e.g., O'Donnell 1994; McSherry 1997). In other cases, electoral democracies are simply removed from the category of democratic and relabeled as "competitive authoritarian" (Levitsky and Way 2002; Puddington 2015). If concerning signs were acknowledged earlier, the accumulation of negative trends in recent years has triggered alarm.

Puzzlingly, democratization in practice has revealed more complex dynamics and a convoluted progression. While electoral democracies have expanded, rights and liberties have suffered in recent years. Major indicators of human rights, freedom, and the state of democracy show consistent losses over the last decade (Puddington 2015; Clark 2014). A similar crisis affects democratic values and institutions. "Acceptance of democracy as the world's dominant form of government—and of an international system built on democratic ideals—is under greater threat than at any point in the last 25 years," asserts a recent Freedom House report (Puddington 2015). More specifically, one scholar notes that there is "a genuine crisis of liberal democracy" in both new democracies as well as Europe and the United States (Krastev 2016, p. 36).

Recent comparative studies of the global course of democratization, liberties, and human rights offer a nuanced, unsettling perspective. Amidst rising state security measures (often undermining fundamental guarantees), in parallel with expanding nationalisms, liberal democracy has been described as undergoing a "normative retreat" and "an international backlash" (Cooley 2015). Restrictions on freedom of expression and movement, increased state surveillance and violations of privacy, attacks on internet freedom, and the return of traditional forms of media censorship around the world, epitomize a decline of democracy giving rise to a debate on a reverse wave. No handful of new electoral democracies can compensate for the significant decline of political and civil rights around the world over the last decade, as shown by Freedom House, among others. For every country that records improvements in the quality of democracy, two others show signs in the opposite direction (Puddington 2015).

As democracies lose substance and exhibit cracks in matters of rights and freedoms, leaders in authoritarian regimes, such as Russian president Vladimir Putin, show scorn for liberal democracy and denounce it as "a cover for U.S. and Western geopolitical interests" (Puddington 2015; Cooley 2015, p. 50). Governments that at the peak of democratization used to at least keep a semblance of civil rights, "now resort to violent police tactics, sham trials, and severe sentences as they seek to annihilate political opposition" (Puddington 2015).

Accompanying a resurgence of coups and involvement of the military in politics, a still unfolding global War on Terror allows governments to justify abuses (Puddington 2015). Thus, while research and reports about the decay of democracy or about the "reverse wave" are not specifically about the police, policing lies at the center of these processes as a main medium through which the state imposes order and governs the population's access to rights.

At the same time, evidence on the decay of democracy has led political scientists to interrogate the links between democracy, freedom, and human rights. Along these lines, drawing on ratings on governance, human rights, and political and civil liberties from the Freedom House, Polity IV, the Political Terror Scale and the Cingranelli-Richards Index, Clark (2014) revisits the relation between democracy and human rights over the period 1981–2010. Comparing the worldwide yearly average ratings for each of the four indexes, the study shows that over the three decades "democracy ratings have risen" but human rights scores have gone down (Clark 2014, p. 403). Since the 1980s, democracy rapidly expanded and democratic performance improved across regions, as reflected in a 20–25% rise in average Freedom House ratings and in 45–60% rise in Polity IV scores worldwide (Clark 2014, p. 400). Significant gaps between established and newer democracies notwithstanding, democracy ratings show analogous patterns and trends. Yet, regardless of how formally "democratic" countries may be, human rights practices tend to diverge in distinct ways across countries and regions, Clark notes, and governments' respect for human rights shows signs of decay even in established democracies (Clark 2014, pp. 404, 407). Overall deterioration is shown by data on state abuses of physical integrity, as measured by the Political Terror Scale, and on 15 fundamental human rights including physical integrity, freedom of speech and movement, or electoral self-determination assessed by the Cingranelli-Richards index, with net losses of 7.5% in the former and 10.8% in the latter between 1981 and 2010 (Clark 2014, p. 401).

Democracy has spread globally at the same time that human rights protection has declined and become less uniform, a trend that puts into question the widespread assumption that democratization would bring improvements in terms of human rights. While positively related, "democracy ratings and human rights ratings are clearly distinct," Clark concludes (2014, p. 399). Other researchers claim that human rights and the quality of democracy have not been eroded in older democracies, only in new ones (Møller and Skaaning 2013, p. 98). Yet, while older democracies are more respectful of civil liberties generally, there is significant reason for concern as regards specific freedoms, such as "freedom of expression and the freedom of assembly/association" (Møller and Skaaning 2013, p. 83). More research is needed about the bonds between democracy and rights and the meaning and prospects of signs of democratic decay. Yet, given the central role of the police in citizens' experience of rights, it is important that policing be a part of this research.

All in all, two decades after Diamond questioned whether the wave of democratization was starting to face "death by a thousand subtractions" (Diamond 1997, p. 40), seemingly far from these concerns, the literature on police democratization remains mostly unchanged. It continues to rely on generic premises and assumptions that seem at best ungrounded, and problematic—if not flawed—at worst. Not only has the literature assumed the existence of models of democratic policing, taking for granted that policing in established democracies *is* by definition democratic, but it also advocates for transferring such models to other countries (Müller, Chapter 9). In this we agree with Krastev's (2016, p. 36) critique of some of the democratization literature, which, he argues, assumes "consolidated democracy cannot backslide and that at the heart of the current crisis is a failure of liberal pedagogy." Instead, we need to better conceptualize the relationship between democracy and the police.

Police abuse is defined and constrained by particular conceptions of democracy. Without taking this connection seriously we risk widening the gap between theories of democracy and people's lived experience. This gap can best be mended not merely by convincing marginalized communities to trust in liberal democratic institutions or tweaking their procedures, but by integrating policing and police abuse into the concept and structures of democracy as a whole. Across political science subfields, the inclusion of policing into studies of democracy can build more robust understandings of inclusion, rights, participation, procedures, and institutions. In the next section, we look more closely at how this can be achieved.

RETHINKING DEMOCRACY WITH POLICE ABUSE IN MIND

When police abuse is introduced to studies of democracy in political science a richer analysis of democracy is possible. With this reinterpretation of democracy we are in a better position to understand both the persistence of hybrid democracies as well as the global decline in democracy (Plattner 2015). For example, the erosion of democratic rights can be more precisely linked to the structural role of police in particular and shifting concepts of democracy. In what follows we consider how police abuse affects three key concepts of democracy—citizenship, accountability, and socioeconomic (in)equality—and draw attention to the questions that emerge that require more rigorous academic debate. While these elements overlap and are interdependent, the two former relate to process—how is membership in the democratic community determined and how are democratic rights and duties exercised and protected—while the latter, tied to questions of political economy, concerns the substantive outcomes of democratic processes.

Citizenship

Expanding the franchise and guaranteeing fundamental protections to life, equality, and freedom of expression have been staples of ideal citizenship under liberal democracy. In turn, theorists of participatory democracy have emphasized the intrinsic value of citizen involvement and deliberation (Pateman 1970). Only active participation and the protection of rights, it is the consensus, can prevent democracy from undermining itself (Schwartzberg 2014). However, participation requires admission and the recognition of political membership.

Citizenship involves full membership in a political community, with duties and entitlements to participate in decisions determining a people's fate (Bellamy 2008, p. 3). Definitions of who counts as a polity's full member lie at the heart of the citizenship puzzle, one that continues to be given contingent, "pragmatic" solutions (Dahl 1990, p. 45). While a necessary condition, the formal recognition of citizenship is not sufficient for the effective exercise of its duties and entitlements, as myriad obstacles make it difficult for the poor, or members of religious or ethnic minorities, or people with certain political perspectives to have their voices respected (see Schneider, Chapter 2; Seri and Lokaneeta, Chapter 3; Dupuis-Déri, Chapter 4). Theorists have promoted alternative mechanisms to make representative democracy more inclusive of minorities (Kymlicka 1995). Still, as in the experience of countless black, Latino, and native American victims of police abuse in the US attests, racism, structural inequalities, and the provision of public order by the police stand in the way of participating in politics and fully enjoying the legal protections of citizenship (see Davenport et al., Chapter 7).

The study of expressions of citizenship in political science tends to encompass legal traditions and classical forms of political participation—from street protests to voting. For students of the police, it is easy to see the preeminent role that policing plays in alternatively protecting or undermining people's rights, voices, and lives, and their access to citizenship and political participation, democracy's foundational elements.

Often the first point of contact between citizens and the judicial system, police officers make discretionary decisions by distinguishing between citizens deserving protection and others perceived as suspect and as a threat to the former (Waddington 1999). The poor, members of indigenous, ethnic and religious minorities, or transgender citizens often find themselves dismissed, criminalized, or subjected to violence, as police considerations of worth and dangerousness mirror society's ste-reotypes. Police categorizing stands as the final, street line recognition of rights and political membership. On a one-to-one basis, police agents define who counts as a full citizen and the proper spaces and modalities through which citizens can express their grievances (della Porta 1998; Hall et al. 1978).

The concept of citizenship meaningfully links the macro structures of government to governing practices shaping individuals' daily lives and access to rights. Police practices constantly delimit and redefine the internal and external borders of the polity in distinct ways by allowing and restricting the exercise of rights. While mainstream political science tends to see the rule of law as a binary category (it exists or does not on the national and/or subnational levels), when police governance is con-sidered, questions of unequal citizenship are raised that go beyond for-mal legal exclusions. In Chapter 3, Seri and Lokaneeta argue that police governance in India and Argentina results in violent exclusions from and hierarchies of citizenship based on ascriptive categories such as race, caste, religion, class, and gender. By comparing these otherwise very different countries, they reveal many similar practices, including police use of torture and extrajudicial and custodial killings, which in both cases disproportionately affect those from lower socioeconomic classes and marginalized communities. Such practices benefit from other state actors' acceptance of police explanations and, consequently, impunity. These practices exist in tension with other democratic gains.

In Chapter 4, Dupuis-Déri reveals that, in addition to identity, police abuse can also define the boundaries of citizens' rights based on polit-ical orientation—even in established democracies. He identifies the emergence of the concept of "political profiling" of social movements actors in public spaces in Montréal, Québec and how the term has highlighted the limits this police practice places on selective citizens' freedom of assembly and expression. He argues that police use arrests and mass arrests, both preemptively and during protests, to silence political perspectives they perceive as illegitimate or criminal. This police repression, he shows, corresponds with the protesters' political perspectives, not their tactics. It has disproportionately affected anarchist and alter-globalization protesters.

In addition to the policing of certain categories of citizens, with the number of world migrants and refugees at its global historical peak, liberal democracies now host millions of foreign residents, many without a legally recognized status, excluded from the protection of the law. Intertwined with domestic forms of exclusion, visible and invisible barriers target immigrants and refugees or those deemed to be "immigrants." Whether it is Mexicans in the United States, or North Africans in Europe, racialization and criminalization keep many in a legally hybrid territory or directly outside the law.

In Chapter 2, Schneider examines this "policing of racial boundaries" in France. Her chapter reveals the colonial and racialized roots of police abuse aimed at "immigrants," particularly (but not exclusively) Algerians. She traces the shifting legal status and policing practices aimed at these communities through the colonial period, World War Two, the postwar/Algerian independence period, to the present day politics of anti-immigration and insecurity. The police abuse she finds includes examples of torture, arbitrary beatings and killings, and racialized incarceration, all of which have involved significant impunity for the police. Through this history she shows how police abuse defines the form of citizenship and democracy experienced by those communities deemed "immigrant" (even if born in France) and, referencing recent terrorist attacks, potentially for many other people in France.

As Schneider's chapter shows, states have perfected legal and policing mechanisms that lead to the criminalization of asylum seekers and refugees, despite the progressive recognition of their rights by international law, excluding millions of people from basic legal protections. As millions survive in a legal no man's land, at the mercy of police, border patrol, or military agents, the "inadequacy" of current conceptions and policies regarding citizenship come to the forefront (Arnold 2007), as do the challenges of political membership and "the rights of others," as they relate to migrants and refugees (Benhabib 2004). As the nuanced access to citizenship in the hands of the police makes clear, policing needs to be included as a dimension that can alternatively strengthen or hollow out citizenship in current democracies—particularly at a time when police powers and jurisdictions are expanded in the name of protecting citizenship and national identity.

Accountability

Linked to the lived experience of citizenship and democracy is accountability. When police abuse their authority and are not held to account, the boundaries of democracy become apparent for those people and communities affected. It reveals democratic accountability to be an institutional act used to mediate legal transgressions between those with power. In contrast, those who are politically, socially, or economically marginalized find they are "policed" with authoritarian practices, which, as noted in our definition of "police abuse," may or may not be defined as illegal, but certainly limit selective citizens' rights.

The dominant political science literature is primarily concerned with the manner in which state institutions check government power. Concepts such as "delegative" or "hybrid" democracy and "competitive authoritarianism" refer to elected governments that, between elections, are subject to few institutional checks on their power (O'Donnell 1994; Levitsky and Way 2002). Similarly, studies of the global decline in democracy hinge their evaluation on government accountability (Plattner 2015; Fukuyama 2015, p. 12). This is because accountability is fundamental to the rule of law, and the rule of law is regarded as a defining feature of liberal democracy.

In theory, the law holds all citizens to account under the "rule of law." Ideally, this refers to accountability to "democratic" laws, in the sense that they uphold political and civil rights and do not disproportionately punish the poor and marginalized (Pinheiro 1999; O'Donnell 1999). Unsurprisingly then, in the political science literature, the judiciary becomes a central institution of accountability, as it is charged with the responsibility to determine wrongdoing and punish those who break the law. Political scientists also concentrate their studies on the most democratic options for the wording of constitutions and laws, which the judiciary is to enforce. If mentioned at all, police are portrayed as a bureaucratic institution that must be "useable," follow directions from the elected government in power, and are confined in their powers by the rule of law. The legislature and the judiciary presumably hold the police accountable for the protection of civil and political rights.

However in practice, for most people, the police are the first arbitrators of the application and interpretation of the rule of law. At the same time, in most democracies, police are not, themselves, fully subject to the rule of law, as the norms that pertain to police powers and their execution rely heavily upon police discretion and acceptance of police justifications. Most political science studies assume that the government controls the police in much the same way as they do other branches of the bureaucracy, and thus governments are held accountable for police actions, and police answer to the government and the judiciary. This then frees political science studies of democracy to focus their attention on the legislature and judiciary, with little attention to the police.

Yet, the policing literature tells us that the police have considerable discretion in how they function. They might choose to apply the law (or not) based on race, sexual identity, or class, or more positively, in one study of protest policing in Great Britain, police refrained from enforcing many laws during protests in order to avoid inciting violence (Waddington 1998, p. 119). In some countries, police have a great deal of autonomy from civilian control (Marenin 1996, pp. 10–13). In Chapters 5, 6 and 7, Bonner, Squillacote and Feldman, and Davenport, McDermott, and Armstrong examine how we can better understand democratic accountability with police abuse in mind. While the chapters raise diverse issues, they all highlight one key question: Are liberal democratic institutional mechanisms of accountability sufficient for democracy? The chapters in this volume argue that, in the case of police abuse, they are not.

First, ideas matter. Judicial and government accountability require, as a prerequisite, that both the state and society agree that police abuse or wrongdoing has occurred. If police actions (regardless of how brutal outsiders might perceive them) are not viewed by the state and society as excessive, then it is unlikely that police will be held accountable. As Janet Chan (1996) explains, drawing on Bourdieu, police culture and abuses (habitus) reflect in part what society will tolerate (the "field" of policing). This is particularly true when such actions are considered within the realm of police discretion, limited only by the officer's ability to justify her or his actions. Beginning with the issue of police abuse we see that "discursive accountability" is as important as institutional accountability (Bonner 2014). Discursive accountability is when state, media, or civil society actors or all three discursively define an action or inaction as wrongdoing, identify who among the possible actors is most responsible, and define the corresponding solutions or remedies. Dominant discourses contribute to police knowledge regarding what actions in which situations will cause them "trouble" and which will be accepted, facilitating police abuse in democracy (della Porta 1998, p. 229; Waddington 1998, pp. 119–120).

In Chapter 5, Bonner explores the dominant political and media narratives around accountability in the Chilean case of the police killing of 16-year-old Manuel Gutiérrez. The chapter argues that the manner in which dominant narratives narrow the definition of accountability, and the purpose it is to serve, limits the scope of actions that can then be taken as a remedy. More specifically, the chapter shows how dominant public narratives on police accountability in the Gutiérrez case aim to reinforce police legitimacy. This central and narrow goal then results in the marginalization or dismissal of calls by other political actors for the pursuit of broader definitions of accountability, including substantial police or political reforms that might better prevent repetition. That is, reducing police abuse includes rethinking the primary goal of accountability.

Similarly, in Chapter 7, Davenport, McDermott, and Armstrong use an experimental method to reveal the importance of observers' subconscious ideas about race on their attribution of responsibility in the case of protest policing in the United States. Given the role that public moral outrage can have on the activation of mechanisms of institutional accountability, this is an important question. They find that blacks are less likely to blame protesters when protesters are black and police are white. In turn, whites are less likely to blame the police in the same situation. Thus one's perception of police wrongdoing and the need or not for accountability is not neutral or color blind. Nor is it simply a response to police or protester actions. There are racial limits to accountability. As the authors point out, these limits pose a significant challenge to achieving a shared democratic notion of acceptable policing practices and when police accountability is needed. Thus if police abuse is to be reduced, closer attention is needed to how conscious or unconscious bias can be reduced in the pursuit of accountability.

Second, social movements are an important venue of accountability. As Enrique Peruzzotti and Catalina Smulovitz (2006) argue, civil society organizations provide social accountability. They do so by shaming wrongdoers, demanding answers for the wrongdoing, and activating institutional mechanisms of accountability, such as courts and oversight commissions. In Chapter 6, Squillacote and Feldman combine political theory with an examination of the situation in the United States to draw our attention to social movement organizations such as Cop Watch. They reveal the distinct role such organizations play in accountability compared to state-organized deliberative processes such as public fora linked to community policing or practical reforms such as police body cameras. As they highlight, police led deliberation with civil society often takes police abuse off the discussion table and instead aims to reinforce or rebuild public trust in the police. Police body cameras similarly emphasize police perspectives.

In contrast, civil society organizations provide what Squillacote and Feldman call "agonistic surveillance," which is independent of the state and offers a pluralistic perspective on police accountability that emanates from "the people." They challenge the idea that such organizations are unrepresentative or could be replaced by institutional mechanisms of accountability. Instead, they argue that Cop Watch type organizations and their protection are a fundamental part of police reforms that could curb police abuse.

In sum, while accountability is central to the definition of liberal democracy, police abuse encourages us to rethink the limits of accountability, who is affected depending upon where those limits are placed, and, how democratic accountability can be made more inclusive.

Socioeconomic (In)Equality

While not central to all definitions of democracy, many scholars of liberal democracy argue that at least a certain degree of socioeconomic equality is needed in order to maintain democracy (e.g., Linz and Stepan 1996; Beetham 1999, p. 63). Scholars of social democracy go further, arguing that greater socioeconomic equality is a central goal of democracy because it is necessary in order to ensure that all citizens have the ability to participate in politics (Bobbio 1996). Yet there is no consensus on the appropriate levels of socioeconomic equality needed for democracy or how inequalities (and the tensions they provoke) should be managed.

Similar to citizenship and accountability, police abuse plays an important role in reinforcing the dominant understandings of the boundaries of socioeconomic inequality in democracy and in particular political economies. Using the tools of political economy, this section examines socioeconomic inequality and policing through the lens of (post)colonialism. This then provides insight into the national and transnational dynamics of the decline of democracy and the connection of democratic policing policies to the democracy promotion agenda.

At the crux of the relationship between the citizen and the state and its economy, policing institutions embody and strengthen the values and practices of the dominant political-economic order. In the first instance, the police are the practical enforcers of a state's formal legal rules and dominant mores—as such, they can guarantee or frustrate the realization of the extent of the rights that are on offer within a particular political-economic regime. More deeply, the police agency is the figurative embodiment of the ways of looking at the world that inform a political economic approach; they are like social mirrors that reflect the worldviews—most especially the "proper" roles of states and markets—that are contained in our systems of codified law and governance.

As highlighted in studies of political economy, most scholars of democratization recognize that the contours of national level democracies are shaped in part by the international context within which they find themselves. In recent years, the relationship between democracy and post or neocolonialism has been the subject of a great deal of debate in political science. Studies have examined how to establish new power arrangements that put aside a colonial past or renegotiate power relations with a neocolonial power, or both. Policing is a part of these colonial and neocolonial structures that need to be rethought. In Chapter 2, Schneider, while focusing on citizenship, highlights the legacies of colonialism that shape how "Algerians," "Arabs," and "immigrants" are policed in France. Similarly, in Chapter 8, Clarke explores the legacy of colonial and apartheid policing in South Africa, revealing how neoliberal economic policies have reshaped these policing practices in remarkably similar ways. Indeed she argues that police abuse plays an important role in the wider social conflict over the limited nature of South Africa's transition and the place of neoliberal economic policies within it. As with Algerians in France, Clarke shows that in South Africa, the "blacks" of colonial South Africa remain the primary targets of new "tough on crime" policies aimed to control crime and those excluded by or who oppose neoliberalism. As these chapters highlight, police abuse played an important role in disciplining colonial subjects as it continues disciplining neocolonial subjects (also see McCoy 2009; National Advisory Commission on Civil Disorders 1968; Thomas 2008).

Postcolonial and neocolonial power dynamics permeate global pursuits such as democracy promotion and its ancillary "democratic policing" policy community. They shape hybrid democracies and offer insights into the global decline of democracy. In Chapter 9, Müller critically examines Brazil's Pacification Police Units (UPPs), which scholars and practitioners have celebrated as a largely successful project of "democratic urban security" with "the potential of becoming 'a model for the region and the world'" (Chapter 9). Instead, Müller demonstrates how the UPPs constitute the reimport of urban counterinsurgency practices from Haiti (where Brazil is in charge of the military component of the UN-peacekeeping mission MINUSTAH) and Colombia. These counterinsurgency practices, and their application in Brazil through the UPPs, have changed the nature of police abuse and increased the militarization of urban security governance in democratic Rio de Janeiro. Moreover, the chapter shows how this reimport of counterinsurgency practices to Brazil is embedded within a larger colonial institutional legacy of racialized police repression in the name of pacifying the racialized and marginalized "urban other." In teasing out these connections, and the role they play in maintaining a particular political economy, the chapter draws our attention to the (post)colonial and international dimension of police abuse in democracy promotion and the perpetuation of violent order-making in the name of protecting democracy.

Police abuse can also place important limits on public protest in democracy and the ability of citizens to oppose certain political economic systems. Indeed, democracy promotion strategies advanced by the United States' government through the National Endowment for Democracy and similar initiatives seek to "suppress popular democratization, which is a threat to elite status quos and the structure of an asymmetric international order" (Robinson 1996, p. 625). Instead, the version of democracy being promoted by the United States and its allies is a procedural one following the outlines of Dahl's (1971) polyarchy (Robinson 1996; McFaul 2004; see also Müller, Chapter 9). The limits police abuse places on protest as a part of the workings of democracy are seen in many of the chapters in this volume, but most notably in those by Dupuis-Déri (Chapter 4) and Clarke (Chapter 8). As both these chapters highlight, in the very different contexts of Canada and South Africa, public protests that oppose neoliberal economics are more likely to face police repression.

Engaging critically with the political economy, postcolonial, and neo-colonial horizon reveals the role of policing and law and (dis)order in state-making, reinforcing mechanisms of social control over histori-cally colonized peoples—not only in the Global South. The established democracies of North America and Europe have their "own 'south,' a racialized world of the poor, excluded, and criminalized" (Comaroff and Comaroff 2006, p. 37). When new security threats are identified, the nature of policing and justifications for police abuse expand, as do its threatening implications for democracy.

The US-led shift of security paradigms from warfighting to crime-fighting leads to a qualitative change in the nature of policing. Thus, "the 'state monopoly of murder' of the warfare state becomes the state monopoly of global discipline and surveillance of the crimefare state" (Andreas and Price 2001, pp. 51–52). With this renewed focus on crime, liberal democracies legitimize neocolonial ways of intervening widely through nonlethal forms of discipline, which turn increasingly lethal for those labeled as "criminal," as the chapters by Schneider, Seri and Lokaneeta, Clarke, and Müller in this volume illustrate. This is especially the case during neoliberalized "moral panics," to borrow from Stuart Hall et al. (1978), when the state (or its police agents) perceives the social order being challenged—as the increasing number of police kill-ings of African Americans in the United States demonstrates. This raises questions such as: How do those most affected by police abuse react and assert agency? and what are the consequences, both for the victims and for democracy?

Linking together our reconceptualizations of citizenship, accountabil-ity, and socioeconomic (in)equality, we find that the often interconnect-ing objectives of particular political economies, (neo)colonial projects, state building, and security threats require specific roles for the police. In turn, these expectations for police play a fundamental role in defining that which is considered police abuse, and thus the boundaries of citi-zenship (rights and political participation), as well as the reach of formal and informal mechanisms of accountability. From this perspective, reduc-ing police abuse as we have defined it in this volume, requires reflection on the types of political-economic systems and associated (neo)colonial practices that may encourage or discourage it. Additionally, it is necessary to expose the mechanisms of accountability, often grounded in implicit biases regarding threats posed by "the dangerous classes," which allow for exclusionary policing practices.

CONCLUSION

Police abuse has been curiously absent or marginalized in most of the political science literature on democracy, where it remains treated mostly as instrumental, neutral law enforcement. Yet cases such as Michael Brown's pose important disciplinary challenges. Policing should not be left to analysis by criminologists and sociologists alone; policing is fundamental to political science, a fact acknowledged in the earlier science of government, the police science, seminal works in political science in the 1960s through the 1980s, and yet ignored or forgotten. As a discipline, we work to categorize and conceptualize ideal and practical forms of democracy that are inclusive, effective, durable, and just. However, without an assessment of police abuse such studies remain incomplete. This then limits our ability to adequately understand ongoing crises in established democracies, democracy's hybrid forms, and the global decline of democracy. As we have shown, police abuse plays a central role in the construction and lived experience of citizenship, accountability, and socioeconomic (in)equality—all key aspects of democracy.

In the chapters that follow we explore these issues further, drawing on case studies and examples from countries around the world. Together this book is a call to political scientists, from all our subfield perspectives, to integrate and take seriously police abuse as a defining feature of democracy affecting its forms, reach, and boundaries. For nonpolitical scientists, these chapters aim to contribute to the already rich discussions of the relationship between policing and democracy.

REFERENCES

Andreas, Peter, and Richard Price. 2001. "From War Fighting to Crime Fighting: Transforming the American National Security State." *International Studies Review* 3 (3): 31–52.

Arnold, Kathleen. 2007. "Enemy Invaders! Mexican Immigrants and U.S. Wars Against Them." *Borderlands* 6 (3). http://www.borderlands.net.au/vol6no3_2007/arnold_invaders.htm.

Bayley, David H. 2006. *Changing the Guard: Developing Democratic Police Abroad*. Oxford, UK: Oxford University Press.

Beetham, David. 1999. *Democracy and Human Rights.* Cambridge: Polity Press.

Bellamy, Richard. 2008. *Citizenship: A Very Short Introduction.* Oxford, UK: Oxford University Press.

Benhabib, Seyla. 2004. *The Rights of Others. Aliens, Residents, and Citizens.* Cambridge, UK: Cambridge University Press.

Bermeo, Nancy. 2016. "On Democratic Backsliding." *Journal of Democracy* 27 (1): 5–19.

Bobbio, Norberto. 1996. *Left and Right: The Significance of a Political Distinction.* Chicago: University of Chicago Press.

Bonner, Michelle D. 2014. *Policing Protest in Argentina and Chile.* Boulder, CO: First Forum (Lynne Rienner).

Chan, Janet. 1996. "Changing Police Culture." *British Journal of Criminology* 36 (1): 109–34.

Clark, Rob. 2014. "A Tale of Two Trends: Democracy and Human Rights, 1981–2010." *Journal of Human Rights* 13 (4): 395–413.

Comaroff, John L., and Jean Comaroff. 2006. "Law and Disorder in the Postcolony: An Introduction." In *Law and Disorder in the Postcolony*, edited by Jean Comaroff and John L. Comaroff, 1–56. Chicago and London: The University of Chicago Press.

Cooley, Alexander. 2015. "Countering Democratic Norms." *Journal of Democracy* 26 (3): 49–63.

Coppedge, Michael, John Gerring, Staffan I. Lindberg, Svend-Erik Skaaning, Jan Teorell, David Altman, Michael Bernhard, M. Steven Fish, Adam Glynn, Allen Hicken, Carl Henrik Knutsen, Kyle L. Marquardt, Kelly McMann, Valeriya Mechkova, Pamela Paxton, Daniel Pemstein, Laura Saxer, Brigitte Seim, Rachel Sigman, and Jeffrey Staton. 2017. "V-Dem Codebook v7.1." Varieties of Democracy (V-Dem) Project.

Dahl, Robert A. 1971. *Polyarchy: Participation and Opposition.* New Haven: Princeton University Press.

Dahl, Robert A. 1990. *After the Revolution? Authority in a Good Society.* New Haven: Yale University Press.

Daleiden, J. Robert. 2006. "A Clumsy Dance: The Political Economy of American Police and Policing." *Policing: An International Journal of Police Strategies and Management* 29 (4): 602–24.

della Porta, Donatella. 1998. "Police Knowledge and Protest Policing: Some Reflections on the Italian Case." In *Policing Protest: The Control of Mass Demonstrations in Western Democracies*, edited by Donatella della Porta and Herbert Reiter, 228–52. Minneapolis, MN: University of Minnesota Press.

Diamond, Larry. 1997. "Is the Third Wave of Democratization Over? An Empirical Assessment." Working Paper #236, Helen Kellog Institute, March.

Diamond, Larry. 2015. "Facing Up to the Democratic Recession." *Journal of Democracy* 26 (1): 141–55.

Dubber, Markus Dirk. 2005. *The Police Power: Patriarchy and the Foundations of American Government*. New York: Columbia University Press.

Foucault, Michel. 1977. *Discipline and Punish: The Birth of the Prison*. New York: Vintage Books.

Fukuyama, Francis. 2015. "Why Is Democracy Performing So Poorly?" *Journal of Democracy* 26 (1): 11–20.

Hall, Stuart, Chas Critcher, Tony Jefferson, John Clarke, and Brian Roberts. 1978. *Policing the Crisis: Mugging, the State, and Law and Order*. London: MacMillan.

Hinton, Mercedes S., and Tim Newburn, eds. 2009. *Policing Developing Democracies*. London and New York: Routledge.

Hunter, Virginia J. 1994. *Policing Athens: Social Control in the Attic Lawsuits: 420–320 B.C.* Princeton, NJ: Princeton University Press.

Huntington, Samuel P. 1996. "Democracy's Third Wave." In *The Global Resurgence of Democracy* (2nd edition), edited by Larry Diamond and Marc F. Plattner, 3–25. Baltimore: Johns Hopkins University Press.

Isaac, Jeffery C. 2015. "The American Politics of Policing and Incarceration." *Perspectives on Politics* 13 (3): 609–16.

Jones, Trevor, Tim Newburn, and David J. Smith. 1994. *Democracy and Policing*. London: Policy Studies Institute.

Krastev, Ivan. 2016. "Liberalism's Failure to Deliver." *Journal of Democracy* 27 (1): 35–38.

Kymlicka, Will. 1995. *Multicultural Citizenship: A Liberal Theory of Minority Rights*. Oxford: Oxford University Press.

Levitsky, Steven, and Lucan Way. 2002. "The Rise of Competitive Authoritarianism." *Journal of Democracy* 13 (2): 51–66.

Levitsky, Steven, and Lucan Way. 2015. "The Myth of Democratic Recession." *Journal of Democracy* 26 (1): 45–58.

Linz, Juan J., and Alfred Stepan. 1996. *Problems of Democratic Transition and Consolidation: Southern Europe, South America, and Post-communist Europe*. Baltimore: Johns Hopkins University Press.

Lipsky, Michael. 1980. *Street-Level Bureaucracy: Dilemmas of the Individual in Public Service*. New York: Russell Sage Foundation.

Marenin, Otwin. 1985. "Police Performance and State Rule: Control and Autonomy in the Exercise of Coercion." *Comparative Politics* 18 (1): 101–22.

Marenin, Otwin. 1996. "Policing Change, Changing Police: Some Thematic Questions." In *Policing Change, Changing Police: International Perspectives*, edited by Otwin Marenin. New York: Garland Publishing.

McCoy, Alfred W. 2009. *Policing America's Empire: The United States, the Philippines, and the Rise of the Surveillance State*. Madison: The University of Wisconsin Press.

McFaul, Michael. 2004. "Democracy Promotion as a World Value." *The Washington Quarterly* 28 (1): 147–63.

McSherry, Patrice. 1997. *Incomplete Transition: Military Power and Democracy in Argentina*. New York: St. Martin's Press.

Møller, Jørgen, and Svend-Erik Skaaning. 2013. "Autocracies, Democracies, and the Violation of Civil Liberties." *Democratization* 20 (1): 82–106.

Muir Jr., William Ker. 1977. *Police, Streetcorner Politicians*. Chicago: The University of Chicago Press.

Munck, Gerardo. 2007. "The Study of Politics and Democracy: Touchstones of a Research Agenda." In *Regimes and Democracy in Latin America. Theories and Methods*, edited by Gerardo Munck, 25–37. Oxford, UK: Oxford University Press.

Munck, Gerardo. 2009. *Measuring Democracy: A Bridge between Scholarship and Politics*. Baltimore, MD: Johns Hopkins University Press.

National Advisory Commission on Civil Disorders. 1968. *Report of the National Advisory Commission on Civil Disorders*. Washington, DC: The US Government Printing Office.

Neocleous, Mark. 1998. "Policing and Pin Making: Adam Smith, Police and the State of Prosperity." *Policing and Society* 8: 425–49.

Neocleous, Mark. 2000. *The Fabrication of Social Order: A Critical Theory of Police Power*. Cambridge: Pluto Press.

O'Donnell, Guillermo. 1994. "Delegative Democracy." *Journal of Democracy* 5 (1): 55–69.

O'Donnell, Guillermo. 1999. "Horizontal Accountability in New Democracies." In *The Self-Restraining State: Power and Accountability in New Democracies*, edited by Andreas Schedler, Larry Diamond, and Marc F. Plattner, 29–51. Boulder, CO: Lynne Rienner.

Pateman, Carole. 1970. *Participation and Democratic Theory*. Cambridge, UK: Cambridge University Press.

Peruzzotti, Enrique, and Catalina Smulovitz. 2006. *Enforcing the Rule of Law: Social Accountability in the New Latin American Democracies*. Pittsburgh, PA: University of Pittsburgh Press.

Pinheiro, Paulo Sérgio. 1999. "The Rule of Law and the Underprivileged in Latin America: Introduction." In *The (Un)Rule of Law and the Underprivileged in Latin America*, edited by Juan E. Méndez, Guillermo O'Donnell, and Paulo Sérgio Pinheiro, 1–8. Notre Dame, IN: University of Notre Dame Press.

Plattner, Marc F. 2015. "Is Democracy in Decline?" *Journal of Democracy* 26 (1): 5–10.

Puddington, Arch. 2015. *Discarding Democracy: A Return to the Iron Fist*. Washington, DC: Freedom House. https://freedomhouse.org/report/freedom-world-2015/discarding-democracy-return-iron-fist.

Robinson, William I. 1996. "Globalization, the World System, and 'Democracy Promotion' in US Foreign Policy." *Theory and Society* 25 (5): 615–65.

Schmitter, Philippe C., and Terry Lynn Karl. 1991. "What Democracy Is ... And Is Not." *Journal of Democracy* 2 (3): 75–88.

Schumpeter, Joseph A. 1943. *Capitalism, Socialism and Democracy.* London: George Allen & Unwin.

Schwartzberg, Melissa. 2014. "Democracy." In *The Encyclopedia of Political Thought*, edited by Michael T. Gibbons, 851–62. Malden, MA: Wiley.

Sklansky, David Alan. 2008. *Democracy and the Police.* Stanford, CA: Stanford University Press.

Thomas, Martin. 2008. *Empires of Intelligence: Security Services and Colonial Disorder after 1914.* Berkeley: University of California Press.

Ungar, Mark. 2011. *Policing Democracy: Overcoming Obstacles to Citizen Security in Latin America.* Baltimore: Johns Hopkins University Press.

Waddington, P.A.J. 1998. "Controlling Protest in Contemporary, Historical and Comparative Perspective." In *Policing Protest: The Control of Mass Demonstrations in Western Democracies*, edited by Donatella della Porta and Herbert Reiter, 117–40. Minneapolis: University of Minnesota Press.

Waddington, P.A.J. 1999. "Police (Canteen) Sub-culture. An Appreciation." *British Journal of Criminology* 39 (2): 287–309.

Williams, Randall. 2003. "A State of Permanent Exception: The Birth of Modern Policing in Colonial Capitalism." *Interventions International Journal of Postcolonial Studies* 5 (3): 322–44.

PART I

Citizenship

CHAPTER 2

Police Abuse and the Racialized Boundaries of Citizenship in France

Cathy Lisa Schneider

The late great sociologist and social historian Charles Tilly believed that civilian control of the coercive apparatus was key to democratic development and stability. In contrast, the political science literature on democracy barely mentions police (see Bonner et al., Chapter 1). Yet, as Tilly has shown us, democracy requires that states exert control over the repressive apparatus and do so as impartial arbiters between competing networks of individuals. The less impartial, the more bound to particular trust networks, the more likely a democratic state is to experience democratic reversals. Even in stable democracies, some categories of citizen remain more exploited and stigmatized than others (see also Seri and Lokaneeta, Chapter 3 and Dupuis-Déri, Chapter 4). Members of more privileged categories of citizens often favor punitive policing of the most exploited and stigmatized groups. States dependent on the financial

Approximately half of this chapter is taken from various parts of the author's book: Schneider, Cathy Lisa. 2014. *Police Power and Race Riots*. Philadelphia, PA: Pennsylvania University Press. Reprinted with permission of the University of Pennsylvania Press.

C. L. Schneider (✉)
School of International Service, American University, Washington, DC, USA

© The Author(s) 2018
M. D. Bonner et al. (eds.), *Police Abuse in Contemporary Democracies*,
https://doi.org/10.1007/978-3-319-72883-4_2

resources and voting preferences of dominant groups consequently pursue policies that weaken police accountability and in so doing undermine democratic governance.

Like police in other countries, police in democratic France are more likely to use violence against members of stigmatized and exploited groups, in particular, against descendants of colonial subjects (particularly Arabs from North Africa and blacks from Africa and the Antilles) and Roma. Most French citizens believe that racial exploitation, while rife in the colonies, has been absent in France itself. This collective amnesia ignores the 130 years that Algeria was a district of France (composed of three departments). Europeans and their descendants had full voting rights and representation, and after 1870, so did Algerian Jews, few of whom had European ancestry. Algerian Arabs, in contrast, were disenfranchised, in both Algeria and mainland France. In 1945, Algerians on the mainland were granted citizenship rights, but were still required to carry identity cards marking them as "French Muslims," and singling them out for higher levels of police abuse. In this chapter, I examine the legacy of the racialized boundaries of citizenship in Algeria on the policing of stigmatized minorities in France. Through historical process tracing and ethnography, I show how policing and police abuse (as defined in the introduction to this volume), is central to both democratic governance and to democratic decay.

There are several unique aspects of French policing. First, France rejects racial and ethnic categorization. The French believe racial and ethnic constructions poison the relationship between citizens and the state. Minority groups that mobilize for civil rights are often accused of creating racial divisions. That has narrowed the options for stigmatized minorities to address discrimination and police violence. Second, the official role of the French police is to defend the state, not to protect and serve the community. Third, French police are centralized and recruited nationally. They answer to the minister of interior (until 2012, the gendarmes answered to the minister of defense) rather than to local authorities.

It was the Nazis that first centralized the French police, to facilitate the pursuit of Jews and resistance fighters. During Nazi occupation, only Paris retained a separate police force. The Nazis gave French fascists a degree of power they had only dreamed of in democratic France. The French secret police—the *Milice*—was more feared than the Gestapo, while the venal and corrupt North African police brigade (charged during the interwar years with policing Arab neighborhoods in Paris) compelled detained and brutalized French Arabs to act as informants

(Rosenberg 2006, p. 207). The deportations of Communists, resistance fighters, Popular Front leaders (including the Prime Ministers Leon Blum and Édouard Daladier) and above all Jews to extermination camps exceeded the numbers requested by their German superiors. Of the 75,721 people the French rounded up and deported, only 2567 survived. Another 4000 died in camps located inside France.

After Liberation, as Jim House and Neil MacMaster note, most "senior police officers or administrators during Nazi occupation retained their posts," and were assigned to counterinsurgency efforts both in the colonies and continental France (House and MacMaster 2006, p. 35). These officers were "involved in both forms of repression, drawing on a shared body of practice. Playing a key role, the Interior Ministry constantly circulated top officials between the Maghreb and Metropolitan France" (House and MacMaster 2006, p. 35). Such officers brought with them knowledge of key features of the Vichy system of control, including:

- The creation of specialized intelligence agencies of the policing of target groups (Jews, Algerians)
- The total control of minority populations
- Elaborate card-index files (*fichiers*) to identify and locate individuals
- Mass round-up operations involving street level stop and search checks or the surrounding and isolation of urban sectors, with house to house searches
- Special police investigative units
- Mass holding centers and camps for those rounded up, often with screening identification units
- Exceptional and discriminatory legislation aimed to identify and detain minorities (night curfews, special identity cards, administrative arrest) (House and MacMaster 2006, p. 35)

Maurice Papon, for instance, eventually imprisoned for his role in the arrest and deportation of 1560 Jews, was appointed the head of police in Constantine, Algeria; Rabat, Morocco; and later Paris. Other Nazi collaborators given important posts include Maurice Sabatier (a *pied-noir*, who should have stood trial with Papon, had he not died in 1989), Jean Chapel (appointed superprefect in Constantine, Algeria), Pierre Garat (head of Jewish Services during the occupation, transferred to Algeria in 1945), Pierre Somville (Papon's right-hand man and cabinet head, transferred to Algeria in 1945), and Pierre-René Gazagne (a vicious anti-Semite *pied-noir*) (House and MacMaster 2006, p. 35).

POLICING PARIS DURING THE ALGERIAN WAR

On July 14, 1953, the Parisian police opened fire on 4500 Algerians marching in a Communist demonstration at Place de la Nation. Six Algerians and one French trade unionist died, and another 150 were wounded (House and MacMaster 2006, p. 40). Jean Baylot, the head of the Paris Police, claimed Algerians had rushed the police. He used the conflict to reconstitute the North African brigade under a new moniker, the *Brigade des aggressions et violences* (BAV), or "anticrime task force" (Rosenberg 2006, p. 207). From that time forward the BAV performed hundreds of identity checks at night, often engaging in neighborhood sweeps and mass arrests (Blanchard 2006, p. 63). In August 1955, Algerians protested at the Goutte-d'Or police station against a police officer's use of a firearm while interrogating a pickpocket. The police accused Algerians of rioting, sealed the neighborhood, and engaged in a massive roundup. As the press noted that this operation marked "the purification of the North African milieu in the capital," four hundred of the detained Algerians were summarily deported (Blanchard 2006, pp. 63–64; 2012, 2013).

In March 1958, members of the Parisian police stormed the National Assembly shouting anti-Semitic slogans. To appease the police, Baylot, now Minister of Interior, invited Maurice Papon back from Morocco and appointed him head of the Paris police force. Papon brought with him "extensive experience of colonial intelligence and policing operations against the nascent insurrectionary nationalists" in Algeria and in Moroccan shantytowns (Blanchard 2012, p. 44). Papon mastered "the sociological profiling of urban populations, which involved the use of census data to map the location of particular classes and ethnic groups" (Blanchard 2012, p. 44). He brought both experiences to bear as head of the Paris police.

When Papon took office, over 180,000 Algerians were living slums and shantytowns in greater Paris. "The impenetrable warren of lanes provided a natural redoubt for FLN militants [the Algerian resistance Front de Libération Nationale, or National Liberation Front], a place in which arms and documents could be concealed, while leaders could avoid police raids by escaping through secret exits or by constantly moving residence between townships," note Jim House and Neil MacMaster (2006, p. 98). To weaken this network, the government began razing the shantytowns and replacing them with worker hostels (Société nationale

de construction de logements pour les travailleurs), temporary housing estates (*cités de transit*), and public housing projects (Habitations
à loyer modérées [HLMs]) (House and MacMaster 2006, p. 99). The
construction of HLMs in distant suburbs contributed to increasing racial
and spatial polarization. The government also agreed to Papon's request
to eliminate restrictions on the police's ability to penetrate Algerian
networks. An ordinance of October 7, 1958, allowed police to hold
Algerians for 15 days without charges and then deport them to army-run
camps in Algeria (Prakash 2010, p. 194).

As torture and extrajudicial killings grew, the FLN responded with
targeted killings of several police officers. In June 1961, however, as the
FLN unilaterally called a cease-fire, Papon expanded the police counterinsurgency offensive. Killings of North Africans increased to thirty-seven
(to seventy-five, according to Jean Luc Einaudi) in September, up from
seven in August and three in July (Prakash 2010, p. 107; Einaudi 2001,
pp. 363–65; House and MacMaster 2006, p. 107). On October 5,
Papon called for a citywide curfew for all Algerians and warned:

> In view of bringing an immediate end to the criminal activities of Algerian
> terrorists, new measures have just been taken by the Prefecture of the
> Police.... Muslim Algerian workers are advised most urgently to abstain
> from walking about during the night in the streets of Paris and in the
> Parisian suburbs, and most particularly during the hours of 8:30 p.m. to
> 5:30 a.m. (Ross 2002, p. 43)

In response, the FLN convoked an act of nonviolent civil disobedience.
Algerian families, including women and children, would march peacea-
bly but in direct defiance of the curfew. They chose October 17, 1961,
as the date. Papon preemptively ordered police to arrest all young men
who looked Algerian or whose identity cards indicated they were Muslim
(Gordon 2000, p. 2). He visited police precincts imparting the following messages: "Settle your affairs with the Algerians yourselves. Whatever
happens you are covered"; "For one blow give them ten"; "You don't
need to complicate things. Even if the Algerians are not armed, you
should think of them always as armed" (Ross 2002, p. 43).

On the evening of October 17, thirty thousand to forty thousand
unarmed men, women, and children, many in their best Sunday attire,
were met by about seven thousand police and members of special republican security forces, armed with heavy truncheons or guns. Police "let

loose on demonstrators in, among other places, Saint Germain-des-Prés, the Opéra, the Place de la Concorde, the Champs Elysée, around the Place de l'Étoile and, on the edges of the city, at the Rond Point de la Defense beyond Neuilly" (Napoli 1997): "At one end of the Neuilly bridge police troops and on the other," noted several police officers who witnessed the events, "CRS riot police slowly moved towards one another. All the Algerians caught in this trap were struck down and systematically thrown in the Seine. At least a hundred of them underwent this treatment. The bodies of the victims floated to the surface daily and bore traces of blows and strangulation" (Ross 2002, p. 43). Police continued to round up protestors, holding many in police stations, and as many as six thousand in sports stadiums. The protestors were shot, beaten, garroted, forced to run a gauntlet of police clubs, or thrown half alive and hogtied along with the dead, into the Seine. The arrests and killings continued throughout the month (Kedward 2005; Einaudi 1991; Ferrandez 2012).[1]

Journalists were warned against covering the demonstrations and kept away from the detention centers (Napoli 1997). Police reports describing Algerians as having opened fire were distributed to the media. Only after Papon was arrested in 1999 for complicity in the 1942 deportation of Jews from Bordeaux did the Lionel Jospin government acknowledge the police's excessive behavior and post a plaque to commemorate the killing of forty protesters. Although there has never been a complete accounting of the dead, most scholars put the number closer to two hundred, and some far higher (House and MacMaster 2006, p. 107; Einaudi 2001, pp. 347–70; Gordon 2000, p. 36; Ross 2002, p. 43; Rosenberg 2006, p. 19; Napoli 1997, p. 36).[2] Seven hospitals reported that 448 had been seriously wounded. The FLN's own inquiry recorded 2300 injuries, many of those rescued from the Seine (House and MacMaster 2006, p. 134). One survivor, who lost an eye and a testicle from a beating at the police station, recalled hearing Papon's words, "Liquidate this vermin for me, these dirty rats. Get to work. Do your business" (House and MacMaster 2006, p. 134).

Weeks later, the Communist Party marched in protest against terrorist actions by the paramilitary settler Organisation Armée Secrete, OAS, which had planted several bombs in metro stations in Paris and one in André Malraux's apartment, which blinded a four-year-old girl. The police shot at the demonstrators, killing eight people, three of them women and one a child. The "political and public outcry against these French deaths at Charonne, contrasts starkly with the absence of major public protest at the deaths of Algerians on October 17, 1961," notes one historian, when twenty times that number were killed (Kedward 2005, p. 345).

Racial Boundaries in the Aftermath of the Algerian War

On March 16, 1962, leaders of organizations representing the two sides of the Algerian War met in Évian to finalize peace plans. The terms of the agreement were, notes Todd Shepard, based on the claim—advocated by the FLN, its sympathizers in France, de Gaulle, the OAS, and the far right—that "Algerians as a group were so different ... from other French citizens, that they could not be accommodated within the French Republic" (Shepard 2006, p. 6). The new French consensus appeared to be expressed by de Gaulle to General Marie Paul Allard in 1959: "You cannot possibly consider that one day an Arab, a Muslim, could be the equal of a Frenchman" (Shepard 2006, p. 75).

By "inventing decolonization," in Shepard's words, French authorities retreated into the comfortable certainty that France had always lived up to its republican ideals (Shepard 2006, p. 75). France was free of the troublesome, racist, backward, and reactionary terror-wielding colony, and with it any recognition of, or policies to abate, racial discrimination in France. Yet classifying all Muslims as Algerians and all Jews and Algerians of European descent as French was not only contrary to republican values and everything France had argued for thirteen decades; it also welcomed into France the very same people, the so-called pied noirs, whose terrorist actions had turned the French public against the war. And it left those Algerians who had served in the French army in mortal danger. As Sartre put it in a scathing essay titled "The Sleep Walkers": "All anyone wanted to hold onto was this: It's over with Algeria, it's over.... We gave all power to a dictator so that he could decide, without asking us, the best means to end the affair: genocide, resettlement, and territorial partition, integration, independence, we have washed our hands, it is his deal" (Shepard 2006, p. 194).

Algerians as New Immigrants in France

At the end of the war, Algeria's economy was in ruins. The colonial government had driven two and a half million peasants into Centres de Regroupements, surrounded by barbed wire and mined mortifications.

When they were released in 1962, they lacked even the most basic resources for living off the land. Another migrant interviewed by Abdelmalek Sayad recalled,

> Algeria, land of unemployment. Algeria, no work, no factories. Algeria, where there are lots of hands, so many hands that there is no work for them. When you have nothing in your hands, no trade, and don't know how to do anything, you're not going to turn up in Algiers looking for work.... You come to France. There is work in France, everyone knows that. You never hear it said that so and so, that this one or that one has left, isn't working, is unemployed. It just doesn't happen. (Sayad 2004, p. 44)

Between 1962, when the war ended, and 1965, a total of 111,000 Algerians entered France. "No other European society had received such a large settler community from its colonial empire," notes Perry Anderson. "A million pieds-noirs expelled from the Maghreb, with all the bitterness of exiles," plus over two million Algerians, a combination that was "likely to release a political toxin," Anderson concludes (2004, p. 14).

On April 10, 1964, Algeria and France signed an agreement limiting migration and establishing a trimester review of the permitted quota based on the economic situation in both countries. The agreement was similar to those signed in 1963 between France and Tunisia and between France, Mali, and Mauritania, and the 1963 agreement between France and Senegal. But these agreements did not prevent the number of immigrants from continuing to grow, rising from 1,574,000 at the end of 1955 to 2,323,000 at the end of 1965. Between 1966 and 1975, three times as many immigrants arrived in France as had in the preceding decade. In 1972, the number of foreigners in France reached 6% of the population, or 3.6 million. The number of North Africans alone reached 1.1 million, including nearly 800,000 from Algeria (Bennoune 1975, p. 3).

Employers desperate to fill large labor shortages and impatient with formal paperwork skirted official channels and recruited labor directly. They sought legal recognition after the fact if at all. The number of migrants who came through formal channels fell to 21% in 1965 and 18% in 1968. In contrast, 65% of the new migrants were recruited directly by firms seeking cheap labor, and regularized after the fact (Silverman 1992, p. 43). This pattern was the reverse of that of previous waves of European immigration. It deprived the new migrants of access to government services and housing that had previously facilitated integration and assimilation. Making matters worse, violence against Algerians, in particular, reached such crisis proportions that when faced with the unwillingness of French authorities to prosecute the perpetrators, the Algerian government (fearing for the safety of its citizens) suspended further immigration to France.

The French police, for their part, kept the same system and personnel, including Papon. Although the BAV (anticrime task force) was merged into the regular police force, most of its members were deployed to North African neighborhoods (Prakash 2010, p. 291). A police report written by Papon's lieutenant, Pierre Someveille, laid out their concerns:

> The presence of nearly 200,000 persons originally from Algeria and African countries of French expression in the Paris region…. poses a problem to the public authorities whose solution should be to deploy a policy limiting entries combined with expulsion measures and systematic repatriation of all inadaptable or undesirable elements…. The control of these ethnic groups in the social, sanitary, administrative and political domains proves more urgent each day. (Prakash 2010, p. 293)

On July 1, 1968, France limited the number of Algerian immigrants to eleven hundred a month, and in December the country signed another agreement with Algeria making employment a condition of entry and capping immigration at thirty-five thousand a year (Bennoune 1975, p. 3). The twin issues of immigration and racism moved rapidly up the political agenda (Silverman 1992, p. 52). Most notably, 1965 marked the rise of Jean-Marie Le Pen as manager of the presidential campaign of the far-right candidate Jean-Louis Tixier-Vignacour. Tixier-Vignacour had been a member of Action Française in the 1930s, a veteran of the Vichy propaganda ministry in the 1940s, a supporter of the neo-fascist journal *Défense de l'Occident* in 1952, and an advocate for the OAS, General Raoul Salan, and Jean-Marie Bastien Thiry. Thiry was executed in 1962 for attempting to assassinate General de Gaulle after Algeria was granted independence. Le Pen had been a fascist street brawler in Paris in the 1940s and a torturer in Algeria in the 1950s (Gourevitch 2011). In the 1964 presidential race, Tixier-Vignancour pulled 5%. Later, he and Le Pen had a falling-out, as Tixier-Vignancour believed that the party needed to reach out to mainstream conservatives to survive, but Le Pen disagreed and broke the alliance.

In October 1969, a new right-wing party emerged out of the ashes of the now-banned fascist political group Occident. The new party, or *Ordre nouveau* (new order), included an array of Vichy leaders, many of who openly expressed nostalgia for German occupation. In addition to the Nazi collaborator, Vichy leader, and Holocaust denier François Duprat, the National Front included Victor Barthélomy, the former general secretary of Jacques Doriat's Parti Popular Français, who played a leading role in efforts to form a single Fascist Party during the occupation and establish a Nazi Europe after working with Mussolini in Italy. Doriat and Barthélomy were critical to the establishment of "a press, a cadre and a structure with a degree of local implantation" (Fysh and Wolfreys 2003, p. 109). Together with Tixier-Vignancour, Maurice Bardeche (a leading French fascist intellectual before and during the war and Holocaust denier after), and Oswald Mosley (the founder of the British Union of Fascists), formed the Mouvement social Européen before collaborating with Le Pen in the Algérie Francaise and Tixier-Vignancour campaigns.

Other members of the national leadership of the new front included François Brigneau, former member of Marcel Déat's Collaborationist National Popular Rally (RNP); Roger Holeindre, former member of the OAS; Roland Gaucher, former member of Déat's RNP; Léon Gaultier, former general secretary of the Waffen SS Division Charlemagne; Gilbert Gilles, former adjutant in the Waffen SS Division Charlemagne and former OAS member; Pierre Bousquet, former corporal in the Waffen SS Division Charlemagne; André Dufraisse, former member of the Parti Populaire Français, who also served in the Division Charlemagne; Jacques Bompard, former OAS supporter; and others of similar background. Concerned that their National Front's Nazi and Vichy origins would isolate them, Duprat advised that "explicit references to National Socialism be dropped" (Fysh and Wolfreys 2003, p. 110).

The Ordre Nouveau used the increased visibility of North African immigrants, the bitterness many French felt over the Algerian war, and the May 1968 uprising to reach out to conservative voters. The most influential Ordre Nouveau leader was the Nazi collaborator François Duprat. Duprat claimed that the "time was right to set up a National Front, open to all extremist sects which would contest elections on a program somewhere short of fascist revolution as a means of putting fascists in contact with potential recruits" (Fysh and Wolfreys 2003, p. 108). But the National Front was not fully formed until 1972, one year before the Ordre Nouveau was banned. To insulate the National Front from accusations of participation in the Nazi genocide, Duprat organized the publication and distribution of the basic texts of Holocaust denial. After Duprat's violent death from a car bomb in 1978, Jean-Marie Le Pen emerged as head of the National Front. In place of appeals for racial purity, Le Pen spoke of Europe's superior culture and civilizing mission and advocated the "humanitarian" repatriation of immigrants.

In 1973, Le Pen called "for a tough regulation of foreign immigration and in particular of immigration from outside Europe," blaming Arabs for falling wages, rising unemployment, increased crime, and the oil crisis (Ellinas 2010, pp. 174–75). Although Le Pen received only 0.74% of the vote in the next year's presidential election, the immigration issue moved up the political agenda. Anxious not to be upstaged by Le Pen, the newly elected president, Valéry Giscard d'Estaing (1974–1981), designated a new cabinet position: secretary of state for foreign workers. The first to hold this position, André Postel-Viney, suspended both primary immigration and family reunification before leaving office six months later, reducing the number of permanent immigrant workers from 204,702 in 1973 to 67,415 in 1975 (Ellinas 2010, p. 172). The ban on primary immigration was never lifted. The ban on family reunification was lifted after being ruled unlawful by France's highest administrative court, the Conseil d'état, in 1978.

D'Estaing's third secretary of state for foreign workers, Lionel Stoléru, argued that immigration was antithetical to the interests of the nation and offered immigrants ten thousand francs each to return to their country of origin (Silverman 1992, p. 57; Weil 1988, p. 10). While the offer was intended for North and sub-Saharan Africans, only the Spanish and Portuguese took Stoléru up on his offer (both groups were happy to return home after the fall of their nations' respective dictatorships). Stoléru also passed a circular (the Marcellin-Fontanet) permitting the police to expel any immigrant who failed to furnish proof of active employment or decent housing. "Police stepped up their presence in the ZUPS [*zones à urbaniser en priorité* or vulnerable neighborhoods] where these young people lived. Thousands of them would soon see the inside of police stations, courts and prisons. Many were expelled from France to the 'home' country of their parents, where they had never set foot. Most came back to France illegally, living clandestinely in their hometown" (Begag 2007, p. 12).

Immigrants protested these measures with hunger strikes in Valence, Toulouse, Paris, La Ciotat, Lyon, Bordeaux, Strasbourg, Mulhouse, Lille, Nice, Montpellier, Aix-en-Provence, and St. Etienne; walked off the job at the Boulogne-Billancourt factory of Renault (outside Paris) in April 1973; and with marches in Paris. "These were the first signs of a widespread mobilization," notes Silverman, "by foreign workers against discriminatory legislation and racism" (Silverman 1992, pp. 49–50). In the universities, North African students created the *Mouvement des travailleurs Arabes* (MTA) in 1972. Begag notes,

> Relations with law enforcement worsened. This degradation was further aggravated by the racism of the policemen 'repatriated' from Algeria after independence in 1962, many of whom had been recruited into the law enforcement services of metropolitan France, where they set about settling scores with the Arabs who had launched a war to gain independence and had then come and installed themselves in France. (Begag 2007, p. 13)

In 1977, approximately thirty young people in Vitry-sur-Seine, a southern suburb of Paris, attacked three policemen. D'Estaing convened the Peyrefitte Commission to report on violence. He began the report with a warning: "a feeling of *insécurité* (insecurity) … can itself engender violence in a society where the rule of law is no longer upheld" (Peyrefitte 1977, qtd. in Terrio 2009). Police commissioners blamed "the ecology of public housing projects marked by social anomie and class segregation" and deplored the immense bleak towers and lack of green spaces. "The city today has its Indians and its reservations," they warned (Peyrefitte 1977, qtd. in Terrio 2009, p. 69).

The commission's use of the word "insecurity" to refer to the feeling of unease provoked by a lawless society became standard political parlance. Over time the term grew in political significance, even when it did not correspond to actual crime. Between 1959 and 1979 penal sentences for juvenile offenders doubled, rising from 15 to 32% (Peyrefitte 1977, qtd. in Terrio 2009, p. 70). In June 1979, the police in Nanterre, a northern suburb of Paris, arrested dozens of young North Africans in a sweep that did not include a single white French youth. A group of young lawyers expressed outrage at the incident (Begag 2007, p. 13). The same year, a terrible incident of police brutality in the Lyon suburb of Vaulx-en-Velin further enraged Maghrébin youths. Seventeen-year-old

Abdelkrim Tabert had developed a strategy for taunting police, winning the admiration of other neighborhood youths. He would steal a moped and deliberately drive past the police. On September 15, 1979, a police patrol tried to arrest him. They surrounded him at a friend's apartment. Realizing that he was trapped, he slit his wrists. A shot was fired and rumors spread rapidly throughout the *banlieue*. As the police dragged Abdelkrim wounded and bleeding, his brothers and friends ran behind them. Soon several hundred North African youths surrounded the police holding Abdelkrim. Fighting broke out and a police superintendent was beaten. Police reinforcements arrived along with firemen, and protesters responded by throwing bottles, stones, garbage, and bicycle parts (Begag 2007, p. 15). Throughout 1979, confrontations between young people and police in the *banlieues* of Marseille, Paris, and Lyon were frequent. In 1980 the "Rock against Police" movement was created in Paris. On April 19, 1980, over one thousand young people assembled in a small plot in the twentieth arrondissement to dance to music and vent their hatred of police (Begag 2007, p. 15).

Segregation and the Politics of Policing in Paris

Housing emerged as a major issue in the 1970s, especially after the deaths of five African workers in apartment fires. Fifteen thousand residents of immigrant hostels marched in 1975, protesting rents and the rigid rules governing life in the hostels. The strike lasted until 1980, becoming the longest strike ever outside the workplace (Silverman 1992, p. 55). Most hostels were located in dilapidated inner-city neighborhoods and were often run by speculators, slumlords, and racketeers. In other cases, workers moved into bidonvilles or shantytowns to make room for arriving family members. Most homes in these areas were little more than shacks, lacking basic sanitary facilities, sewers, running water, and electricity. In the mid-1960s, over seventy-five thousand people were still officially classified as living in these bidonvilles (and most estimate the actual number to be as much as three times that), and the numbers continued to grow throughout the early 1970s (Hargreaves 1995, p. 69). The hostel-style accommodations created in 1956 to house Algerian workers were woefully insufficient as family members began to join the workers in Paris. In 1975, the French government shifted its strategies toward the housing crisis. It stopped investing in the construction of hostels and began investing considerable funds in the construction of better-quality public housing for immigrant families (Hargreaves 1995, p. 70).

However, construction lagged far behind the phasing out of the existing housing. The impetus behind building *Habitations à Loyer Modéré* (HLMs, or housing projects) in distant suburbs was fear of the threat posed by the network of Algerian bidonvilles inside Paris. Granted, some more benevolent public officials believed that placing HLMs in the *banlieues* near the factories where the workers were employed would reduce overcrowding in the city and give workers access to greenery and open spaces. In practice, however, there was little greenery and few parks were created. The construction of HLMs in the *banlieues* moved immigrants from the city center. One Algerian woman, I spoke to in Aubervilliers remembered her childhood in Paris with nostalgia: "I could walk for hours and hours. Paris is such a beautiful city to walk in, and everything was accessible. Out here in the *banlieues* there is nothing. It is ugly here, and it takes so long to get to Paris. I never seem to have the time." Another French Algerian woman I spoke with remembered the move quite bitterly: "I grew up in the Marais. It wasn't till we moved to the *banlieue* that I learned I was different. There I learned that foreigners are poor."

By the 1970s, the economic downturn had led to the closing of most factories in the *banlieues*. As the HLMs filled with immigrants, French tenants abandoned the area. "The French whose standard of living had been improving began to leave the suburbs," note Renee Zauberman and René Lévy, and "the public agencies responsible for the allocation of public housing filled them with former shantytown and slum-dwellers, along with new immigrants and large families, thus encouraging spatial and social segregation" (Zauberman and Lévy 2003, p. 1065). The problem was accentuated by the distance of the *banlieues* from the city center and the government's failure to build adequate public transportation to the area, pairing, as Paul Silverstein notes, "socioeconomic marginalization … with spatial isolation" (Silverstein 2006). The urban transportation network failed to keep pace with the growth of the suburban population. The metro reached a small minority of the closest suburbs, while the farther suburbs were served, if at all, by local train service. As was the case with the urban renewal policies pursued in the United States, the result was the increased segregation of poor immigrants and racial minorities in areas of concentrated poverty.

Police Reform and the Activation of Racial Boundaries in the First Socialist Administration

In 1981, the Socialist candidate François Mitterrand swept into office promising, among other reforms, to legalize immigrant organizations and grant residency permits to all foreign workers who had entered France before January 1, 1981. His election ended a hunger strike of several clergy members begun the previous month in the Lyon *banlieue* housing project Les Minguettes to protest the deportation of youths of North African origin. Mitterrand also vowed to abolish capital punishment, maximum-security quarters in prison, and deportation laws, and to enact sweeping revisions of the Penal Code and Code of Criminal Procedure. Last, he pledged to drastically reform the police force.

Many of Mitterrand's supporters had been students in 1968, and police reform was high on their agenda. The last wave of recruitment of police had been during the Algerian war, when the sole actual qualification was hatred of Arabs. The lack of accountability and professional standards had led to massive corruption: "Many policemen were involved in illegal activities," notes Bonelli; "some were pimps and most of them usually drunk during their service" (Bonelli 2012, p. 5). The director of the national police told him that "when he arrived to Paris in the early 80's, as a young officer, he was the only one not drinking and making sport of his service" (Bonelli 2012, p. 5). The government (taking advantage of a wave of retirements) implemented two major reforms. First, it institutionalized professional standards for the selection and training of new recruits. Second, it purchased new, more modern office equipment, vehicles, and weapons. "It is almost impossible to compare police behavior in the 70's with that of today," Laurent Bonelli insists. "This does not mean that there is no racism or alcoholism anymore in the police; but they have disappeared as structural factors" (Bonelli 2012, p. 6; 2008). Police reform, however, was stymied by the National F ront's stoking of racial fears and resentments. As National Front support grew, even in some traditional working class neighborhoods, mainstream parties were put on the defensive.

National Front leaders attacked the government for being soft on crime and immigration and for pursuing policies that threatened the security of middle- and working-class French families. Didier Fassin notes,

> The historic victory of the left in the general elections of 1981, after 23 years of conservative domination, provoked the restructuring of the French political landscape, with the rapid rise of the far right and the

weakening of the traditional right. The National Front built its success principally on two issues, immigration and security, often mixing the two by presenting immigrants, or their children, as the major source of insecurity. (Fassin 2013, p. xiv)

To maintain relevance the traditional right took up both issues with increased fervor. Even some Communist mayors, anxious to avoid being out-segued on immigration and crime, accused immigrants of engaging in drug trafficking (Ellinas 2010, pp. 172–73). Communist leaders that had been among the staunchest defender of immigrant rights, issued a call for the repatriation of immigrants and rejected proposals to grant them voting rights in national elections (Fassin 2013, p. 173). As politicians scrambled to out-tough each other on crime and immigration, police reform was jettisoned in favor of a crack down on crime in immigrant neighborhoods. For Algerians and other former colonial subjects, the attacks bore the familiar stain of colonial oppression. Fassin notes,

> In mid-twentieth-century Paris, the Algerian population, in spite of being French nationals, were seen as undesirables, and well documented raids on the neighborhoods where they were concentrated went along with a whole trail of violence, harassment, racist insults and illegal detentions. The continuity running through these repressive practices towards certain sectors of society, from laboring classes to working-class populations, and from colonial subjects to immigrants and minorities, should not be underestimated: the activity of law enforcement has always been focused on groups whose economic and social vulnerability was easily inverted into the threat of crime and a peril to security. (Fassin 2013, p. 216)

In the Les Minguettes suburb of Lyon, youths devised a game they called a *rodeo*. They would taunt the police, steal a car, provoke a chase, and, just as the police came near, jump out, set the car aflame, and run. In the summer of 1981, there were 250 *rodeos*. When the police killed a young man during such a *rodeo*, the neighborhood reacted forcefully. One young man told Silverstein, "It was from the moment of police provocations that the youth began to become aggressive.... The rodeos were to respond to everything they had undergone, they and their parents.... The rage they had in themselves was directed at the cars" (Silverstein 2005). Similarly, Fassin points out, "what is manifested in these frantic flights is past experience of interactions with the police, and their occasionally playful aspects should not mask the real base of irrepressible fear. In short, a sort of immune reaction which, unlike that produced by vaccination, allows the danger to which one is exposed to be recognized, but does not protect one from it" (Fassin 2013, p. 9).

THE PERSPECTIVE OF RESIDENTS OF THE *BANLIEUES*

During a meeting that I attended in Aubervilliers in 2002, a young Muslim (of Algerian descent) angrily accused France of hypocrisy: "We demand 'Republican' *flics* (cops) to give the same discourse and attitude [to everyone], not to treat us as slaves. The young respond [to this unfair treatment]. We don't have a Republican system of justice or Republican police.... Justice does not take care of poor people like us. I am boiling with hatred." Another, interviewed in December 2001, noted, "A foreigner has a state of exception from all the rights guaranteed the French—a different set of statutes for those who come from the colonies—racist laws, a different set of laws, a different justice." In a workshop that a researcher conducted with police and prisoners, one prisoner turned to the police and said, "It is you who has made me a criminal."[3]

French youths of Algerian descent saw continuity between police repression in colonial Algeria and that in Paris. According to a religious young Muslim man in Garges-lés-Gonesse,

> All the major political figures in France were colonial army officers in Algeria. Those experiences are fresh in their minds. Here it is just Algeria in France. France's record is worse than Israel's. In the National Assembly there are 560 deputies, and not one Muslim, Arab, or African. [There are some in the indirectly elected, less powerful senate]. Even in Israel there are Arab deputies.... Here there is continuity from colonization. It has only been 40 years since the independence of Algeria in 1962. Someone like Chirac was a soldier in Algeria. It is still fresh in their minds.... To them we are still immigrants.... When the right won, the police told young people here, OK, the party is over.

Algerians also saw continuity in the forms of violence directed against them. A religious young woman of Algerian descent said,

> There is a long history of police violence directed at Algerians. My grandfather was tortured in Algeria. All our grandfathers were tortured in

Algeria. It is what we all share.... [In France] we have a government that funds police to repress us. There are fewer and fewer teachers, more and more police. Young people face very aggressive police. It has gotten worse and worse every day.

Another young Muslim woman noted, "The police arrive in our neighborhood in large groups and are very aggressive and disrespectful. They ask everyone for IDs." One time she saw a boy take out his papers and the police purposely open them and drop them on the pavement. It was raining, so the papers got wet. He picked them up and gave them back to the officer. "Again, the officer tried to push the young person to react, but the boy didn't say anything. The policeman got more aggressive and asked for papers again. Then the police took one of the boys with him. When this boy was released from *garde à vue*, he had been beaten." The young people in the *banlieue*, another young Muslim woman told me: "no longer respect the law, so they break the law.... There is an institutionalization of abuse by the police. The police are supposed to represent the law but they break the law."

A press secretary to the Green Party presidential candidate in 2002 spoke at an event in a banlieue on the anniversary of Malcom X's birthday. The event was designed to bring together blacks, of which the speaker was one, and Arabs or Muslims in poor suburbs. He noted:

> Twenty years ago, they didn't speak of Islam; they spoke of Arabs, or Beurs. It is ethno/racial exclusion.... Now Islam is viewed as leading to terrorism. So, the discussion has changed to religion. But it is the same politics, the same carrot and stick.... The French Left are so generous, they defend the *sans papiers* (undocumented immigrants), never the Arabs or blacks, never those who have citizenship. They mobilize for the *sans papiers*. Among all the children of immigrants educated, with diplomas, none have a position of power in France ... Until you show force you will not have a political voice, and nothing will change.

CONCLUSION

On October 25, 2005, police chased three black and Arab youths in a poor suburb into an electric substation and abandoned them there, to the death of two of them. Two days later, police shot a tear gas canister into a mosque in the same neighborhood, after two youths they were pursuing ran inside and the guards refused to allow police to follow.

Hundreds of worshippers, most of them women and children, gasped for air, many hospitalized. After both incidents, the Minister of Interior, Nicolas Sarkozy, defended the police. After the second incident, Clichy-sous-Bois exploded. Riots spread to the neighboring banlieue (suburb), then the next, until 280 towns were consumed by flames. After three weeks, the government took the extraordinary measure, not taken since the Algerian War, of imposing a nationwide curfew to quell the fires. "Some people in pain, cut themselves," one neighborhood organizer told me, "these kids took all this pain and threw it outside. It was like externalizing their internal explosions."

In 2007, Sarkozy used his tough on crime mantle to successfully run for president. During the following ten years, notes Malek Boutih, an MP and former head of SOS Racism, the situation has grown worse: "There has been a decline that is approaching irreparable. In the last ten years, the suburbs stopped producing rioters. Now they are producing terrorists" (McPartland 2017). On November 13, 2015, at 9:40 p.m. gunman entered the Bataclan Theater and opened fire on the audience gathered to hear a death metal band. The massacre at the Bataclan Theater was the highest death toll that night: 90 of the 130 dead were killed there. Hundreds more were severely injured in simultaneous attacks on the Le Carillon bar, Le Petite Cambodge Restaurant, La Cas Nostra Pizzeria (17 died in the 3 attacks) and La Belle Epoque (where 19 died). The five sites were located in Paris's most diverse neighborhood: within a ten block radius of the apartment where I was living, and where I had gone home early that night to rest. I heard the ambulances, but it was not until a friend from the United States called to let me know what had happened that I thought I also heard screams and cries. Two assassins blew themselves up outside the St. Denis football stadium where a guard had blocked their entrance, killing one unfortunate bystander. In Paris, the dead were as diverse as the city itself and hailed from 20 countries. In the wake of the bloodiest terrorist attack in Parisian history, the government imposed a three-month state of emergency.

On December 6, 2015, the National Front won 6 out of 12 regions in the first round of regional elections. In the second round, the Socialists withdrew its candidates from regions where it ran third, and prevented the National Front from winning a single region. Nonetheless, the Socialist president embraced the National Front agenda. Under the state of emergency, extended for an additional three months, both the

Minister of Interior (in charge of police) and local police chiefs were granted exceptional powers, including the power to regulate or forbid circulation and gathering in some areas, impose a curfew, close places of gathering, impose house arrest, authorize administrative searches and seizures, day and night, without judiciary oversight. Police conducted 4292 warrantless raids, 612 house arrests, and 1657 identity and vehicle control stops. These measures led to only 61 terrorism-related criminal investigations, including only 20 under France's broadly defined offense of "criminal association in relation to a terrorist undertaking" (Amnesty International 2016). The other 41 resulted in lesser charges of glorifying terrorism. While the government's attempt to alter the constitution to make the State of Emergency permanent failed, continual renewals of the three-month state of siege turned, notes one Amnesty International Report,

> the generalized security threat into grounds for a constant state of emergency. The ongoing use of disproportionate sweeping executive powers, with few checks on their use, is resulting in a host of human rights abuses. In the long run, the choice between rights and security that the French people are being presented with is a false one. (Amnesty International 2016)

The French commission of inquiry into the November 2015 attacks concluded in July 2016, that the state of emergency had "limited impact" on improving security. Farhad Khosokravar, who spent decades working in French prisons observes: "For some inmates, especially those who were only nominally Muslim and non-practicing, violent aspirations emerge first, with religiosity—and often a very approximate understanding of Islam—grafting itself onto to them later" (Khosokrovar 2015). Amal Bentounsi, whose younger brother was fatally shot in the back by police, and who organized a massive nonviolent March for Dignity on the 10th anniversary of the deaths of the two youths electrocuted in 2005, concurs: "I do not wish to justify what Amedy Coubali did [the man who shot the people in the kosher supermarket in January 2015] but it is not mere coincidence that when he was younger his best friend was shot in the head by police. This is what happens when there is no justice." It is impossible to understand the current wave of terrorist violence in France without accounting for the impact of discrimination, racial profiling, and police violence, and abuse.

Yet, the response of the government has been to double down on more of the same. In the third week of September, 2017, President Emmanuel Macron, a former Socialist, proposed new antiterrorism measures that would, for millions of French citizens in urban areas, in the words of Patrick Weil (a French scholar long opposed to the recognition of racial distinctions), resemble "a precedent in our history: The Native Code" (Weil 2017), the most hated and discriminatory anti-Arab legislation in Algeria.

If political scientists are to better understand democratic governance, they must put policing at the heart of the discussion. As this chapter demonstrates, unless police are deployed impartially to serve and protect the rights of all its citizens, democracy is hollow. How political authorities choose to deploy the police and how the police in turn exercise power, does more than delineate the boundaries of citizenship. It also determines the durability of democracy itself.

NOTES

1. Kedward estimates the number killed at two hundred (2005, p. 345). Einaudi estimates the number killed at 325 (2001, pp. 347–56, pp. 349–70). He includes legally registered deaths, legal claims pursued for those missing, and deaths listed by medical-legal authorities. Fernandez estimates the number at 200 dead (2012, museum exhibit).
2. House and MacMaster document 105 North Africans violently killed that month but estimate that the number was at least 121 given the large number who never reached the morgue (2006, 160).
3. These were a series of focus groups conducted with prisoners in the juvenile detention center Bois d'Arcy.

REFERENCES

Amnesty International. 2016. "France: Renewal of State of Emergency Risks Normalizing Exceptional Measures." *Amnesty*, December 15. https://www.amnesty.org/en/latest/news/2016/12/france-renewal-of-state-of-emergency-risks-normalizing-exceptional-measures/.

Anderson, Perry. 2004. "Union Sucreé." *London Review of Books* 18. http://www.lrb.co.uk/v26/n18/perry-anderson/union-sucre.

Begag, Azouz. 2007. *Ethnicity in the Balance*. Omaha: University of Nebraska Press.

Bennoune, Mahfoud. 1975. "Maghribin Workers in France." Middle East Research and Information Project Reports 34.

Blanchard, Emmanuel. 2006. "Police Judiciaire et Pratiques d'Exception Pendant la Guerre d'Algéri." *Vingtiéme Siècle: Revue d'Histoire* 2: 61–72.

Blanchard, Emmanuel. 2012. "La Goutte d'Or, 30 Juillet 1955: Une Émeute au Coeur de la Métropole Coloniale." *Actes de la Recherche en Sciences Sociales* 5: 98–111.

Blanchard, Emmanuel. 2013. "La Goutte d'Or, 30 July 1955: A Riot in the Heart of the Colonial City." *Les Mots son Importants.* http://lmsi.net/La-Goutte-d-Or-30-juillet-1955.

Bonelli, Laurent. 2008. *La France a peur.* Paris: La Découverte.

Bonelli, Laurent. 2012. "Governing the Police: Political Bargaining and Organizational Outputs in the French Police Reforms (1982–2010)." Presented at the International Political Science Association Annual Conference, Madrid.

Einaudi, Jean Luc. 1991. *La bataille de Paris, 17 Octobre 1961.* Paris: Seuil.

Einaudi, Jean Luc. 2001. *October 1961: Un massacre á Paris.* Paris: Librarie Arthéme Fayard.

Ellinas, Antonis A. 2010. *The Media and the Far Right in Western Europe: Playing the Nationalist Card.* Cambridge: Cambridge University Press.

Fassin, Didier. 2013. *Enforcing Order: An Ethnography of Urban Policing.* Cambridge: Polity Press.

Ferrandez, Jacques. 2012. "Algérie 1830–1962, with Jacques Ferrandez." *Exhibition at the Musée de l'Armée,* Paris.

Fysh, Peter, and Jim Wolfreys. 2003. *The Politics of Racism in France.* New York: Palgrave Macmillan.

Gordon, Daniel A. 2000. "World Reactions to the 1961 Pogrom." *University of Sussex Journal of Contemporary History* 1: 1–6.

Gourevitch, Philip. 2011. "No Exit: Can Nicolas Sarkozy—And France—Survive the European Crisis?" *New Yorker,* December 12. http://www.newyorker.com/reporting/2011/12/12/111212fa_fact_gourevitch?currentPage=all.

Hargreaves, Alec G. 1995. *Immigration, "Race" and Ethnicity in Contemporary France.* New York: Routledge.

House, Jim, and Neil MacMaster. 2006. *Paris 1961: Algerians, State Terror and Memory.* New York: Oxford University Press.

Kedward, Rod. 2005. *France and the French: A Modern History.* Woodstock and New York: Overlook.

Khosokrovar, Farhad. 2015. "The Mill of Muslim Radicalization in France." *The New York Times,* January 25. http://www.nytimes.com/2015/01/26/opinion/the-mill-of-muslim-radicalism-in-france.html.

McPartland, Ben. 2017. "Why the French Banlieues are Ripe for a Repeat of the 2005 Riots." *The Local,* February 14. http://www.thelocal.fr/20151027/france-ripe-for-repeat-of-2005-riots.

Napoli, James J. 1997. "A 1961 Massacre in Paris: When the Media Failed the Test." *Washington Report on the Middle East Affairs* 36. http://www.wrmea.

org/wrmea-archives/185-washington-report-archives-1994–1999/march-1997/2464-a-1961-massacre-of-algerians-in-paris-when-the-media-failed-the-test-.html.

Peyrefitte, Alain. 1977. Réponse à la violence. Rapport à M. Président de la République présenté par le Comité d'Etudes sur Violence, la Criminalité, et la Délinquance.

Prakash, Amit. 2010. *Empire on the Seine: Surveillance, Citizenship, and North African Migrants in Paris (1925–1975)*. New York: Columbia University Press.

Rosenberg, Clifford. 2006. *Policing Paris*. Ithaca: Cornell University Press.

Ross, Kristin. 2002. *May '68 and Its Afterlives*. Chicago: University of Chicago Press.

Sayad, Abdelmalek. 2004. *The Suffering of the Immigrant*. London: Polity Press.

Schneider, Cathy Lisa. 2014. *Police Power and Race Riots*. Philadelphia: Pennsylvania University Press.

Shepard, Todd. 2006. *The Invention of Decolonization: The Algerian War and the Re-making of France*. Ithaca, NY: Cornell University Press.

Silverman, Maxim. 1992. *Deconstructing the Nation: Immigration, Racism and Citizenship in Modern France*. London: Routledge.

Silverstein, Paul A. 2005. "Urban Violence in France." *Middle East Report Online*, November. http://www.merip.org/mero/interventions/urban-violence-france.

Silverstein, Paul A. 2006. "Postcolonial Urban Apartheid." Presented at the Social Science Research Council [SSRC] Conference on "Riots in France," New York City.

Terrio, Susan. 2009. *Judging Mohammed: Juvenile Delinquency, Immigration and Exclusion at the Paris Hall of Justice*. Palo Alto, CA: Stanford University Press.

Weil, Patrick. 1988. "La Politique Française d'Immigration." *Pouvoirs* 47: 45–60.

Weil, Patrick. 2017. "Le projet de loi antiterroriste rappelle le code de l'indigénat." *Le Monde*, Septembre 26, 2017. http://www.lemonde.fr/idees/article/2017/09/27/patrick-weil-le-projet-de-loi-antiterroriste-rappelle-le-code-de-l-indigenat_5191957_3232.html.

Zauberman, Renee, and René Lévy. 2003. "Police, Minorities and the French Republican Ideal." *Criminology* 41 (1): 1065–100.

CHAPTER 3

Police as State: Governing Citizenship Through Violence

Guillermina Seri and Jinee Lokaneeta

"We say that governments go by, and repression stays." CORREPI

On January 2, 2017, major Indian national newspapers reported that a 25-year-old man, Sompal, had died under mysterious circumstances, falling from the terrace of the Adarsh Nagar Police Station in the capital of India, Delhi. The police detained Sompal on December 28, 2016 in relation to a quarrel. Subsequently, his body was found 5 kilometers (about 3 miles) from the police station in a bloodied condition. The ensuing scandal exposed a police cover-up of Sompal's death, to escape scrutiny and accountability. As the story unfolded, it emerged that the Station House Officer (SHO) in charge of the police station along with five others transported Sompal's body in an official car and dumped it near a Metro Station where it was spotted by a passerby. The SHO initially denied his role, alleging that he went on leave right after the incident, but later was

G. Seri
Union College, Schenectady, NY, USA

J. Lokaneeta (✉)
Department of Political Science and International Relations,
Drew University, Madison, NJ, USA

© The Author(s) 2018
M. D. Bonner et al. (eds.), *Police Abuse in Contemporary Democracies*,
https://doi.org/10.1007/978-3-319-72883-4_3

55

implicated by others who admitted having followed his orders to clean up the blood stains from the police station courtyard where Sompal fell.[1] The family remains unconvinced that Sompal, the sole breadwinner in a household with aging parents who migrated to Delhi from the state of Madhya Pradesh in search for a better living, would jump from the terrace of the police station. Evidence that Sompal was detained and tortured by three constables gives support to their skepticism.

Unfortunately, the death of Sompal is far from exceptional. If visible police and other state abuses in authoritarian regimes concentrate global media and scholarly attention, the conditions of law, human rights, and citizen guarantees in democracies should contribute to make them a rare occurrence. That state abuses are not a rare occurrence define a problem that has only recently been examined. Even in societies in which democratic institutions and the rule of law have been well established for decades, the poor and members of non-hegemonic religious and other groups often find their rights ignored, abandoned in a borderland "between minimal rights (or 'resistance') and a straight denial of rights," as Etienne Balibar (2008) observes (also see Schneider, Chapter 2; Dupuis-Déri, Chapter 4). Those hundreds of millions referred to as the new "precariat," that neoliberalism leaves "without an anchor or stability," as Guy Standing (2011) describes them, seem most likely to experience abuses. Echoing this volume's concern with the worldwide decay of democracy, this chapter explores one of democracy's pillars: the conditions of, and exclusions from citizenship, and the ways in which police abuse erodes fundamental citizen rights and protections in democracy (Maranhão Costa 2011).

With a long pedigree in political theory, the study of citizenship has mostly focused on formal legal institutions and procedures, suggesting the progressive expansion of rights and franchise. No less consequential, however, the grassroots, daily governing practices that shape effective access to and exclusions from rights have only recently begun to be explored. Policing is one such salient practice as it is part of the administrative state apparatuses that categorize individuals and filter experiences of citizenship. Police and administrative mechanisms of exclusion are at play in democracies, from India and Argentina to France or the United States (see Schneider, Chapter 2; Squillacote and Feldman, Chapter 6; Davenport et al., Chapter 7). In France, the police have been strategic in stigmatizing, criminalizing, and excluding citizens of North African descent, as Cathy Schneider shows in this volume (Chapter 2). In the United States, an "unprecedented" expansion of criminalization and imprisonment since the 1970s, known in no other full democracy, has led to the rise of what Lerman and Weaver (2014, p. 5) characterize as "custodial citizenship." At a time when over a third of the population, especially young African American males and poor citizens are caught up in the criminal system, with over five million citizens having lost their voting rights, citizenship is losing strength.

Acknowledging that exclusion from citizenship may adopt various forms, in this chapter, we are interested in violent, deadly exclusions in the modality of custodial deaths. Policing enacts technologies of governance through which, as Michel Foucault noted, power "reaches into the very grain of individuals, touches their bodies and inserts itself into their actions and attitudes, their discourses, learning processes and everyday lives" (Foucault 1980, p. 39). The reach of police agents in everyday interactions with citizens, backed with the use of force, makes the police one of the most widespread and decisive organs of government and an extended node of stateness. Through localized, individualized police interventions, the state not only asserts itself but also categorizes individuals and groups, alternatively shaping and protecting, taking life and letting some die—along the biopolitical rationale of modern governance conceptualized by Foucault (2003). Yet the administrative rationale transpiring in these processes, while disciplining targeted populations, is at odds with the rationale of self-governing citizens and can lead to their violent exclusion—as in the extreme case of custodial deaths.

Despite the remarkable expansion of rights in Argentina and judicial independence and progressive practices in India, everyday grassroots governance tells a story in which historic forms of exclusion are perpetuated most violently and visibly through policing. In this regard, a subject of concern for activists and scholars alike is the tension between liberal constitutional provisions—both in India and Argentina, and progressive judicial rulings in India—versus the lack of implementation such that they often end up being symbolic acts. Showing a stubborn persistence, police abuses, torture, extrajudicial killings, and deaths in prisons and police stations take place routinely in democratic India and Argentina, gaining visibility only as communities mobilize and reach out to the media. Thus, beyond significant differences in historical and institutional trajectories, forms of social and political organization, state–society relations, and policy constraints, similarities and parallels in patterns of custodial deaths seem remarkable in democratic India and Argentina.

While rooted in political theory, the chapter draws loosely on what comparative politics refers to as the method of most different systems comparison. We show how police governance in very different social and political contexts contributes to reproduce internal exclusions from citizenship. Our findings highlight parallel mechanisms of both formal and informal, legal and extralegal state violence, institutional practices, and public discourse through which states regulate access to rights and citizenship in ways that tend to remain concealed and tolerated. More broadly, approaching the state as a series of mobile, dynamic, reconstituting governing networks, we address the persistence of police abuses and extrajudicial killings in democracies, and the ways in which these practices regulate and reshape identities, access to rights, state power, and the experience of citizenship.[2]

Violent exclusions from citizenship adopt different modalities and traditions, often involving the definition of areas, zones, or pockets of formal or informal suspension of the law that restrict access to the protections of rights and citizenship. While police abuses have far from vanished from the wealthier democracies in the global North, their pervasiveness and consequences for citizenship seem evident across the global South. An extreme manifestation of the dynamics of police governance, deadly police abuses expose the police's imperviousness to the egalitarian principles and practices of democracy and their role in reinforcing societal inequalities and inscribing citizenship's boundaries.

Only in cases of outrageous evidence, after communities and civil and human rights groups mobilize along with family members, do the media and the authorities pay attention to custodial deaths and abuses that otherwise remain in the dark. In what follows, we first revisit the main components of citizenship and the role of policing in granting or denying access to the actual enjoyment of rights. Next, we characterize policing and judicial institutions, the status of democracy and rights, and similar patterns of custodial deaths in India and Argentina. As other chapters in this book show, the modalities of violent exclusion from citizenship revealed in India and Argentina seem to be present more broadly across the democratic world. Our chapter draws together its implications for the status of rights and citizenship.

CITIZENSHIP AND VIOLENT EXCLUSIONS

Citizenship carries full membership in political communities, with civic duties, protections, and rights to participation and self-determination, freedom of expression, movement, assembly, and access to a fair trial and legal redress. Whether based on birth, blood ties, or naturalization, states stipulate different conditions to recognize individuals as citizens. Such definitions, historical and contingent, pose structural limits to membership in a political community, without which political philosophers from Aristotle to Arendt agree that human life cannot be fully realized. Along these lines, at the core of citizenship, Balibar (2008, p. 530) highlights the possibility for individuals to "claim rights in the public sphere" or at least not to be excluded from the exercise of rights.

A formal and legal category, citizenship's key components expand into collective identities, political membership, and social rights, which can develop together or separately (Benhabib 2004). The comparative experience of citizenship suggests that different categories of rights may alternatively expand and contract, as well as undergo decay. This insight elaborates upon, and qualifies, T.H. Marshall's original view of civil, political, and social rights as progressive, accumulated sets of rights (Marshall 1992). Acknowledging gaps between the formal recognition and effective enjoyment of rights, the possibility of reversals makes citizenship a project under permanent construction, with access mediated by identities and social hierarchies. While poor citizens living in ghettoes or shantytowns are entitled to the formal protections of citizenship, internal forms of exclusion persist as a result of "representations, social conditions, and political practices" (Balibar 2008, p. 530).

In conditions of abandonment heightened by a shrinking public sphere, job market, and social policies associated with neoliberalism, citizens experience "a double bind situation" (Balibar 2008, p. 536). Entitled to speak up and fight for their rights and recognized as political agents yet also "excluded from the possibility of active political participation" (Balibar 2008, p. 536) various forms of exclusion—often violent—tend to cancel the formal recognition of their status. Contemporary analyses of citizenship such as Balibar's, as we can see, complicate the progression of rights earlier described by Marshall (Balibar 2008, p. 536).

This is where policing enters the picture, we argue, carrying out visibly exclusionary practices. Often dismissed as instrumental, yet authorized to enforce laws and regulations and maintain order, police officers have in their hands unique prerogatives including the power of arrest and the use of force. In their everyday search to distinguish between "productive," "decent" citizens and criminals, police agents help to construct them by imposing social hierarchies and identities onto people's bodies.

Through myriad interventions, police agents place people along contingent categories of race, caste, religion, class, or gender allowed access to different levels of citizenship, or none, in ways that echo dominant social hierarchies. These categories allow us to understand how democracies can at once formally acknowledge and informally undermine citizen rights. Recalling Iris Marion Young's (1989) notion of differentiated citizenship, Anupama Roy (2017) also points to the ways in which a universal conception of citizenship and equality fails to recognize the membership of a group that actually mediated such an experience. In other words, belonging to a marginalized religious minority group in India, for instance, may transform the very experience of citizenship despite formal equality. Filtered by interventions that tend to criminalize the lifestyles of the poor and the socially vulnerable, individuals are selectively recognized for access to rights and citizenship or abandoned outside the law, on a case-by-case basis. Guillermina Seri (2012), in her previous work on Argentina, has noted the ways in which the police categorize people to sort out or construct criminals, thus separating the worthy people to protect—*la gente* (the people)—from those both portrayed and treated as threats—*delincuentes* (criminals). Upendra Baxi (2002) has revisited hierarchies of citizenship in ways relevant to our study. Baxi characterizes three sections of marginalized citizens who he calls subject, insurgent, and gendered citizens. These groups, unlike the super citizens who are beyond the law and the negotiating elite citizens, represent the impoverished majority of the population: subject citizens

> (…for whom the law applies relentlessly and for whom the presumption of innocence stands inverted); insurgent citizens, often *encountere*d or exposed to vicious torture, whose bodies construct the expedient truths of the security of the state; *gendered citizens* (women, lesbigay, and transgender people, recipients, and often receptacles, of inhuman societal and state violence and discrimination) and finally (without being exhaustive) the PAPs-citizens, the project affected peoples who remain subjects of state practices of lawless development. (Baxi 2002, p. 59, fn 30)

While the police may not create the societal hierarchies themselves, they do play a role in determining the targets of their violence. Thus, while recent critiques of citizenship have rightly pointed to ways in which citizenship is mediated by particular group identities, Baxi helps us think about how such definitions of citizenship actually become the basis of their interaction with the police.

How can we explain the persistence of grassroots state abuses alongside decades of democratization and the expansion of citizenship rights? Not just a legacy of military dictatorships or colonialism, abusive police practices appear as "part of a model of social control" with long-lasting historical roots (Maranhão Costa 2011; also see Schneider, Chapter 2; Clarke, Chapter 8). Supported on tacit acceptance, it serves to discipline those deemed undesirable—such as the poor and indigenous, or other marginalized identities, and to prevent them from full access to the exercise and protections of citizenship. Abusive policing also targets immigrants, who tend to be denied citizenship and legal and occupational status, which places them into extremely vulnerable conditions, as part of the *precariat* (Standing 2011, p. 96).

While policing is not the only arena in which exclusions of rights occurs, judicial and political actors being significant players as well, the police do play a major role in creating and perpetuating the experiences of exclusion from citizenship, often with deadly consequences. Going further, we contend that this is not just about ineffectiveness but also about exclusionary governmental regimes awkwardly overlapping with and utilizing the institutions of liberal democracy.

Along these lines, Daniel Brinks has conjectured the existence of informal, unwritten rules encouraging the police to kill "perceived violent criminals" and providing them with immunity in the performance of such a "social cleansing function" (2006, p. 232). Thus, Brinks (2006, p. 224) notes,

> An informal institution that permits the killing of perceived violent criminals is the operative rule in Buenos Aires and Sao Paulo. The rule of conduct included in this institution is applied by actors within the legal system—including the police, prosecutors, and judges—as evidenced by cases in which clear violations of the law come to the attention of the legal system and are not punished. The police enforce the rule through the use of violence against complainants and witnesses, and by withdrawing cooperation from the courts that are supposed to supervise them. (...) For all practical purposes, then, the rule that governs is one of impunity for police officers who kill, at least so long as they are seen to be carrying out their social cleansing function.

Markus Dubber (2005), in turn, has traced the history of the police as a patriarchal modality of governance, based not on rights but on force, in which police agents operating in the way of a head of the household exert violence over members of the community perceived not as resources but as nuisances, unproductive, or insurgent. Whether an informal institution, or a parallel modality of governance, police, then, enact distinct governmental practices that are incompatible with the principles of democracy and citizenship but are sought to be made compatible.

In this perspective, a major dimension of policing, we argue, is to put individuals into different categories such as those identified by Baxi, only some of whom are de facto recognized for citizenship protections. As the most pervasive state organ, the police make visible a biopolitical mechanism administering both access to and violent exclusions from citizenship.

The persistence of violent exclusions from citizenship reflects gaps, losses, and reversals in the actual recognition of access to rights. If citizen exclusions of members of vulnerable groups may be more apparent in India and Argentina, these societies are far from outliers. Growing disenfranchisement in the United States reveals a similar trend, where a number of poor "custodial citizens" are stripped of political rights through criminalization, and others learn to "stay invisible" to avoid police harassment (Lerman and Weaver 2014; also see Squillacote and Feldman, Chapter 6; Davenport et al., Chapter 7 in this volume).

Our research exposes modalities of accommodation of violence within liberal democratic institutions even as formal rights and safeguards expand. As Jinee Lokaneeta (2011) has shown in her previous work on torture in India and the United States, even Supreme Court discourses in both contexts have been ambivalent about the use of excess violence by police, facilitating their persistent use of torture. We make the argument here that while legal discourses may enable torture to some extent by not defining it precisely or allowing for gaps within the law (Lokaneeta 2011), the police ultimately govern the everyday experience of such a regime of violence. Such violence manifests most starkly in its use against those marginalized in society, without necessarily affecting the formal institutional democratic and citizenship framing in India or Argentina.

We review the main traits of policing in each country next in order to better understand how these exclusions occur. Beginning with a brief introduction to the structure of policing in each of the countries to give a sense of the extent of police interaction with citizens and citizens' attitudes toward them, we then explain the patterns of custodial deaths in both contexts and consider the judicial and civil society response to the patterns of police violence and abuse that remain as challenges in both countries. In conclusion, we analyze the role of the police in enabling the violent exclusions in the practice of citizenship.

POLICING IN INDIA AND ARGENTINA

After achieving independence from Britain in 1947, India became a democratic constitutional republic in 1950. The Indian constitution, progressive and democratic, enshrines fundamental rights, including those related to liberty and equality, as well as a visionary section defined as Directive Principles, which are gradually legislated as rights such as education and employment guarantees.

In article 246, the Indian Constitution "assigns the responsibility of policing" to the 29 states. Each state can set its own rules for police recruitment and governance. In turn, a central police governs seven additional union territories, while the central/federal government can send other armed guards to the states, from time to time. As there is no national or federal police, the upper ranks of the state forces come from the central government. Once recruited through the Indian Police Service Examinations, new members of the police are sent to the states.

Despite states' autonomy to organize their policing, police bodies in India remain modeled on the 1861 Police Act introduced by British colonial rule. Neither the various police commission reports, nor the work of committees, or the recent efforts on the part of the Supreme Court have altered the structure and functioning of the Indian police, which has undergone little change since its creation.

Similar to India, Argentina not only has 23 autonomous provincial forces and the Metropolitan Police in the city of Buenos Aires but also has the Federal Police to deal with federal crimes throughout the national territory and the recently created Aeronautic Police, which patrols airports. In addition, in recent years, terrestrial and naval border patrols (the Gendarmería and Prefectura) have also been put in charge of policing protests and poor neighborhoods.

In 2014, the Indian police had just over 1.7 million agents. For a population of 1.22 billion, this leaves a ratio of one police officer for every 708 people (Commonwealth Human Rights Initiative 2015, p. 46; Police Organisation in India 2008). Relatively higher in Argentina, with one police agent for every 155 people, or 558 police agents per hundred thousand, in the early 2000s, the number of police agents ranged from 215 to 245 thousand and private security guards from 75 to 200 thousand (Pontón 2007, p. 174). While the lower number of police agents in India may contribute toward the abuse, as we point out, the patterns of abuse are actually similar in both Argentina and India thereby suggesting that increasing the number of police agents alone may not lead to decline in state violence.

Despite the much higher ratio of police to citizens in Argentina, 62.4% of Argentine 2015 Latinobarometro survey respondents did not acknowledge the police as efficient, transparent, well trained, or as respecting human rights, and 63.6% of respondents expressed little to no trust in the police.[3] Distrust seems higher among citizens from vulnerable groups, as 70.6% of respondents self-identified as black and 71.7% of respondents self-identified as indigenous had little to no trust in the police.

Distrust of the police has deep roots in Argentina. Already in the early twentieth century, torture of criminal suspects was known as a police routine (Rejali 2008). Police abuses targeted immigrants, the poor, and political dissidents (Kalmanowiecki 2000; Caimari 2009). Starting in 1930, a series of coups d'états opened half a century of military rule and states of emergency. Conditions worsened in the 1960s, as the National Security Doctrine encouraged the identification of some individuals as "internal enemies." Placed under military control, police forces participated in kidnappings, torture, and killings. Abuses with police participation in Argentina escalated under the 1976–1983 military dictatorship, reaching genocidal proportion with 30 thousand forced disappearances, hundreds of clandestine death camps, and hundreds of thousands of exiles. Understandably, decades after the return of democracy, citizen distrust of the police continues in Argentina.

In the 2010–2014 World Values Survey, 23.2% of Indian respondents report to trust their police "A great deal," in contrast to only 4.1% of Argentines (World Values Survey 2012, 2013). Yet on other measures Indians have similarly negative evaluations of their police forces. Reports by human rights groups have noted high levels of distrust in the Indian police, including a 2005 survey in which 87% of respondents said the police were corrupt and 75% reported to have received poor quality service (Human Rights Watch 2009, p. 18). Custodial abuses and violence disproportionately affect the poor and socially vulnerable, including migrants, religious minorities (Muslims and Christians), lower castes, women, and tribals. Along these lines, three Directors General of Police, Sanjeev Dayal (Maharashtra), Deoraj Nagar (Uttar Pradesh), and K Ramanujam (Tamil Nadu) recently admitted that minorities, in particular Muslims, have a "trust deficit" toward the police. Muslims, a newspaper report notes, "see them [the police] as 'communal, biased and insensitive…. ill-informed, corrupt and lacking professionalism.'"[4]

Despite such negative evaluations of current policing practices, democracy and the rule of law made a significant, positive difference in Argentina since 1983 and in India after the emergency period (1975–1977). After enduring the longest and most brutal military dictatorship, Argentine citizens saw the 1983 redemocratization as a sign of hope to end state abuses, linking democracy to the rule of law, justice, and human rights. Following his inauguration, President Raúl Alfonsín summoned a group of notables to investigate abuses, kidnappings, murders, and forced "disappearances" carried out by the dictatorship. Supported with testimonies and evidence gathered in the commission's final report, *Nunca Más*, by the mid-1980s, historic human rights prosecutions of members of the 1976–1983 military juntas raised expectations that state abuses would become a bad memory from the past.

In the following years, Argentine law redefined security as the protection of the Constitution and human rights, while the 1994 constitutional reform incorporated international human rights agreements into the constitution. Over the last two decades, historically marginalized groups, including women, citizens of indigenous descent and other ethnicities, linguistic minorities, regional migrants, gay, lesbian, bisexual, and transgender citizens all made significant strides in gaining legal protections, a process in which Argentina has been at the forefront (see Fig. 3.2).

India's recent experience with democracy and human rights abuses has been somewhat different than Argentina's. One way to think of state abuses in postindependence India is in terms of three main phases. First, in the immediate aftermath of freedom and partition (that was an extremely violent event), there was a lot of support for the Indian state to respond to the challenges of the new postcolonial state (1947–1960s), even if challenges to the new state continued in parts of the country. However, by the 1960s, faith in the government was challenged by the Naxalite movement inspired by the Maoists that gained some support among students and intellectuals alongside peasants and the anti-inflation, anticorruption Total Revolution–Jay Prakash Narain Movement that almost directly led to the imposition of Emergency in 1975–1977 by the then Prime Minister Indira Gandhi.

This period (the second phase) is particularly important for understanding human rights abuses that led to institutional demands for police accountability. While torture and custodial deaths/extrajudicial killings have been a part of postcolonial India, the emergency formally allowed for the suspension of the key, fundamental rights of life and liberty enshrined in the Constitution, thereby making it substantively easier to commit human rights abuses of the most brutal kind. In the post-emergency period (1980s–today), there are areas of the country which have experienced high levels of conflict, such as the North East, Kashmir (since independence), and parts of Central India (since the 1980s–1990s), that often report a complete flouting of the rule of law and constitutional protections, either through specific exceptions or extraordinary laws (many of which have been upheld by the Indian Supreme Court, thereby mediating its role in upholding rights and the rule of law) (Singh 2007; Lokaneeta 2011). Yet, more than just an issue in conflict areas, or a memory from colonial times, the use of torture and custodial deaths in routine criminal cases have continued throughout independent India.

Despite decades of democratization, human rights policies, and—in the case of India—reaffirmation of an autonomous, democratic, postcolonial state, in both Argentina and India policing remains linked to torture, extrajudicial killings, and custodial deaths. No doubt the institutional legacies of colonial and authoritarian violence run deep. Still, considering the significant transformations and reforms over recent decades, these legacies cannot explain the persistence of state abuses, whose manifestations lie in the modalities of exclusion from citizenship in democracy.

Reform and enforcement attempts in both countries with regard to torture and abuse have been clearly insufficient, while patterns of abuse suggest the existence of formal and informal mechanisms of violent exclusion from citizenship, as we see next.

CUSTODIAL DEATHS IN INDIA AND ARGENTINA

The individual stories and public data on the scope of police killings and custodial deaths in both countries are available to us because of the work of local and national activists. Sompal's case mentioned at the beginning of the chapter is a reflection not only on state violence in India but also on the responsiveness of civil liberty and democratic rights groups, as well as on state initiatives such as the National Human Rights Commission (NHRC) and the jurisprudence on custodial deaths. Only rarely do custodial deaths of migrant fruit sellers dominate the national media or garner prompt attention of the NHRC or the police. Unusual aspects of Sompal's case include receiving front-page coverage in national newspapers after a whistleblower from within the police department leaked the news of the cover-up. The case became known after a passerby found Sompal's body and the Investigating officer (IO) discovered that Sompal was last seen in the custody of the police.

Sompal is believed to have escaped to the terrace of the police station and from there, the official investigations remain unsure about whether he jumped to avoid further torture or was pushed by the police; the family suspects the latter. Sompal's elder brother Deena Zamadar reportedly told the newspapers, "We suspect that the policemen threw him down from the terrace due to which he died. The final probe report is still awaited."[5]

The IO informed the higher police officials who confirmed the role of the police through an internal investigation. Amazingly, the police department took immediate action. Six police officers were suspended, and cases were filed against them for charges including wrongful confinement and murder.[6] In addition, the main human rights complaints and monitoring committee, the NHRC, took up the case *suo moto* on January 2 and asked the Delhi Police Commissioner to submit a detailed report including postmortem, inquest, and video CD of the postmortem magisterial inquiry report within six weeks.[7]

Less unusual in the Sompal case, however, is its routine character, side by side with a number of custodial deaths of suspects for theft or minor quarrels. This seems clear in the study of custodial death cases since 1980 done by People's Union for Democratic Rights (PUDR), a democratic rights group. In this light, Sompal's death personifies the routineness in this modality of state violence excluding certain kinds of individuals—poor and migrant—from citizenship. Indeed, in news reports regarding Sompal, journalists mentioned two other cases from 2014 to 2015 in Delhi. In 2014, Manoj died of asphyxia while being tortured for confession related to a firing incident, and in 2015, Shahnawaz Chudhury died due to police beatings and resulting asphyxia in a police van after intervening in a fight between a couple and the police.[8]

A concerted effort by national and international human rights groups to monitor human rights violations in India expanded during the emergency (1975–1977) and post-emergency years. Indeed, the documenting of custodial deaths in Delhi by groups such as the PUDR and the People's Union for Civil Liberties (1981) appears to be a result of such an impulse. Data is available only for deaths in police stations and prisons, as the Asian Centre for Human Rights collated the NHRC data on torture and deaths in custody between 2001 and 2011. The report notes that about 1504 persons died in police custody during this period (over 150 per year) and that 12,727 died in judicial custody between 2001–2002 and 2009–2010 (1414 per year) (Asian Centre for Human Rights 2011).

Such attempts to collect data and demand accountability clash against the official denial of the role of torture in custodial deaths. The police, as the PUDR 1980–2004 reports show, often create myths about how people died while in custody (PUDR 1994, 2000, 2004). Often, they claim that the person escaped and died in an accident or committed suicide on the railway tracks. As in the Argentine case discussed below, the police come up with improbable stories of suicides of people in custody. Thus, Vikal Kumar Adhana's death, a PUDR report noted, was characterized as a suicide despite the fact that he was tied to "a rope fashioned from a floor mat and suspended from a vertical bar of the cell" (PUDR 2000, p. 10). Illness is also a major reason offered to justify deaths, even though family testimonies and fact-finding reports by PUDR and others show that the victims were perfectly healthy before being detained or under medical treatment, with medication that should have been administered by the officers in charge.

Cases of torture, custodial deaths, and extrajudicial killings in India take place in routine criminal cases, as well as in conflict areas fighting for autonomy or basic rights, and in situations where citizens, often religious minorities, are subject to extraordinary laws as terror suspects. In this regard, Indian constitutional provisions enabling the use of preventive detention, extraordinary laws upheld by the Supreme Court as necessary for dealing with terrorism and conflicts, and ambiguities in routine law are all conducive to abuses.

Custodial deaths are also frequent in Argentina, where community organizing and media scandals following police killings of the young and poor have given abuses visibility. One of the first milestones, in this regard, was the Ingeniero Budge massacre, when police officers executed three youths in May 1987 in Greater Buenos Aires. Another case, which took years and had important institutional repercussions, was the murder of teenager Walter Bulacio in Buenos Aires, after his detention outside a rock concert in 1991.

Like countless other youths, Walter was detained in a *razzia* or police raid, in a surprise, preventive roundup for background checks. His death in custody triggered massive protests and demands for reform. Kafkaesque, the near 200 courthouse steps and 22 years undergone for the Bulacio case to reach trial, with its myriad judges, courts, and prosecutors, is dismal (Verdú 2009; CORREPI 2012; CELS 2013). Considering that the Bulacio family was sponsored by major human rights organizations and their lawyers, it is hard to imagine that anyone other than extremely privileged Argentine citizens would be able to afford the time and resources involved in seeking redress when one looks at what Verdú rightly describes as "Walter's labyrinth."

Arbitrary detentions, the use of police stations to hold prisoners, citizens held in prison without a judicial sentence, and extrajudicial killings by the police have been repeatedly reported in Argentina by human rights organizations, especially the Center for Legal and Social Studies (CELS) and the Coordinator against Police and Institutional Repression (CORREPI). The latter, in particular, was established in 1996 with the purpose to document and resist forms of police and institutional violence in democracy. One distinctive contribution made by CORREPI has been documenting deaths at the hands of police, from an initial list of names in a notebook gathered by the mother of one of the victims to the current database with national scope and recognition. Drawing on media reports and testimonies, CORREPI's archive includes over 4600 documented arbitrary deaths since the start of redemocratization in 1983. Listing the names of the victims and circumstances of their death brings light to the otherwise opaque state violence targeting vulnerable citizens. If sobering, the list is incomplete, just the most visible layer of a mass of killings by state agents that the organization describes as "enormous" (CORREPI 2015a). Killings by the police and prison guards often go unreported or recorded under generic data on homicides (CELS 2016, pp. 95, 169–72). Reporting is more accurate in larger cities with stronger human rights organizations and traditions, while "entire provinces" remain mostly in the dark, as only a handful of resonating cases become known through the media (CORREPI 2015b).

A cursory look at cases in the database assembled by CORREPI (2015b) reveals patterns of violent forms of exclusion from citizenship that parallel those in India. Thus, we learn that on October 26, 2013, 17-year-old Jorge Daniel Reyna was found dead in the police station of Capilla del Monte, Córdoba, the same day he was arrested. The police report described Jorge as having committed suicide by hanging with his jacket. Both his mother and friends, however, found hematomas in Jorge's eyebrows, cheeks, shoulders, arms, and legs, as well as scars and other signs of having been beaten up. Just days before his death, Jorge had declared at the local courthouse that the police forced him and others to steal. As elsewhere in Argentina, the police are known for forcing poor teenagers to steal and sell drugs, both to profit from the activities and then to arrest and torture the youths to prove their efficiency in fighting crime. Differently from India, where judges and prosecutors exhibit significant independence, independent judicial actions are the exception in Argentina. In this case, the prosecutor who took Jorge's testimony had personal ties with the governor (CORREPI 2013). Protests following Jorge's death were met with police repression and arrests, as his friends underwent harassment and threats by the police (CORREPI 2013). Yet, protests continued, demanding the prosecution of those responsible for the death of Jorge and others.

Jorge's case is not isolated. CORREPI records similar deaths, all of them badly disguised as suicides, in the province of Córdoba alone. The pattern extends to those in prisons and juvenile detention centers. For example, in 2013, 17-year-old Guillermo Palleres was found dead in a juvenile detention center, and both Verónica Castaño, a young woman, and 23-year-old Iván Rivadero were found dead in their prison cells. In all of these cases, the authorities alleged suicide whereas relatives and human rights organizations insisted that these deaths followed beatings and torture. Thus, in Argentina, as in India, torture and custodial deaths are symptomatic of larger patterns of police abuse that continue with impunity.

Characterizing "everyday repression as state policy," CORREPI's database offers a sense of the scope of violent exclusions from citizenship in Argentina. Main forms of violence include trigger happy killings or extrajudicial executions (46%), the death of persons in custody— often following torture (39%), killings of protesters (2%), the murder of family members by state agents with weapons provided by the state, staged shootings and other crimes (1%), and forced disappearances (4%) (CORREPI 2016). Routine repressive modalities include political policing, the policing of protests, arbitrary detentions, the use of police stations to hold prisoners, and citizens held in prison without a judicial sentence.

In ways paralleling India's Sompal case, only under public pressure will the state acknowledge cases of abuse. While killings by the Argentinian state intensify during crises, as in 2001, 2009, 2010, and 2014, and there is a deep continuity between governments, some of them have administered more deadly violence. Over 3000 deaths, 65% of CORREPI cases, took place during the presidencies of Nestor Kirchner and Cristina Fernandez de Kirchner (2003–2015), accompanied by dozens of forced disappearances and protesters killed. In Argentina, deaths while in custody take place in prisons, police stations, police vehicles, and other improvised sites of detention and amount to 39% of the cases documented by CORREPI. Following beatings, torture, or fires set to protest or ask for assistance, similar to India, these deaths are often staged as suicides (CORREPI 2016; CELS 2016, p. 194).

ACCOUNTABILITY FOR POLICE ABUSE AND DEMANDS FOR CHANGE

Reproduced and amplified by the media, the employment of myths in police reports to deny the use of torture is common in both Argentina and India. If some reporting suggests that it is becoming increasingly difficult for the Indian police to sustain these narratives in custodial death cases, this has not yet helped to eliminate a pattern of impunity.[9]

Both in India and Argentina, the institutional response to abuses following demands of civil society groups and movements has been significant though inadequate. In post-emergency India (1977), the rise of civil liberties and democratic rights groups systematically took up the issue of custodial deaths, especially extrajudicial killings or fake encounters (where the police portray the killings as the result of a shootout between them and the escaping or attacking militant). The passage of the Human Rights Act in 1993 and the creation of the National Human Rights Commission in 1994 (and subsequently State Human Rights Commissions) initiated a visible state response in favor of rights protection. Regarding torture and custodial deaths, the NHRC mandated that every custodial death was to be reported to the Commission within 24 hours of its occurrence, along with a subsequent enquiry report into the custodial death and video of the postmortem. The number of deaths in

Fig. 3.1 Judicial independence in Argentina and India (*Source* CIRI Dataset, Cingranelli et al. 2014)

police and judicial custody appear in an annual report of NHRC. This directive has led to the creation of an archive on custodial deaths but not to the decline in the cases, as discussed below. The 1990s also saw the creation of a custodial jurisprudence on torture and custodial deaths that highlighted the continuing challenge for the judiciary of how to address the question of torture.

The role of the judiciary in investigating and denouncing police abuse has been significant in India, favored by the country's tradition of judicial independence. As we can see (Fig. 3.1), the CIRI index captures the judges' independence from the executive power or the military, including dimensions such as job stability, the possibility for the judiciary to challenge other government branches in court, or lack of corruption, where a score of 2 represents independence and a score of 0 conveys strong obstacles to the independent action of the judiciary.

Echoing these trends, 30.5% of Indian World Values Survey respondents report trusting their judges "A great deal," a view shared by only 2.9% of Argentines. A telling though not surprising gap, considering how decades of military dictatorships undermined judicial independence in Argentina. Never fully recovered, judicial independence deteriorated during the 1990s under the pressure of the executive power and then, again, in the 2000s, as reforms of the Judicial Council made Argentine judges more dependent on political authorities and limited their checks on the executive. In recent years, designations of new judges stalled, leading to over a 20% rise of temporary "surrogates" whose job stability depends on political authorities. Unfortunately, surveys suggest that judicial independence has been steadily deteriorating in India as well since the turn of the century and the court occasionally refers to its own failure in certain areas. Regarding abuses, even the Indian Supreme Court has accepted the fact of high levels of custodial deaths and its own inability to check them. In the oft-cited DK Basu case in 1996, the Court notes:

> Experience shows that worst violations of human rights take place during the course of investigation, when the police with a view to secure evidence or confession often resorts to third degree methods including torture and adopts techniques of screening arrest by either not recording the arrest or describing the deprivation of liberty merely as a prolonged interrogation. A reading of the morning newspapers almost everyday carrying reports of dehumanising torture, assault, rape and death in custody of police or other governmental agencies is indeed depressing. The increasing incidence of torture and death in custody has assumed such alarming proportions that it is affecting the credibility of the Rule of Law and the administration of criminal justice system. The community rightly feels perturbed. Society's cry for justice becomes louder.[10]

Such a judicial assessment remains relevant today.

Several commissions have examined the issue of police reform in India; national police commissions brought out eight reports between 1977 and 1981, the fourth of which focused on torture.[11] The reports recommended structural reforms of the police, including making appointments and transfers politically independent; increasing infrastructure and facilities; reducing the caseload of the police; providing efficient supervision over the lower rungs; and training officers in human rights. In 2006, the Supreme Court also accepted a Public Interest Litigation (PIL)—a mechanism through which the higher courts are approached for advancing fundamental rights of citizens and issues of broader public concern—and called for immediate changes to strengthen police independence and accountability.[12] The Court recommended the creation of local and state public complaints authorities to receive and investigate complaints from the public about custodial violence, arbitrary arrest and detention, rape in custody, and police excesses. Noting that "the basic and fundamental problem regarding the police [was] how to make them functional as an efficient and impartial law enforcement agency fully motivated and guided by the objectives of service to the public at large, upholding the constitutional rights and liberty of the people," the Court ordered that its recommendations should be instituted within the same year (2006).[13] Overall, however, the police reform process in the postindependence period has been largely unsuccessful.

In 2013, an amicus curiae petition raised questions about whether Court interventions have been useful since "despite the repeated judgments and directions passed by this Hon'ble court … the implementation by various States appears to be lax, resulting in a steady stream of cases of gross custodial violence."[14] Thus, when acknowledging custodial deaths, the police and official versions treat them as a result of anything other than torture. For example, the National Crimes Research Bureau, an official body, reports that deaths in police custody are primarily due to suicides (25%), hospitalization/treatment (27%), illness (18.8%), and occurring during the production process in courts/journey connected with investigation (15.6%) (Lokaneeta and Jesani 2016). In such a context, the relationship of police to violence and torture is often lost and the reasons for custodial deaths never fully investigated. Even landmark cases in the Indian Supreme Court regarding the issue of custodial torture and deaths failed to translate into prosecutions of police or other state officials or a decline in the numbers of deaths each year. The main areas of intervention have been compensations for custodial deaths by the NHRC, state human rights commissions, or the courts, rather than recommending prosecution (Lokaneeta and Jesani 2016; Ramakrishnan 2013).

In the meantime, protections from killings and political torture by the government, captured here by the V-Dem Physical Violence index, illustrate the dramatic, positive impact of Argentina's redemocratization in 1983 in terms of access to rights, as well as India's drop and recovery after the emergency period. The Varieties of Democracy database defines physical integrity as "freedom from political killings and torture by the government," which stands as the most important of all liberal rights in explaining conditions of political competition and government accountability (Coppedge et al. 2017). While, as the graph below shows, Argentine physical integrity protections are now higher than India's and closer to OECD countries standards (included for comparative purposes), both countries show some decline over the last decade, as the cases and trends discussed in this chapter illustrate (Fig. 3.2).

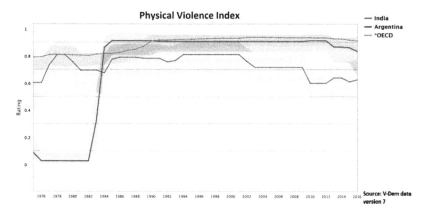

Fig. 3.2 Physical violence index for Argentina and India (*Source* Varieties of Democracy (V-Dem) [Coppedge et al. 2017])

In cases such as Sompal's, the actual working of the police, the judiciary, and the state in the context of torture and custodial deaths becomes apparent both in India and Argentina. It reveals the ways in which, despite institutional initiatives, the police still determine how the citizen/subject are treated in their everyday functioning and the exclusions and violence that they are able to initiate and accommodate.[15]

Concluding Remarks

Exposing a generally neglected dimension in the study of citizenship, the police play a decisive role in the de facto inclusion or exclusion of individuals from access to rights and citizenship. In their everyday search to distinguish between "productive citizens" and criminals, police agents impose social hierarchies and identities onto people's bodies, differentiating between higher and lesser forms of life and making decisions on their fate. Through distinct forms of governance, part of a biopolitical mechanism through which the state sorts out individuals prior to the legal recognition of rights, formal and informal police rules and protocols tend to criminalize the lifestyles of the poor and the socially vulnerable. Thereby, cases such as Sompal's—young, male, poor migrant—have to be understood not as isolated instances but as emerging out of the role that police play as a site of state power in enacting hierarchies of citizenship shaped as much by law and society as by unwritten rules. Only those ranking higher in the hierarchy are granted full rights in a biopolitical device implicitly allowing for the annihilation of those deemed worthless or dangerous.

In a way that questions beliefs regarding the progress of democracy and rights, patterns of custodial deaths, and other modalities of police abuse expose how citizen rights can be significantly eroded even when the formal, legal guarantees of citizenship are in place. In patterns that are replicated across countries, in this case, the most different examples of Argentina and India, police practices help to classify people into worthy members of the community whose lives deserve to be protected and others deemed worthless or a threat. Violent police practices need to be scrutinized for their consequences for citizenship. As Lerman and Weaver show for the United States, repeated experiences of neglect or mistreatment by state institutions teach citizens about their precarious standing and the behaviors that should be "off-limits to 'people like them'," with dire consequences for citizenship (Lerman and Weaver 2014, p. 15).

Echoing broader concerns with exclusions from citizenship in the literature (e.g., Balibar 2008; Baxi 2002; Lerman and Weaver 2014; Brinks 2006; Maranhao Costa 2011; as well as Schneider, Chapter 2; Dupuis-Déri, Chapter 4), this chapter argued that police agents administer access to rights and citizenship by bypassing the formal recognition of citizen rights and protections, using their impressive prerogatives, which include recognizing or denying rights and taking life. While citizenship studies have in recent years pointed to the exclusionary practices of citizenship enacted on certain sections of society, this chapter focuses on the role of the police in enabling such practices in everyday governing manifesting at times in custodial deaths. The particular trajectories of institutional frameworks and activist initiatives in Argentina and India determine the distinct ways through which such practices occur in these two contexts but they both reflect similar patterns of custodial violence in democracies. The mechanisms through which that happens are more fluid in democracies, where formal institutions have at once the ability to accommodate violence even as they deny or control it. The police help govern these practices along existing citizenship hierarchies.

NOTES

1. Singh, Karn Pratap. "Six Cops try to hush up death of vendor in custody at Adarsh Nagar Police station, suspended." *Hindustan Times*, January 1, 2017. http://www.hindustantimes.com/delhi-news/six-cops-try-to-hush-up-death-of-vendor-in-custody-at-adarsh-nagar-police-station-suspended/story-RbtARLC6MGv64yeFDsDu4J.html (last accessed November 13, 2017); Sikdar, Shubhomoy. "Man falls to death at Delhi police station." *The Hindu*, January 2, 2017; Singh, Karn Pratap, and Snehal Tripathi. "Delhi custodial death: Body was dumped in cop's official car." *Hindustan Times*, January 4, 2017.
2. In this chapter, for purposes of comparison between India and Argentina, we focus on police forces and not on militarized or paramilitary bodies often used in borders areas (e.g., Border Security Force in India, Gendarmería and Prefectura in Argentina), or conflict zones (e.g., Assam Rifles in north east India), which can be mobilized in other contexts.
3. Latinobarometro survey, question: "¿Cuál de las siguientes características cree Ud. que tiene la policía de (país) o cree Ud. que no tiene ninguna de estas características?" "Which of the following characteristics do you believe the police of (country) have or do you believe they don't have any of these characteristics?"
4. Nair, Smita. "Muslims think we are communal, corrupt: Police." *The Indian Express*, July 14, 2014.
5. Singh, Karn Pratap. "Six Cops try to hush up death of vendor in custody at Adarsh Nagar Police station, suspended." *Hindustan Times*, January 1, 2017. http://www.hindustantimes.com/delhi-news/six-cops-try-to-hush-up-death-of-vendor-in-custody-at-adarsh-nagar-police-station-suspended/story-RbtARLC6MGv64yeFDsDu4J.html (last accessed November 13, 2017).
6. Manral, Mahender Singh. 2017. "Custody death: Five Delhi cops booked, suspended." *The Indian Express*, January. http://indianexpress.com/article/cities/delhi/custody-death-five-cops-booked-suspended-in-delhi-4454894/ (last accessed November 13, 2017); Chand, Sakshi. 2017. "Custodial death case: Discrepancies in FIR put cops in the soup." *DNA India*, January 4. http://www.dnaindia.com/delhi/report-custodial-death-case-discrepancies-in-fir-put-cops-in-the-soup-2289100 (last accessed November 13, 2017).
7. NHRC issues notice to the Delhi Police Commissioner on the reported death of a vendor in custody (02/01/2017). http://nhrc.nic.in/disparchive.asp?fno=34162 (last accessed October 1, 2017).
8. Human Rights Law Network. "'Custodial deaths ... a convoluted manifestation of the darker side of the guardians of civil liberties:' Delhi HC remarks in latest judgment." 2015. http://www.hrln.org/hrln/

reproductive-rights/pils-a-cases/1749-qcustodial-deaths-a-convoluted-manifestation-of-the-darker-side-of-the-guardians-of-civil-libertiesq-delhi-hc-remarks-in-latest-judgment.html (last accessed November 13, 2017).

9. Dey, Abhishek. "Police lies and unidentified bodies: The story of two custodial deaths in Delhi two years apart." Scroll.in, January 9, 2017. https://scroll.in/article/825905/police-lies-and-unknown-bodies-the-story-of-two-custodial-deaths-in-delhi-two-years-apart (last accessed November 13, 2017).

10. *D.K. Basu vs. State of West Bengal*, and *Ashok K. Johri vs. State of Uttar Pradesh* (1996).

11. These reports include the National Police Commission Report (1977–1981), the Ribeiro Committee (1998), and the Padmanabhaiah Committee (2000).

12. *Prakash Singh & Ors vs Union Of India & Ors* (2006).

13. The current PIL related to the Anti-torture Bill in the Supreme Court will reveal what the judiciary and other institutions do in relation to torture in the future. In addition, there has also been the Police Act Drafting Committee (2005–2006), and most recently, the 2014 Model Police Act Review Committee that have focused on the creation of new legislation.

14. Amicus curiae petition by Senior Advocate A.M. Singhvi, 22 November 2013. https://www.scribd.com/fullscreen/188522776?access_key=key-rt2fk5wvpsvs10brytu&allow_share=true&escape=false&view_mode=scroll (last accessed August 15, 2016).

15. *Hindustan Times*. "Anti-torture law in India's interest, says SC." April 24, 2017. http://www.hindustantimes.com/india-news/anti-torture-law-in-india-s-interest-says-sc/story-mi7uoq3jUJRTaVxzj1vODJ.html.

References

Asian Centre for Human Rights Torture in India. 2011. Delhi: ACHR.

Balibar, Etienne. 2008. "Historical Dilemmas of Democracy and Their Contemporary Relevance for Citizenship." *Rethinking Marxism* 20 (4): 522–38.

Baxi, Upendra. 2002. "The (Im)possibility of Constitutional Justice." In *India's Living Constitution. Ideas, Practices, Controversies*, edited by Zoya Hasan, E. Sridharan, and R. Sudarshan, 31–63. New Delhi: Permanent Black.

Benhabib, Seyla. 2004. *The Rights of Others: Aliens, Residents, and Citizens*. Cambridge: Cambridge University Press.

Brinks, Daniel M. 2006. "The Rule of (Non)law: Prosecuting Police Killings in Brazil and Argentina." In *Informal Institutions & Democracy: Lessons from Latin America*, edited by Gretchen Helmke and Steven Levitsky, 201–26. Baltimore: The Johns Hopkins University Press.

Caimari, Lila. 2009. *La ciudad y el crimen. Delito y vida cotidiana en Buenos Aires, 1880–1940*. Editorial Sudamericana.

Centro de Estudios Legales y Sociales (CELS). 2013. "Caso Bulacio: 22 años para llegar a juicio." September 24. www.cels.org.ar/web/2013/09/caso-bulacio-22-anos-para-llegar-a-juicio/.

Centro de Estudios Legales y Sociales (CELS). 2016. *Derechos humanos en la Argentina Informe 2016*. Ciudad Autónoma de Buenos Aires: Siglo Veintiuno Editores.

Cingranelli, David L., David L. Richards, and K. Chad Clay. 2014. "The CIRI Human Rights Dataset." http://www.humanrightsdata.com. Version 2014.04.14.

Commonwealth Human Rights Initiative. 2015. *Rough Roads to Equality: Women Police in South Asia*. Delhi.

Coppedge, Michael, John Gerring, Staffan I. Lindberg, Svend-Erik Skaaning, Jan Teorell, David Altman, Michael Bernhard, M. Steven Fish, Adam Glynn, Allen Hicken, Carl Henrik Knutsen, Kyle L. Marquardt, Kelly McMann, Valeriya Mechkova, Pamela Paxton, Daniel Pemstein, Laura Saxer, Brigitte Seim, Rachel Sigman, and Jeffrey Staton. 2017. "V-Dem Codebook v7.1." Varieties of Democracy (V-Dem) Project.

CORREPI. 2012. *Boletín informativo* n° 654, April 23.

CORREPI. 2013. "Jorge Daniel Reyna, como Walter, pero hoy." *Boletín informativo* n° 704, November 17.

CORREPI. 2015a. *Boletín informativo* n° 746, January 14.

CORREPI. 2015b. *Antirrepresivo 2015. Los gobiernos pasan, la represión queda*.

CORREPI. 2016. *Archivo 2016. Recopilación de casos de personas asesinadas por el aparato represivo del estado 1983/2016*. https://correpi.lahaine.org/archivo-2016/.

Dubber, Markus Dirk. 2005. *The Police Power: Patriarchy and the Foundations of American Government*. New York: Columbia University Press.

Foucault, Michel. 1980. *Power/Knowledge*. New York: Pantheon.

Foucault, Michel. 2003. *Society Must Be Defended*. New York: Picador.

Human Rights Watch. 2009. *Broken System: Dysfunction, Abuse, and Impunity in the Indian Police*. New York, NY: Human Rights Watch.

Kalmanowiecki, Laura. 2000. "Origins and Applications of Political Policing in Argentina." *Latin American Perspectives* 27: 36–56.

Lerman, Amy E., and Vesla M. Weaver. 2014. *Arresting Citizenship: The Democratic Consequences of American Crime Control*. Chicago and London: University of Chicago Press.

Lokaneeta, Jinee. 2011. *Transnational Torture: Law, Violence and State Power in the United States and India*. New York: New York University Press.

Lokaneeta, Jinee, and Amar Jesani. 2016. "Torture and Detention in India: Challenges to Prevention." In *Does Torture Prevention Work?* edited by

Richard Carver and Lisa Handle, 501–47. Liverpool: Liverpool University Press.

Maranhão Costa, Arthur. 2011. "Police Brutality in Brazil." *Latin American Perspectives* 38 (5).

Marshall, T.H., and Tom Bottomore. 1992. *Citizenship and Social Class.* London: Pluto Press.

People's Union for Civil Liberties. 1981. "Deaths in Police Custody." PUCL Bulletin. http://www.pucl.org/from-archives/81oct/deaths.htm.

People's Union for Democratic Rights. 1994. *Custodial Rape: A Report on the Aftermath.* Delhi.

People's Union for Democratic Rights. 2000. *Dead Men's Tales: Deaths in Police Custody.* Delhi.

People's Union for Democratic Rights. 2004. *Custodial Deaths in Delhi, 2003.* Delhi.

Police Organisation in India. 2008. *Commonweath Human Rights Initiative.* Delhi.

Pontón, Daniel. 2007. "Recursos Humanos de la Fuerza pública en América Latina." *Urvio* 2.

Ramakrishnan, Nitya. 2013. *In Custody: Law, Impunity and Prisoner Abuse in South Asia.* New Delhi: Sage.

Rejali, Darius. 2008. *Torture and Democracy.* Princeton: Princeton University Press.

Roy, Anupama. 2017. *Citizenship in India.* Oxford: Oxford University Press.

Seri, Guillermina. 2012. *Seguridad: Crime, Police Power, and Democracy in Argentina.* New York: Bloomsbury.

Singh, Ujjwal K. 2007. *The State, Democracy and Anti-Terror Laws in India.* New Delhi: Sage.

Standing, Guy. 2011. *The Precariat. The New Dangerous Class.* London and New York: Bloomsbury.

Verdú, María del Carmen. 2009. *Represión en Democracia.* Buenos Aires: Herramienta ediciones.

World Values Survey, 2012 India and 2013 Argentine Surveys. http://www.worldvaluessurvey.org/WVSOnline.jsp.

Young, Iris Marion. 1989. "Polity and Group Difference: Critique of the Ideal of Universal Citizenship." *Ethics* 99 (January): 250–74.

CHAPTER 4

Development of the Concept of "Political Profiling": Citizenship and Police Repression of Protest in Quebec

Francis Dupuis-Déri

Translated by Sarah Igelfeld

Within contemporary liberal states, police practices raise many questions about democracy, citizenship, and fundamental rights often overlooked in political science studies of democracy. One particular area of concern, increasingly present in public debates and academic reflections, has been the degree to which police actions correspond with the liberal democratic ideal of police neutrality with respect to diversity of racial, social, and political categories (the problem of discrimination or "profiling") (Jones et al. 1996; Ward and Stone 2000; Sklansky 2008; see also Bayley

---

This text is a slightly revised and updated version of the author's article published in French: "Émergence de la notion de 'profilage politique': repression policière et mouvements sociaux au Québec," *Politique & sociétés*, vol. 33, no. 3, 2014, pp. 31–56.

F. Dupuis-Déri (✉)
Department of Political Science, Université du Québec à Montréal, Montréal, Canada

81
M. D. Bonner et al. (eds.), *Police Abuse in Contemporary Democracies*,
https://doi.org/10.1007/978-3-319-72883-4_4

2006; Schneider, Chapter 2; Seri and Lokaneeta, Chapter 3; Davenport et al., Chapter 7). This issue is even more significant at a time when police interventions have become more numerous and more repressive, as has been the case in established liberal democracies over the last fifteen years or so, in response to waves of mobilization and protest, in particular, by the alter-globalization movement (Fillieule and della Porta 2006; Waddington 2007; Fernandez 2008; Jobard 2008; Starr et al. 2011; Dupuis-Déri 2013a; Wood 2014). For example, during large international summits, the number of mobilized police is in the thousands (often more than 10,000). They obtain budgets of several hundreds of millions of dollars and regularly carry out hundreds of arrests, even more than a thousand for a single protest event (see Dupuis-Déri 2013a, pp. 261–62, Appendix, tables I and II).

In Canada, like in many other established liberal democracies since the beginning of the 2000s, police have moved from managing protests using the "negotiated management" approach (favoring communication and exchange of information, route negotiation, and putting marshals in place to maintain order), to an approach of "strategic incapacitation" (King 2004; Sheptycki 2005; Shantz 2012; Wood 2014). This new approach to protest management aims to reduce, as much as possible, protesters' capacity for action during mobilizations considered to be "radical," mainly by means of mass arrests, including those made before the beginning of a demonstration (for a more global perspective, see Waddington 2007, p. 118ff). The decision to apply or not apply the label "radical" to a protest is a form of "political profiling" that limits the freedom of speech of some citizens based on their political ideas.

Yet Canada is an established and stable liberal parliamentary democracy, where the police forces are generally respected as a global model of professionalism, efficiency, and probity. Canadian police officers are regularly sent abroad on training missions, under the United Nations' mandate, to countries such as Haiti. Thus while, political profiling can imply much more violent—and even lethal—police actions when it occurs in contexts of armed struggle and civil war (e.g., Schneider, Chapter 2), such is not the case in Canada. In Canada, political profiling and subsequent police repression of selective protests refers to police actions that are not lethal and not even necessarily illegal, but are nevertheless arbitrary, politically motivated, and aim to silence the public voice of some citizens based on their political perspectives.

Moreover, the protesters that police profile and target in Canada are a relatively powerless social movement, despite their claims to be "radical" (i.e., "anticapitalist" or "anarchist"). Yet the new twenty-first century Canadian anarchists are systematically labeled as "violent" by the authorities and the media. For example, while putting together information about people who might protest against the G20 Summit in Toronto in 2010, the Integrated Security Unit Joint Intelligence Group (2009, pp. 6–7) produced *An Investigative Baseline for the Primary Intelligence Investigative Team*, in which "anarchism, anarcho-syndicalism, nihilism, socialism, and/or communism" were identified as the "radical ideologies [embodying] potentially serious public safety challenges," underlining which "it is instructive to note that anarchists pursue a *destruction of law, order and government* as a precursor to the imposition of anarchy" (emphasis added). This is a clear case of "threat amplification" (Monaghan and Walby 2011).

However, no anarchist group in Canada is close to having the capacity to destroy any government. Nor do they have any serious plans that aim toward such a goal. Indeed, they do not even have the capacity to bring more than a few hundred people into the streets. Today Canadian anarchists' so-called violent deeds are limited to: drawing graffiti; dropping banners; toppling road-cones, trash-cans, and street-fences; smashing a few windows of corporate stores; and, sometimes throwing things at police who are in full riot gear (helmet, shield, battle dress, etc.), such as stones, empty bottles, sometimes vegetables, and even ... snowballs. Although all of this is illegal, it is not clear that it justifies mass arrests of hundreds of protesters. Indeed, the disproportionate police repression raises important questions about the political function and motivation of police actions and their implications for citizens' political rights to freedom of assembly and freedom of speech.

It is not only in reaction to this situation, but also in the context of the growth and intensification of mobilizations in Quebec (alter-globalization movement or the student movement), that human rights organizations and militant groups drew on the concepts of racial profiling and social profiling to propose the concept of "political profiling" to both designate and denounce these police practices. According to Goyette, Bellot, and Sylvestre: "profiling is based on stereotypes. That is how these groups are so extensively monitored, inspected, arrested and judicialized, even when there is no criminal behavior involved" (2014, p. 402). It is, therefore, a form of police abuse; that is, "police actions that may or may not be 'illegal' but severely limit selective citizens' rights, receive minimal punishment (limited accountability), and may play a role in maintaining (or promoting) particular political and economic objectives" (Bonner et al., Chapter 1). It raises serious concerns about citizenship since it contradicts fundamental rights, neutrality of law enforcement, and limits freedom of assembly and of speech. In its strongest form, profiling refers to when the police crack down on individuals solely on the basis of their racial, social, or political identity, even if they do not commit any wrongdoing. In its weaker form, it includes when protesters do commit a wrongdoing, yet profiled individuals are more rapidly and more harshly punished than others who commit the same acts, but whom the police are not watching as closely. In both cases, political profiling raises legal, social, and political questions in which police actions expose the boundaries of citizens' rights.

This chapter uses process tracing to examine the emergence of the concept of political profiling in Quebec, with special attention given to the city of Montreal. More precisely, this chapter reveals the kind of relationship that existed between the police and social movements when this new concept was brought forward into the public arena, and how other concepts contributed to the proposal of this term. This discussion will reveal how institutions and actors close to social movements or actively engaged in them, succeeded in changing public discourse by introducing a new concept that widens our understanding of police abuse and its implications for democratic citizenship.

POLICE AND THEIR "CLIENTELE"

Studies and research done on the history of police reveal that their attitudes and behaviors are strongly influenced by their perception of the categories or groups that make up their "clientele." This refers to the categories or groups that require attention because of their racial, social, and political characteristics (real or perceived). The authorities tend to explain that this is a rational attitude, given that these categories of people are presumed to be precisely those that create problems in society, such as higher rates of transgression, crime, violence, etc. Specialists also explain this phenomenon by identifying several factors: The history of the police, for example in colonial and post-colonial contexts (Rigouste 2012, pp. 19–54; Schneider, Chapter 2; Clarke, Chapter 8; Müller, Chapter 9); prejudices of the police officers themselves, and the process of acquiring and confirming those prejudices (Wilson et al. 2004); the categories to which the police officers themselves belong; professional training and organizational structure of the police; relations between the police and other organizations (political power, economic power, the media, etc.); local or national experience and the transfer of knowledge among police forces (van Maanen 1978; Monjardet 1996; Loubet del Bayle 2006; Müller, Chapter 9).

Recent analyses of relations between the police and social movements have shown that police officers make a binary distinction between a "(good) protester and [...] (bad) rioter" (Jobard 2008), or the reasonable and respectable protesters, on the one hand, and protesters who are unreasonable, on the other hand, thus not very respectable and even problematic when it comes to maintaining order (Favre 1990, p. 157; Fillieule 1997, p. 312; della Porta and Reiter 1998, pp. 24–27; Fillieule and della Porta 2006). These stereotypes function as a guide for action. The police generally behave more tolerantly and respectfully toward respectable protests and more intolerantly and repressively toward protesters perceived as being irrational and reprehensible; they see the latter as engaging in straightforward criminality without a political basis (McClintock et al. 1974).

The Relations Between the Police and Social Movements in Canada and Quebec

The police in Canada have always kept potentially subversive groups under special surveillance (Parnaby and Kealey 2003), even though, until the beginning of the twentieth century, it was often the army that was sent into the streets to contain disorderly crowds (Parizeau 1980; Dupont 2011). More recently, two director generals of the Sûreté du Québec (Quebec provincial police) publicly stated that the police distinguish between different categories of protesters. Florent Gagné (in *Courrier international*, April 11, 2001), shortly before the Summit of the Americas in Québec City in 2001, shared his thoughts with the media about three types of protesters

> [T]hese protesters are divided into 3 groups. There are, first of all, the 'traditionals', such as the unions, who respect the democratic regulatory framework that prevails in Canada [...] they are, thank God, the majority. [Then there are] those people who work with concepts of so-called civil

disobedience. Their actions can be anything from the relatively peaceful sit-in to more extreme actions such as pouring cement on themselves [*sic.*] or attaching themselves to buses so that the police cannot tow them away. Lastly, there are the so-called direct action groups. These violent groups do not really have any ideology. They are thugs, anarchists.

Then, Mario Laprise, testifying at the hearings of the Commission spéciale d'examen des événements du printemps 2012 (Special commission examining the events of spring 2012), on September 26, 2012, explained that:

> One must understand that among the groups of protesters in Quebec … there are three categories of protesters. There are the peaceful ones which include the students, which include ordinary people, who come to protest peacefully. We also have, in Quebec, groups that specialize in civil disorder, who are against violence but who commit a certain number of offences and crimes. The management of a crisis… with protesters like these is easier to carry out. But we also have groups who are anarchists, activists and criminals and hooligans…

Thus, according to these two commanders in chief, there are, on the one hand, the "pacifists" and the adherents of civil disobedience that are clearly violating the law. "Managing" them is relatively easy. On the other hand, there are the individuals who are not really protesting; they are "thugs," "hooligans," or criminal anarchists. These public declarations reflect the findings of several studies on the relations between the police and social movements in Canada and Quebec.

One of the first quantitative studies on the topic in Canada examined groups that mobilize and the interactions between them and official institutions, such as the police (Frank and Kelly 1979, pp. 594–95). Based on the data gathered from key newspapers,[1] the study analyzed 281 demonstrations that took place between 1963 and 1975 in Ontario (145 events) and in Quebec (136 events). The goal was to determine, among other things, which variables had a significant impact on the possibility that arrests would be made. The researchers assessed the political status of the mobilizing group, its organizational form, its demands, its forms of collective action (demonstration or strike), and the repression (arrests). In Quebec, arrests were made at 76% of events (demonstrations, strikes) carried out by groups whose status was considered "illegitimate" and which did not have any "friends in high places," as opposed to only 37% of the events associated with groups with an "acceptable" status (ibid., pp. 608–9). The difference is almost 40 percentage points. The researchers concluded that police repression (arrests) in Quebec is moderately influenced by the group's "status in society," that is, by the way that group is "perceived by the authorities" (Frank 1984, pp. 326–27; see also Frank and Kelly 1979, p. 597 [for the hypothesis] and p. 608ff. [for the results]). Frank notes that the groups that seem the least legitimate in the eyes of the police are also those that object to the "dominant values" of society. Their members are seen as "communists" (the study was conducted during the time of the Cold War) or "anarchists," meaning "radicals looking to undermine the established order." Their ideology is "more of a threat to the status of the powers that be—the very structure of the political system" (Frank and Kelly 1979, p. 597; Frank 1984, pp. 348–49). Thus, according to Frank and Kelly, the police distinguish between legitimate and illegitimate demonstrations, and this distinction has a (moderate) influence in terms of repression.

Rafail (2005) offers a more recent quantitative study that examines the period that corresponds to the emergence of the alter-globalization movement. In analyzing three local newspapers,[2] this researcher listed 1152 demonstrations between 1998 and 2004 in three Canadian cities—Montreal (413 demonstrations), Toronto (379), and Vancouver (360). His main goal was to understand which variables diminish or increase the probability of the occurrence of one or more arrests during a demonstration. He identified several variables: police and militant tactics; the size of the demonstration; the intensity of the pre-mobilization; the cause being defended; and, the history of the mobilizing group (past episodes of violence and confrontations with the police). The results of his study indicate that there are almost twice as many events marked by the destruction of public or private property in Montreal than in the other two cities (the number of occurrences is low in all the cities: 13% in Montréal, 7% in Vancouver, 6% in Toronto). However, arrests were somewhat more frequent in Toronto (16% of the time) than in Montreal (14%)[3] and Vancouver (13%). As for the police in Montreal, they carried out mass arrests (30 arrests or more) more frequently, that is, in 22% of the all the demonstrations where arrests were made (10% in Toronto and 4% in Vancouver) (Rafail 2005, p. 24).[4] The author points out that "[a] particularly noteworthy result is the absence of a strong relationship between protester violence and arrests in two of the three cities [Montreal and Toronto], despite its intuitive appeal" (Rafail 2010,

p. 500). He concludes that: "at least in terms of arrests, what the protestors do during a demonstration is not directly linked to arrests in
Montreal" (Rafail 2005, p. 28). He thus confirms that "[p]olice do
appear to use arrests differentially depending on the social movement"
(Rafail 2010, p. 501).

Taking a qualitative approach, I conducted two studies on police
repression in Quebec, the first examines 1990–2011 (approximately
3800 arrests) (Dupuis-Déri 2013b) and the second examines the 2012
student strike in Quebec (around 3500 arrests and almost 1500 the
next year) (Dupuis-Déri 2013b). The studies analyzed media discussions about: the protests that were targets for arrests; the police "logs"[5];
and also police officers' court testimonies. The studies revealed that the
police have a tendency to perceive "anarchists" as a threat and that they
identify them more or less accurately by the appearance of their cloth-
ing or their flags. Because these anarchists have used violence during
some previous protests, it is quite possible that such actions provoke
arrests (Dupuis-Déri 2013c). However, in some of the protests studied, the police carried out mass arrests even though there was no sign
of any wrongdoing; they were sometimes made even before the beginning of the protest marches (surrounding about 500 people, April 26,
2002, before a protest march called by la Convergence des luttes anticapitalistes—CLAC [Anti-Capitalist Convergence]). Communiqués
from the police indicate that on some occasions police were the targets
of projectiles, but no arrests were made, or only one or two protesters
were arrested and those were usually individuals known to have committed wrongdoings during a previous event (Dupuis-Déri 2013b, p. 222).
These findings echo the conclusions of earlier studies, which found that
the actions of protesters do not determine police response. An analysis
of police discourse confirms that the political identity of the protesters is
an important factor in explaining the type of intervention used, a point
admitted to by police officers.

Thus, the level of repression depends on the political identity of the
group that is protesting. During a trial following the "preventive arrest"
of April 26, 2002, before the start of a protest march, a police officer tes-
tified that there were "red flags [sic] representing anarchy and problematic people" in the crowd, which signaled "the potential for violence."[6]
Thus, the anarchist seems so threatening that he or she deserves to be
arrested even before beginning to protest.[7]

In another study of labor union mobilizations in Canada in the early 2000s (especially strikes) that examines 38 cities from 10 different provincial jurisdictions, Hall and De Lint find that: *"[a]s police see it*, the potential for trouble in social protest situations is rarely from union members and more from 'radical' groups that refuse to protest in a lawful manner" (2003, p. 230 [emphasis added]). However, the transgression of the law does not seem to be the factor that explains police intervention. Police officers managing strikers want, above all, to reduce tensions. This includes police discouraging employers or the public from crossing a picket line, even when it is illegal or strikers are not respecting an injunction issued by a judge (ibid., pp. 226 and 228). Thus, police officers believe that the best way to maintain order is to limit the show of force. In conclusion, the researchers note that: "[i]f the contrast between the policing of strikes and anti-globalization protests shows anything, it is not that police reject their role as a force for public order, but rather that they are *selective* about when they use force and on whom they use it" (ibid., p. 232 [emphasis added]). Not all citizens have an equal right to protest.

Together, these studies reveal that since the end of the 1960s, the real or perceived identity of protesters influences the way in which police forces intervene, or not. In the context of the 2000s, police repression is aimed at, above all, the alter-globalization movement and the "anarchists," and this is often unrelated to the type of actions carried out. This can be referred to as discrimination, police abuse, or political profiling and it has important implications for the boundaries of democratic citizenship.

DIVERSITY IN PROFILING[8]

Many people have spoken out in Quebec in the last few years to denounce "political profiling," an expression signifying that the police do not intervene in a neutral and impartial manner when faced with the diverse components of social movements. This concept evokes "racial profiling," a term that appeared in the United States (Skolnick 1966) at the time of escalating conflicts between the police and racialized communities, particularly as part of the "war on drugs" and "the war on terror" (Hoopes et al. 2003; Harris 2011, p. 56). In fact, the term "profiling" comes from the police forces themselves, who introduced the term "criminal profiling." Psychological profiling of common criminals is a policing technique that has existed for more than a century in Great Britain. The investigation of Jack the Ripper is often referred to in the scholarly literature as one of the first cases of criminal profiling. However, even witch hunts are thought to have contributed to the development of techniques to profile suspects (Bartol and Bartol 2013).

Today, a number of agencies specialize in profiling. For example, in Canada, there is the branch of Criminal Investigative Analysis (CIA) of the Royal Canadian Mounted Police (RCMP) and the Service de l'analyse du comportement (Behavioral analysis service) of the Sûreté du Québec (SQ). In its own documents, the Service de police de la Ville de Montréal (SPVM) (The police department of the City of Montreal) explains that "criminal profiling is a legitimate policing practice used to identify a suspect" (SPVM, "Politique Relations avec les citoyens" [Policy of relations with citizens], n° Po. 170, November 24, 2014 [in Okomba-Deparice 2012, p. 42]), and also refers to the definition of Martin Scheinin (2007, §33) who presents it as: "the systematic association of a set of physical, behavioral or psychological characteristics with a certain type of infraction and the use of these characteristics to justify decisions taken by the police services" (Okomba-Deparice 2012, p. 13 note infra 5).

A number of academic studies have discussed and contributed to the development of the concept of criminal profiling and participated in its development. For Muller (2000, p. 236), criminal profiling consists primarily of putting together a hypothetical description of the criminal on the run: Not only personality traits and behaviors, but also indicators of age category, ethnicity, or geographical location (in this last instance, the term "geographical profiling" is also used). At first, criminal profiling was concerned with previously committed crimes that were excessively violent and ritualized, in particular, serial murders and serial rapes. Canter (2004) adds that profiling could also be used in the case of thefts, fires, and terrorism. Yet, criminal profiling is now more commonly perceived as having a prospective value, meaning it could function as an evaluation grid, enabling the identification of potential suspects *before* they commit a crime. This "prospective profiling" (Bourque et al. 2009, p. 6) justifies an increased level of surveillance and the subjection of certain categories of individuals to questioning and body searches before any wrongdoing has been committed.

Muller, a psychologist, questions this development stating that "[t]hose who practice criminal profiling have claimed that it is alternatively a science or an art, depending on who you listen to" (Muller 2000, p. 234; also see Winerman 2004, p. 66). Other scholars raise even more significant concerns: "The critical review of scientific writings has not allowed us to legitimize the practice of prospective profiling on a scientific, legal or moral basis, or on the basis of risk evaluation of statistically extremely rare events" (Bourque et al. 2009, p. 6). Thus, criminal profiling has a number of detractors among those who defend fundamental rights and are critical of police abuse of authority, such as discriminatory attitudes and practices. According to this critical perspective, criminal profiling carries a significant risk of downward spiral and could dissimulate racial, social, and political profiling practices.

Racial profiling was the first concept to gain the attention of those who criticize the discriminatory practices of the police. This term was used for a long time in the United States (Skolnick 1966; Westley 2003 [1950]) before it appeared in the 1990s in Canada and Quebec. For some, "[t]he practice of racial profiling is a disgrace to the policing profession" (Chalom 2011). For others, it is more like a "myth" that would only serve to discredit a rational practice of criminal profiling, since certain racial or ethnic categories really do have a stronger propensity toward crime (MacDonald 2001, p. 1). Jacques Duchesneau, former chief of the Montreal police department and, at that time, president of the Canadian Air Transport Security Authority, explained in 2006, regarding body searches in airports: "We must carry out a certain degree of segregation, whether we like it or not." He then asked a rhetorical question which he promptly answered: "Is this '*racial profiling*'? No, it is '*profiling*'" (in Buzzetti 2006, p. A3).

It is increasingly recognized, even by certain police forces, that racial profiling is a real problem that raises questions about citizenship, rights, justice, freedom, and equality. In a special issue of the journal *Policing and Society* (vol. 21, no. 4, 2011) on police stop-and-search practices, the editors recall that police officers intervene most often based on intuitions or basic suspicions related to "more general views about marginal communities," thus "making suspects out of entire communities." Police officers who stop and question individuals who seem like illegal immigrants to them, will justify themselves by explaining that the suspect "looks foreign," "speaks a foreign language," reads a newspaper in a foreign language, listens to "ethnic music," "smells like an illegal alien," looked dirty or simply "looks like they shouldn't be here" (Bowling and Weber 2011, p. 482).

In Canada, the people who are subjected to racial profiling are mainly those with black or dark skin of African or Latin-American origin, indigenous people (Green 2006; Comack 2012), and people who are perceived to be Muslim or of Arab origin, especially since the air attack against the United States on September 11, 2001. The Ontario Human Rights Commission, having studied this issue since 2003, points out that "criminal profiling is not the same as racial profiling since the former is based on objective evidence of wrongful behaviour while racial profiling is based on stereotypical assumptions" (2003). Furthermore, police forces have a tendency to mobilize more resources to monitor certain populations; this leads to a disproportionate number of interventions, convictions, and incarcerations (Bernard and McAll 2008; for a similar phenomenon in the United States, see Harcourt 2003). In 2004, the Ministère des Relations avec les Citoyens et de l'Immigration (MRCI) (Ministry of citizen relations and immigration) in Quebec set up a task force on racial profiling. The following year, the SPVM unveiled its first policy to internally fight against racial profiling. In 2005, the Commission des droits de la personne et de la jeunesse du Québec (CDPDJ) (Quebec commission for human rights and youth rights) produced an initial document proposing a definition of the phenomenon:

> Racial profiling refers to any action taken by a person or persons in a position of authority towards one person or group of people for reasons of safety, security or protection of the public, that is based on factors of real or presumed affiliation, such as race, colour, ethnic or national origin, or religion, without a real motive or reasonable suspicion, and that results in subjecting the person to a different examination or treatment. (Turenne 2005, pp. 4–5)

The CDPDJ concluded in 2010 that: "[t]he stereotypes associated with racialized people play a key role in provoking a police intervention" (Eid and Turenne 2010, p. 7). This is evident even when the individual seems to belong to privileged professional and financial categories. Judge Juanita Westmoreland-Traoré also pointed this out in a judgment rendered in the Court of Québec: "young Blacks are subject to racial profiling if they are wealthy and are driving luxury cars; they are also subject to racial profiling when they are poor" (in Eid and Turenne 2010, p. 6).

Following the CDPDJ report, the City of Montreal (2011) issued a communiqué acknowledging the importance of "eradicating all forms of discrimination from its territory." The SPVM declared that it reacted positively to the CDPDJ report, recognizing that:

> certain racial profiling problems exist [...]. The position of the SPVM is clear: racial profiling is unacceptable and will not be tolerated. But there is no generalized racial profiling in the SPVM [...]. However, a misconception, either in the policing work or in the local reality, could cause misunderstandings leading to a perception of racial profiling. (Service de police de la Ville de Montréal)

Other police forces also made their position clear, such as in Ottawa (Radio-Canada, 2013). Finally, the term "racial profiling" is now included in jurisprudence. For example, on September 20, 2012, Judge Pierre-Armand Tremblay explained in his judgment of the *City of Longueuil v. De Bellefeuille* case in the Longueuil Municipal Court that: "[t]he doctrine and the jurisprudence submitted to the Court demonstrate that racial profiling is not necessarily intentional and characterized by bad faith."[9]

The concept of racial profiling has served as a model for the development of other concepts that refer to issues both similar and different, namely social and political profiling. In 2004, several groups called upon the CDPDJ due to their suspicion that there was systematic discrimination in the way the police in Montreal treated homeless people. A working group was set up in 2005, and in 2009 the CDPDJ finally produced a document on social profiling entitled *La judiciarisation des personnes en situation d'itinérance à Montréal: un profilage social* (The judicialisation of homeless people in Montréal: a case of social profiling) (Bellot et al. 2005; Campbell and Eid 2009, p. 71; Sylvestre 2009). In this document, Lawyer Christine Campbell and Sociologist Paul Eid provide a history of "social profiling," recalling the practice of hunting down poor people (Chamayou 2010, pp. 114–25) and vagabonds several centuries ago. However, they emphasize the influence of more recent initiatives undertaken in the City of New York in the 1990s where police prioritized the tracking down of uncivil behavior (Wilson and Kelling 1982, pp. 29–38; see also Silverman 2001). Campbell and Eid (2009) explain that the targets of this form of profiling are often homeless people who live in extreme poverty and suffer from alcoholism, drug addiction, and mental health problems.

In 2012, the SPVM produced a *Plan stratégique en matière de profilage racial et social* (Strategic plan regarding racial and social profiling) which stated that:

> [C]riminal profiling is a concept that is quite well understood by the police officers of the SPVM. However, it is necessary to continue to remind them of the importance of intervening on the basis of behaviours [facts, observations, information, descriptions or *modus operandi*, etc.] and not on the basis of the appearance of individuals, to ensure service that is free of discrimination. (Okomba-Deparice 2012, p. 14)

In this document the SPVM affirms that it "endorses the definition of racial profiling of the Commission on the Rights of the Person and the Rights of Youth" (ibid., p. 14) and it also draws upon the work of the CDPDJ when discussing social profiling. The SPVM identify these two types of profiling as problematic in that they hinder the declared efforts "to have a closer relationship with citizens"; they even hinder the "effectiveness of police work" (ibid., p. 15). The action plan identifies "challenges" and proposes "areas of intervention" and "measures" to reduce the risks of racial and social profiling. Political profiling, however, is not mentioned in this document.

POLITICAL PROFILING

Although the concept of political profiling is not as well known as those of racial and social profiling, it has nevertheless been the subject of public debate in the last few years. The emergence in Quebec of the concept of political profiling was influenced by a deeper examination of racial and social profiling as well as the rise of the alter-globalization protest movement. Already in 1998, a report by the Quebec Civil Liberties Union observed that: "the actions of police forces are symptomatic of a phenomenon of denigration, marginalization and criminalization of dissent, particularly among movements fighting against globalization and trade liberalization" (Barrette 2002, p. 23). Lawyers Natacha Binsse-Masse and Denis Poitras were the first (to my knowledge) to define the concept of political profiling. They represented the plaintiff Rachel Engler-Stringer in a class action lawsuit against the City of Montreal following a mass arrest on July 28, 2003, during protests against a ministerial summit of the World Trade Organization (WTO). About 238 people had been surrounded and arrested. Based explicitly on the CDPDJ's definition of racial profiling, the class action presented this statement:

> Political profiling refers to any action taken by a person or persons in a position of authority towards one person or a group of people for reasons of safety, security or protection of the public, that is based on factors such as political opinion, political convictions, allegiance to a political group or political activities, without a real motive or reasonable suspicion, and that results in subjecting the person to a different examination or treatment.[10]

In the end, the class action lawsuit was dismissed, as the limitation period had expired.

The links between the different forms of profiling were discussed during a conference entitled "Le profilage discriminatoire dans l'espace public" (Discriminatory profiling in the public space), organized in honor of lawyer Natacha Binsse-Masse by the Quebec Civil Liberties Union and the Réseau d'aide aux personnes seules et itinérantes de Montréal (RAPSIM) (Montreal aid network for homeless people and people who are alone). The conference was held on June 10 and 11, 2010 in Montreal, several days before the G20 Summit in Toronto, where the police carried out more than 1000 arrests. During the conference, many speakers shared their views on political profiling. That same year, law professor Lucie Lemonde wrote in a Quebec Civil Liberties Union newsletter devoted to profiling:

> Political profiling refers to the different treatment reserved for certain protesters because of their political convictions [...] This type of police intervention in the form of mass and preventive arrests is discriminatory insofar as the police do not act in this way during union demonstrations, for example. They carry out mass arrests during alter-globalization demonstrations, not because of the illegal actions of the demonstrators, but because of their political identity, real or supposed. (Lemonde 2010, p. 7)

The concept was taken up again in 2011 by the activist Alexandre Popovic, who filed a complaint with the CDPDJ against the SPVM after the announcement of the existence of an investigation unit within the organized crime division named Guet des activités et des mouvements marginaux et anarchistes (GAMMA) (Surveillance of marginal and anarchist groups' activities). The complainant had collaborated with the

Collectif opposé à la brutalité policière (COBP) (Collective opposed to police brutality) as well as with the Coalition contre la répression et les abus policiers (CRAP) (Coalition against police repression and abuse). CRAP was founded after the death of Fredy Villanueva, a young man of Latin-American origin killed in Montreal North by a police officer during a routine intervention in a park on August 9, 2009. CRAP declared that this was a case of "racial profiling." Popovic pointed out in his complaint that even the name GAMMA implies that "the convictions expressed by the adherence to a political ideology, such as anarchy and anticapitalism, now constitute a sufficient motive in the eyes of the SPVM for a person to be under surveillance [...] which signifies outright political profiling." The CDPDJ dismissed this complaint. That same year the Convergence des luttes anticapitalistes (CLAC) (Anti-Capitalist Convergence) circulated a Declaration against political profiling in Montreal endorsed by about 40 community and militant groups and about 20 public figures, mainly academics; and the Association pour une solidarité syndicale étudiante (ASSÉ) (Association for Student Union Solidarity) denounced the "GAMMA squad" in the media, accusing it of practicing political profiling (Bélair-Cirino 2011).

During the student strike of 2012, the COBP adopted "political profiling" as the theme for its annual protest march against police brutality on March 15 in Montreal. During the student strike, a number of articles in the media dealt with the question of "political profiling" (among many others: Duchaine 2012; Miles 2012; Santerre 2012), sometimes suggesting a comparison with racial profiling (Elkouri 2012). A study based on more than 300 testimonials signed jointly by the Quebec Civil Liberties Union, l'Association des juristes progressistes (Association of progressive lawyers) and ASSE, documented police repression during the strike, and spoke explicitly about political profiling (Ligue des droits et libertés, Association des juristes progressistes et Association pour une solidarité syndicale étudiante 2013, p. 41).

The perspective on political profiling in the public debate is both descriptive and normative since this term is implicitly critical of the actions of the police. The police, for their part, tried to intervene in the debate to convince the public that they are not practicing political profiling, acknowledging that this is in fact about a problem in liberal regimes where the justice system in general and the police in particular claim to be neutral institutions. Thus, during the long student strike of 2012 in Quebec, the director of the SPVM, Marc Parent, speaking publicly about "racial or political profiling," declared that "there is no way we would accept this kind of intervention based on biases or prejudices" (Duchaine 2012; Miles 2012; Santerre 2012). André Pyton (2012), deputy chief inspector of la Direction des opérations policières du Service de protection des citoyens de Laval (the Directorate of police operations of the citizens protection service of Laval), spoke about "criminal profiling" and a columnist from the *Journal de Montréal* declared that "the police are doing what needs to be done to maintain a semblance of order and security in the city. They are not doing *political profiling*, they know with whom they are dealing" (Aubin 2012, p. 25 [emphasis added]).

Following the wave of mass arrests in Montreal during the student strike of 2012 and the following year, several class action lawsuits were filed, some of which raised the issue of political profiling. Furthermore, "political profiling" was at the center of a trial before Judge Julie Coubertin of the Montreal Municipal Court dealing with two occupations organized by the student movement. The project GAMMA was referred to during the trial (the case conclude October 2015 with a deal, and thus no formal judgment about the issue of "political profiling"). Thus, we find that actors in social and legal realms, as well as in the media, increasingly used the concept.

The term "political profiling" can have several functions when expressed in the public sphere. It can point to the problematic nature of a reality observed by militants and academic studies, including studies done in Canada and Quebec; and it can encourage an understanding that this phenomenon is problematic and a challenge to citizens' rights. However, state authorities still do not recognize the existence of this problem, and the expression itself is taking a long time to become an accepted legal term and enter into jurisprudence.

POLITICAL PROFILING AND THE MODEL OF "SELECTIVE REPRESSION"

A highly publicized and recent sequence of events caused a number of editorialists, journalists, columnists and even the premier of Quebec to observe that the police can intervene (or not) differently according to the social and political identity of those who commit a wrongdoing during a political mobilization. In the summer of 2014, the municipal public sector unions mobilized against Bill n°3, which was perceived as a threat to their pension fund. In Montreal, on August 18, 2014, union members disrupted a hearing of city council. This disturbance was preceded by a demonstration in front of city hall, during which masked protesters placed posters on the walls of the building, just a few feet away from police who were on guard and who stood idly by (with their arms crossed).[11] A few weeks earlier, another demonstration in which police officers participated, ended with a throwing of hats into a fire that had been lit in front of city hall, while firemen hosed down the front of the building. This collective action also attracted the attention of the media and provoked significant public debate.

Clearly, the situation was more complex because the police officers themselves are members of the municipal public sector and were mobilized by their fraternity against Bill n°3. What was particularly noticeable was that a police force (the SPVM) that had been so quick to intervene, often in a brutal manner, during the student strike in 2012, did not react when union members carried out, right in front of them, wrongdoings sometimes even more serious than those committed by nonpolice in 2012. Thus, there seemed to be a clear double standard—and this is not even counting the 1500 arrests in 2013, in Montreal, mostly carried out even before the beginning of the protest marches, under the pretext that the police had not been informed of the itinerary.

In the days after the commotion at city hall, many voices were heard in the media deploring the inaction of the police and pointing out that students and union members had been treated differently. The editor-in-chief of *Le Devoir*, Bernard Descôteaux, recalled that:

> The police officers themselves established a *double standard* towards citizens that was linked to the cause they were defending by marching in the streets. The "guitar scratchers" and the protesting student are vigorously beat up and pepper-sprayed, but not those whose cause is believed to be good and just. This is dangerous. (Descôteaux 2014, p. A6; see also an editorial from *La Presse*: Journet 2014, p. A20 [emphasis added])

Even the columnist Richard Martineau (2014), who had been very critical of the "carrés rouges" (red squares)[12] in 2012, observed in the *Journal de Montréal* that there is a difference in treatment by police officers depending on whether they are dealing with "protesting students" or "municipal employees who are protesting and making a commotion" (see also Payette 2014). François Cardinal, columnist in *La Presse*, used a rather curious expression when writing about this in his blog—he called it "upside-down profiling."[13]

The newspapers published open letters from trade unionists or ex-trade unionists who also observed a certain degree of incoherence by the police force (Patenaude 2014, p. A6; Robert 2014, p. A19). Finally, Premier Philippe Couillard declared, after this event: "A parallel is being made, which I understand, between the events of the spring of 2012, to which law enforcement officers reacted forcefully, and those of yesterday. There cannot be two types of treatment for this kind of behaviour." And to conclude: "[T]his 'double standard' undermines the confidence of the population in the police force" (Radio-Canada 2014).

Under public and political pressure, the police launched an investigation and a number of trade unionists, who had participated in the disturbance, were accused and several were laid off. However, the inaction of the police on the day of the event calls to mind the observations expressed in the studies discussed earlier (Rafail 2010; Dupuis-Déri 2013a; Hall and De Lint 2003). These studies all give examples of illegal union demonstrations that were not targets of police intervention. In fact, the police helped the union members manage traffic during the blockade of a warehouse by locked out employees of the *Journal de Montréal* in December 2009, and calmed impatient people in front of a picket line during the Université du Québec à Montréal [UQAM] (SPUQ), teachers' union strike in March 2009 (Dupuis-Déri 2013a, pp. 26–27). Hall and de Lint state that they witnessed a situation where two employees of a private security agency attempted to cross a picket line with their vehicle. The strikers seriously damaged the vehicle (including the equipment inside), and the police on site arrested only two security agents (2003, p. 230). Rafail (2010, p. 490) recalls that in 2002, in Montreal, police surrounded and arrested 371 people during a demonstration against police brutality after a few windows were shattered. Yet, on November 25, 2003, the police did not intervene when 500 members of the Canadian Union of Public Employees vandalized the building where a member of the executive committee of the City of Montreal lived (dumping barrels of pig manure and activating fire sprinklers). These cases illustrate the general conclusions of the studies: The police proceed by following a "selective repression model" (Rafail's 2005, p. 39) according to the sociopolitical and ideological identity of the protesters, and not according to their actions.

CONCLUSION

The emergence of the concept of "political profiling" in Quebec's public sphere is the result of a combination of factors: (1) a political context marked by the increased activity of social movements; (2) more repressive police interventions; (3) observations made by academics, lawyers, and activists that the police intervene differently depending on the social movement; (4) the proximity in the public vocabulary of "political profiling" to the already familiar concepts of racial and social profiling, which were used and adapted by academic, legal, and militant networks; (5) the role of certain institutional players (the student movement, Quebec Civil Liberties Union, COBP, CRAP, and in the United States, the American Civil Liberties Union), legal experts (jurists and lawyers), and militants (e.g., Alexandre Popovic), who have led this development.

While the emergence of the concept of political profiling is important to expanding our understanding of the different forms police abuse can take in democracy, it also opens an array of new questions for political scientists and others in related disciplines. In what follows, I offer some important paths for future research, relevant not only to the case studies of Quebec or Canada, but also to all contemporary liberal democracies.

To begin, what are the differences between the various forms of profiling from a collective versus individual viewpoint? Political profiling often involves officers of superior rank who are in charge of hundreds of police officers. It targets hundreds of individuals (mass arrests). Police interventions are sometimes planned in advance and in partnership with other services, such as the ambulance services and the fire department. Political profiling can also affect individual militants well known by the police. In Montreal, in the 1990s, Alexandre Popovic (2013), who campaigned against police repression, was arrested on many occasions. The police also targeted the militant anticapitalist Jaggi Singh, the anarchist Katie Nelson during the student strike (Marquis 2012) and Jennifer Bobette, associated with COBP (Lavoie 2014). Thus, it is important to ask: What is the difference between collective and individual profiling and what are the implications for the limits on citizens' right to protest in democracy?

It is also important to understand whether the various forms of profiling influence each other and how. For example, a study on the right to stop and search granted to British police officers by the *Antiterrorist Law* in 2000 (Section 44, *Terrorism Act*) states that the police carried out 100,000 searches in 2009, disproportionately targeting people with dark skin (none of these searches were followed with accusations of terrorism). In this case, political profiling (terrorism) and racial profiling (skin color) intersect (Parmar 2011, p. 370). Indeed, Davenport, McDermott, and Armstrong's findings in Chapter 7 of this volume could be useful to begin such an examination into how race influences politically motivated forms of profiling as well as police and public assessments of wrongdoing.

Likewise, sexual profiling could be studied in conjunction with political profiling. It seems that women generally experience less frequent police interventions and racial or social profiling (Wortely and Owusu-Bempah 2011, p. 398; Campbell and Eid 2009, p. 34). However, when they are apprehended, women are more likely to be victims of sexual harassment and sexual assault, as was reported with respect to the G20 Summit in Toronto (Canadian Civil Liberties Association and National Union of Public and General Employees 2011, pp. 45–46).

Another area of study would be to better understand the perception police have of the individuals targeted by political profiling. One retired police officer, remembering their work in Quebec managing separatist demonstrations around 1970, explained that: "the police were supposed to charge into the crowd and arrest people, mainly those who wore a beard, which, in many people's minds, was a characteristic of real troublemakers" (Côté 2003, p. 134). Here we see how political identity and cultural styles intersect, as well as possibly class. Rather than working class, in Québec, the police are part of the high middle class. The commanders in chief of the Montréal police receive a higher wage than the Québec provincial Premier; the province's police commander in chief is part of the most-wealthy 1%.

We also need to better understand the influence of information services on political profiling (Cyr 2013). For example, a study on the G20 Summit in Toronto, based partly on police documents obtained under the *Access to Information Act*, concluded that the information services had identified "criminal anarchists" as the main threat to security and offered specific training to police officers who were to be deployed in the streets. The authors thus identify a phenomenon of "threat amplification," which had the effect of justifying repression related to political profiling (Monagham and Walby 2011, p. 659). One also could ask whether information service agencies visiting militants (Lévesque 2012; Canadian Press 2012) constitutes a kind of political profiling (in the form of harassment, threat, etc.). It also would be helpful to better understand the influence of the media in political profiling, an issue examined in the United States at the end of the 1970s (Marx 1979; see also Boykoff 2007, pp. 282–83 and 288; also see Bonner, Chapter 5).

Moreover, in a context where security services are increasingly privatized, it would be important to study the potential practice of political profiling by employees of private security agencies, or by police officers whose services have been commercialized (South 1988; Bayley and Shearing 1996, pp. 589–90; Rigakos 2002). Similarly, is political profiling also practiced in the justice system? For example, does it influence judges' sentences and, if so, is it affected by other types of profiling.

Finally, and of particular importance to political scientists, it is important that we better understand the influence that political authorities can exert on political profiling. Indeed, as discussed in the introduction to this book (Bonner et al., Chapter 1), police pay attention to the orientations of the political elite (also see Bonner, Chapter 5). Police knowledge of how to manage protests is derived in part from the political response given to specific movements at the national and international level (Della Porta and Reiter 2002, p. 75; Bonner 2014, Chapter 2).

Together these questions may help us better understand why the political and police authorities in Quebec, who have now recognized the problem of racial and social profiling, are slow to recognize political profiling. Beyond Quebec, the emergence of "political profiling" as a concept in the public sphere encourages us to begin to examine its possibilities and limitations as a tool to name, and thus confront, targeted police abuse. Such profiling affects selective citizens' lived experience of liberal democracy and draws the boundaries of acceptable democratic discourse.

Acknowledgements The author wishes to thank his colleagues Céline Bellot, Paul Eid, and Fo Niemi of the Observatoire sur les profilages racial, social et politique (Observatory of racial, social, and political profiling in the public space) for their help with the research, as well as the master's candidates that he is supervising or co-supervising whose reflections and research enriched the discussion presented in this text and encouraged the continuation of the study of the police: Guillaume Faucher, Lynda Khelil, David L'Écuyer, Tristan Ouimet-Savard, and Bernard St-Jacques. Thank you as well to Pascal Dominique-Legault, doctoral student in sociology at the Université Laval for the very stimulating discussions, as well as for the Observatoire for its financial support for the translation, and the translator Sarah Igelfeld, for her work.

NOTES

1. *The Globe and Mail* for Ontario, *La Presse* for Quebec, and the *Montreal Star* in 1971 when *La Presse* was not published for several months due to a strike.
2. *The Gazette* (Montréal), *The Toronto Star* and *The Vancouver Sun*.
3. The SPVM states that it carried out arrests in only 3% of the "gatherings" in Montreal, but this term includes political demonstrations as well as festivals, parades, fireworks, and outdoor street sales (http://www.spvm.qc.ca/FR/documentation/gd_22.asp), consulted on the Internet February 20, 2013.
4. Let us remember that the study was conducted before the G20 Summit in Toronto (more than 1100 arrests in three days) and the student strike in 2012 in Quebec (more than 3500 arrests in eight months), which was followed by another wave of mass arrests (more than 1500 arrests in 2013, even though there was no large protest movement).
5. Records containing information about an operation noted down during its occurrence, including the number of protesters and their movement and actions. These documents were obtained during trials where they had been entered as evidence.
6. Ruling of September 23, 2004 [998-757-115], Judge Evasio Massignani, Montreal Municipal Court, Johanne Allard, official stenographer, p. 7. Regarding the "black flags," see particularly the testimony of police officer Dominic Monchant (mat. 3822), *R. v. Aubin Jordan et al.* [case nos. 102-075-736 *et al.*], Montreal Municipal Court, Judge Denis Boisvert, April 20, 2004, p. 8.
7. We see here a phenomenon brought to light by the approach of the *labeling perspective*, developed by Becker (1963) and used by other writers to understand the actions of the police when faced with political mobilizations (Schervish 1973; Clinard 1974; Gove 1975).
8. This section is inspired in part by St-Jacques (2016).
9. *Ville de Longueuil v. Joël Debellefeuille.* [case nos. 09-19841], Longueuil City Court, Judge Pierre-Armand Tremblay, September 20, 2012, p. 22 §107.
10. In the document "Demande d'aide financière au Programme de contestation judiciaire (secteur droit à l'égalité)" (Request for financial aid from the collective action program [right to equality section]), September 30, 2005, p. 22.
11. Regarding this stance, see Jacques Nadeau's photo that accompanies Corriveau's article in *Le Devoir* (2014; see also Journet 2014, p. A20).
12. Refers to the student protesters during their strike who wore small red squares pinned to their clothes.

13. http://www.lapresse.ca/debats/chroniques/francois-cardinal/201408/19/01-4792758-invasion-barbare.php, consulted on the Internet October 24, 2014.

References

Aubin, Benoît. 2012. "État Policier? Mon œil." *Le Journal de Montréal*, June 11. http://www.journaldemontreal.com/2012/06/11/etat-policier–mon-oeil (last accessed November 19, 2017).

Barrette, Denis. 2002. "Le Liberté d'Expression dans la Rue: Judiciarisation de la Dissidence et quelques Moyens de Défense." *Bulletin de la Ligue des droits et des libertés*, décembre.

Bartol, Curt R., and Anne M. Bartol. 2013. *Criminal & Behavioral Profiling*. London: Sage.

Bayley, David H. 2006. *Changing the Guard: Developing Democratic Police Abroad*. Oxford, UK: Oxford University Press.

Bayley, David H., and Clifford D. Shearing. 1996. "The Future of Policing." *Law and Society Review* 30 (3): 585–606.

Becker, Howard. 1963. *Outsiders: Studies in the Sociology of Deviance*. New York: Free Press.

Bélair-Cirino. 2011. "Hausse des droits de scolarité—L'ASSÉ se dit victime d'un profilage politique." *Le Devoir*, July 19. http://www.ledevoir.com/politique/montreal/327708/hausse-des-droits-de-scolarite-l-asse-se-dit-victime-d-un-profilage-politique (last accessed November 19, 2017).

Bellot, Céline, Isabelle Raffestin, Marie-Noëlle Royer, and Véronique Noël. 2005. *Judiciarisation et Criminalisation des Populations Itinérantes à Montréal*. Montréal: Secrétariat national des sans-abris.

Bernard, Léonel, and Christopher McAll. 2008. "La Surreprésentation des Jeunes Noirs Montréalais." *Centre de Recherche de Montréal sur les Inégalités Sociales, les Discriminations et les Pratiques Alternatives de Citoyenneté (CREMIS)* 3 (3): 15–22.

Bonner, Michelle D. 2014. *Policing Protest in Argentina and Chile*. Boulder, CO: First Forum.

Bourque, Jimmy, Stefanie LeBlanc, Anouk Utzschneider, and Christopher Wright. 2009. Efficacité du Profilage dans le Contexte de la Sécurité Nationale. Commission Canadienne des droits de la personne/Fondation canadienne des relations raciales.

Bowling, Ben, and Leanne Weber. 2011. "Stop and Search in Global Context: An Overview." *Policing and Society* 21 (4): 480–88.

Boykoff, Jules. 2007. "Limiting Dissent: The Mechanisms of State Répression in the USA." *Social Movement Studies* 6 (3): 281–310.

Buzzetti, Hélène. 2006. "Entretien avec Jacques Duchesneau: Le "Profilage", un Mal Nécessaire." *Le Devoir*, 17 août, A3.

Campbell, Christine, and Paul Eid. 2009. *La Judiciarisation des Personnes Itinérantes à Montréal: Un profilage Social.* Québec: Commission des droits de la personne et des droits de la jeunesse. Cat. 2.120-8.61.

Canadian Civil Liberties Association et National Union of Public and General Employees. 2011. Breach of the Peace: G20 Summit—Accountably in Policing and Governance, Toronto.

Canadian Press. 2012 "Visites à l'Imporviste: La SCRS Estime Agir en toute Légitimité." *Le Devoir*, March 5.

Canter, David. 2004. "Offender Profiling and Investigative Psychology." *Journal of Investigative Psychology and Offender Profiling* 1 (1): 1–15.

Chalom, Maurice. 2011. "La Pratique du Profilage Racial Déshonore la Profession Policière." *Revue Internationale de Criminologie et de Police Technique et Scientifique* 64 (Janvier–Mars): 83–100.

Chamayou, Grégoire. 2010. *Les chasses à l'homme*. Paris: La Fabrique.

Clinard, Marshall B. 1974. *Sociology of Deviant Behavior*, 4e éd. New York: Holt, Rinehart and Winston.

Comack, Elizabeth. 2012. *Racialized Policing: Aboriginal People's Encounters with the Police*. Halifax-Winnipeg: Fernwood.

Corriveau, Jeanne. 2014. "Grabuge à l'Hotel de Ville de Montréal." *Le Devoir*, August 19. http://www.ledevoir.com/societe/actualites-en-soci-ete/416252/grabuge-a-l-hotel-de-ville-de-montreal (last accessed November 19, 2017).

Côté, Robert. 2003. *Ma guerre contre le FLQ*. Montréal: Trait d'union.

Cyr, Marc-André. 2013. "La Délicate Violence du Policier sans Uniforme." In *À qui la Rue? Répression Policière et Mouvements Sociauxed*, edited by Dupuis-Déri. Francis. Montréal: Écosociété.

de Montréal, Ville. 2011. "Dépôt du Rapport de la CDPDJ sur le Profilage Racial—La Ville, le SPVM et la STM Poursuivront Leur Lutte au Profilage Racial." Montreal, May 11. http://ville.montreal.qc.ca/portal/page?_pageid=5798,42657625&_dad=portal&_schema=PORTAL&id=16414 (last accessed November 19, 2017).

del Bayle, Loubet, and Jean-Louis. 2006. *Police et politique: Une approche sociologique*. Paris: Harmattan.

Della Porta, Donatella, and Herbert Reiter, eds. 1998. *Policing Protest*. Minneapolis: University of Minnesota Press.

Della Porta, Donatella, and Herbert Reiter. 2002. "Mouvement 'Anti-Mondialisation' et Ordre Public." *Les Cahiers de la sécurité intérieure* 47 (1): 51–77.

Descôteaux, Bernard. 2014. "Servir et protéger? Police de Montréal." *Le Devoir*, August 20, A6.

Duchaine, Gabrielle. 2012. "La CLASSE Dénonce le Profilage Politique." *La Presse*, June 11. http://www.lapresse.ca/actualites/dossiers/conflit-etudiant/201206/11/01-4533692-la-classe-denonce-le-profilage-politique.php (last accessed November 19, 2017).

Dupont, Benoît. 2011. *Les polices au Québec*. Paris: Presses Universitaires de France.

Dupuis-Déri, Francis, ed. 2013a. *À qui la rue? Répression policière et mouvements sociaux*. Montréal: Écosociété.

Dupuis-Déri, Francis. 2013b. ""Printemps Erable" ou "Printemps de la Matraque"? Profilage Politique et Répression Sélective pendant la Grève Etudiante de 2012." In *À qui la Rue? Répression Policière et Mouvements Sociaux*, edited by Francis Dupuis-Déri. Montréal: Écosociété.

Dupuis-Déri, Francis. 2013c. *Who's Afraid of the Black Blocs: Anarchy Around the World*. Toronto and Oakland: Between the Lines and PM Press.

Eid, Paul, and Michèle Turenne. 2010. *Profilage Racial: Document de Consultation sur le Profilage Racial*. Québec: Commission des droits de la personne et des droits de la jeunesse.

Elkouri, Rima. 2012. "Déni Policier." *La Presse*, June 12. http://www.lapresse.ca/debats/chroniques/rima-elkouri/201206/12/01-4534009-deni-policier.php (last accessed November 19, 2017).

Favre, Pierre. 1990. "Nature et Statut de la Violence dans les Manifestations Contemporaines." *Les Cahiers de la sécurité intérieure. La documentation française* 1 (April–June): 149–62.

Fernandez, Luis A. 2008. *Policing Dissent: Social Control and the Anti-Globalization Movement*. New Brunswick: Rutgers University Press.

Filieule, Olivier. 1997. *Stratégies de la rues: Les manifestations en France*. Paris: Presses de Sciences po.

Filieule, Olivier, and Donatella della Porta, eds. 2006. *Police et manifestants: Maintien de l'ordre et gestion des conflits*. Paris: Presses de Sciences po.

Frank, J.A. 1984. "La Dynamique des Manifestations Violentes." *Revue Canadienne de Science Politique* 17 (June): 325–50.

Frank, J.A., and Michael Kelly. 1979. "'Street Politics' in Canada: An Examination of Mediating Factors." *American Journal of Political Science* 23 (August): 593–614.

Gove, W.R. 1975. "The Labelling Perspective: An Overview." In *The Labelling of Deviance: Evaluating a Perspective*, edited by R. Gove. New York and London: Sage.

Goyette, Martin, Céline Bellot, and Marie-Ève Sylvestre. 2014. "La Gestion de l'Espace Public: De la Confiance des Citoyens à la Méfiance à l'Endroit des Pratiques Répressives." In *Les Défis Québécois: Conjonctures et Transitions*, edited by R. Bernier. Montréal: Presses de l'Université du Québec.

Green, Joyce. 2006. "From Stonechild to Social Cohesion: Anti-Racist Challenges for Saskatchewan." *Revue Canadienne de Science Politique* 39 (3): 507–27.

Hall, Alan, and Willem De Lint. 2003. "Policing Labour in Canada." *Policing and Society* 13 (3): 219–34.

Harcourt, Bernard E. 2003. "The Shaping of Chance: Actuarial Models and Criminal Profiling at the Turn of the Twenty-First Century." *University of Chicago Law Review* 70 (1): 105–28.

Harris, David A. 2011. "Profiling Unmasked: From Criminal Profiling to Racial Profiling." In *Blind Goddess: A Reader on Race and Justice*, edited by Alexander Papachristou. New York: The New Press.

Hoopes, Jennifer, Tara Lai Quinlan, and Deborah A. Ramirez. 2003. "Defining Racial Profiling in a Post-September 11 World." *American Criminal Law Review* 40: 1195.

Jobard, Fabien. 2008. "La Militarisation du Maintien de l'Ordre, entre Sociologie et Histoire." *Déviance et Société* 32 (1): 101–9.

Jones, Trevors, Tim Newburn, and David J. Smith. 1996. "Policing and the Idea of Democracy." *The British Journal of Criminology* 36 (2): 182–98.

Journet, Paul. 2014. "La Clique Policière." *La Presse*, August 20, A20.

King, Mike. 2004. "D'une Gestion Policière Réactive à la Gestion des Manifestants? La Police et les Manifestations Anti-Mondialisation au Canada." *Cultures & Conflits* 56: 209–47.

Lavoie, Sébastien. 2014. "P-6: contesté, contestable... et encore applicable?" *Le journal des alternatives*, July 1. http://journal.alternatives.ca/spip.php?article7875 (last accessed November 19, 2017).

Lemonde, Lucie. 2010. "Le Profilage dans l'Espace Public: Comment Cacher ce que l'on ne Veut pas Voir!" *Bulletin de la ligue des droits et libertés*, Fall.

Lévesque, Claude. 2012. "Le SCRS Montré du Doigt par des Groupes Sociaux." *Le Devoir*, January 30. http://www.ledevoir.com/societe/actualites-en-societe/341383/le-scrs-montre-du-doigt-par-des-groupes-sociaux (last accessed November 19, 2017).

Ligue des droits et libertés, Association des juristes progressistes et Association pour une solidarité syndicale étudiante. 2013. *Répression, discrimination et grève étudiante: Analyse et témoignages*.

Maanen, John van. 1978. *Policing: A View from the Street*. New York: Random House.

Martineau, Richard. 2014. "Se Protéger et se Servir." *Le Journal de Montréal*, August 21, 6.

Marquis, Mélanie. 2012. "6000$ en Contraventions Pendant la Grève: Une Etudiante Commence le Combat." *La Presse*, August 7.

Marx, Gary T. 1979. "External Efforts to Damage or Facilitate Social Movements: Some Patterns, Explanations, Outcomes and Complications." In

The Dynamics of Social Movements, edited by J. McCarthy and M. N. Zald. Cambridge, MA: Winthrop Publishing.

McClintock, F.M., André Normandeau, Philippe Robert, and Jérôme Skolnick. 1974. "Police et Violence Collective." In *Police, culture et société*, edited by Denis Szabo. Montréal: Les Presses de l'Université de Montréal, 91–159.

MacDonald, Heater. 2001. "The Myth of Racial Profiling." *City Journal* 11 (2): 14–27.

Miles, Brian. 2012. "Grand Prix: Pas de Profilage Politique dit le SPVM." *Le Devoir*, June 11.

Monagham, Jeffrey, and Kevin Walby. 2011. ""They Attacked the City": Security Intelligence, the Sociology of Protest Policing and the Anarchist Threat at the 2010 Toronto G20 Summit." *Current Sociology* 60 (5): 653–71.

Monjardet, Dominique. 1996. *Ce que fait la police*. Paris: La Découverte.

Muller, Damon A. 2000. "Criminal Profiling: Real Science or Just Wishful Thinking?" *Homicide Studies* 4 (3): 234–64.

Okomba-Deparice, Herman. 2012. *Des Valeurs Partagées, un Intérêt Mutuel: Plan Stratégique en Matière de Profilage Racial et Social (2012–2014)*. Montréal: Service de police de la Ville de Montréal.

Ontario Human Rights Commission. 2003. *Paying the Price: The Human Cost of Radical Profiling*. Toronto, ON: Ontario Human Rights Commission.

Parizeau, Alice. 1980. "L'armée et la Crise d'octobre." *Criminologie* 13 (2): 47–78.

Parmar, Alpa. 2011. "Stop and Search in London: Counter-Terrorist or Counter-Productive?" *Policing and Society* 21 (4): 369–82.

Parnaby, Andrew, and Gregory S. Kealey. 2003. "The Origins of Political Policing in Canada: Class, Law and the Burden of Empire." *Osgoode Hall Law Journal* 41 (2–3): 211–40.

Patenaude, Alain. 2014. "Nos Policiers et le Projet de Loi 3." *Le Devoir*, August 19, A6.

Payette, Lise. 2014. "Tarzan contre Goliath." *Le Devoir*, August 22. http://www.ledevoir.com/politique/quebec/416469/tarzan-contre-goliath (last accessed November 19, 2017).

Popovic, Alexandre. 2013. "Contre l'Apitoiement: l'Auto-Organisation Face à la Répression Politique." In *À Qui la Rue? Répression Policière et Mouvements Sociaux*, edited by Francis Dupuis-Déri. Montréal: Écosociété.

Pyton, André. 2012. "Du profilage criminel." *La Presse*, February 10. http://www.lapresse.ca/debats/votre-opinion/201202/09/01-4494393-du-profilage-criminel.php (last accessed November 19, 2017).

Radio-Canada. 2013. "La police d'Ottawa commence son projet-pilote surleprofilageracial."May6.http://ici.radio-canada.ca/nouvelle/612483/police-ottawa-profilage-racial-projet-pilote (last accessed October 24, 2014).

Radio-Canada. 2014. "Couillard Déplore le Deux Poids, Deux Mesures du SPVM." August 19. http://beta.radio-canada.ca/nouvelle/680847/philippe-couillard-hotel-ville-montreal (last accessed November 19, 2017).

Rafail, Patrick. 2005. "Is There an Asymmetry in Protest Policing? Comparative Empirical Analysis from Montreal, Toronto, and Vancouver." Montréal, McGill Social Statistics Masters Working Paper Series, August 29.

Rafail, Patrick. 2010. "Asymmetry in Protest Control? Comparing Protest Policing Patterns in Montreal, Toronto, and Vancouver, 1998–2004." *Mobilization* 14 (4): 489–509.

Rigakos, George S. 2002. *The New Parapolice: Risk Markets and Commodified Social Control.* Toronto: University of Toronto Press.

Rigouste, Mathieu. 2012. *La domination policière: Une violence industrielle.* Paris: La Fabrique.

Robert, Jacques. 2014. "Le Respect en Prend un Coup." *La Presse*, August 20, A19.

Santerre, David. 2012. "Le SPVM Dément Faire du Profilage Politique." *La Presse*, June 11. http://www.lapresse.ca/actualites/dossiers/conflit-etudiant/201206/11/01-4533799-le-spvm-dement-faire-du-profilage-politique.php (last accessed November 19, 2017).

Service de police de la Ville de Montréal. "Profilage racial: La position du SPVM." http://www.spvm.qc.ca/fr/Fiches/Details/Profilage-racial (last accessed October 24, 2014).

Scheinin, Martin. 2007. Rapport du Rapporteur Spécial sur la Promotion et la Rotection des Droits de l'Homme et des Libertés Fondamentales dans la Lutte Antiterroriste. Nations Unies. Doc. A/HRC/4/26.

Schervish, Paul G. 1973. "The Labelling Perspective: Its Bias and Potential in the Study of Political Deviance." *The American Sociologist* 8 (2): 47–57.

Shantz, Jeff. 2012. "Protest and Punishment in Canada: From Legislation to Martial Law." In *Protest and Punishment: The Repression of Resistance in the Era of Neoliberal Globalization*, edited by Jeff Shantz, 219–38. Durham: Carolina Academic Press.

Sheptycki, James. 2005. "Policing Political Protest when Politics Go Global: Comparing Public Order Policing in Canada and Bolivia." *Policing and Society* 15 (3): 327–52.

Silverman, Eli. 2001. *NYPD Battles Crime: Innovative Strategies in Policing.* Boston: Northeastern University Press.

Sklansky, David Alan. 2008. *Democracy and the Police.* Stanford, CA: Stanford University Press.

Skolnick, J. 1966. *Justice Without Trial: Law Enforcement in a Democratic Society.* New York: Wiley.

South, Nigel. 1988. *Policing for Profit: The Private Security Sector.* London: Sage.

Starr, Amory, Luis Fernandez, and Christian Scholl. 2011. *Shutting Down the Streets: Political Violence and Social Control in the Global Era*. New York, NY: University Press.

St-Jacques, Bernard. 2016. *Injustice, criminalisation de la pauvreté et profilage social: Regards croisés d'Erving Goffman et de Georg Simmel*. M.A. thesis, Department of Political Science, UQAM.

Sylvestre, Marie-Ève. 2009. "Policing the Homeless in Montreal: Is This Really What the Population Wants?" *Policing and Society* 20 (4): 432–58.

Turenne, Michèle. 2005. *Le Profilage Racial: Mise en Contexte et Définition*. Québec: Commission des droits de la personne et des droits de la jeunesse. Cat. 2.120-1.25.

Waddington, David P. 2007. *Policing Public Disorder: Theory and Practice*. London: Routledge.

Waddington, David, and Mike King. 2007. "The Impact of the Local: Police Public-Order Strategies during the G8 Justice and Home Affairs Ministerial Meetings." *Mobilization* 12 (4): 417–30.

Ward, Heather, and Christopher E. Stone. 2000. "Democratic Policing: A Framework for Action." *Policing and Society* 10 (1): 11–45.

Westley, William A. [1950] 2003. "Les Racines de l'Éthique Policière." In *Connaître la Police: Grands Textes de la Recherche Anglo-Saxonne*, edited by Jean-Paul Brodeur and Dominique Montjardet, 32–47. Paris: IHESI.

Wilson, George, Roger Dunham, and Geoffrey Alpert. 2004. "Prejudice in Police Profiling Assessing an Overlooked Aspect in Prior Research." *American Behavioral Scientist* 47 (7): 896–909.

Wilson, James Q., and George L. Kelling. 1982. "Broken Window: The Police and Neighborhood Safety." *Atlantic Monthly* 249 (3): 29–38.

Winerman, Lea. 2004. "Criminal Profiling: The Reality Behind the Myth." *Monitor on Psychology* 35 (7): 66–9.

Wood, Lesley J. 2014. *Crisis and Control: Militarization of Protest Policing*. London, Toronto: Pluto Press and Between the Lines.

Wortely, Scot, and Akwasi Owusu-Bempah. 2011. "The Usual Suspects: Police Stop and Search Practices in Canada." *Policing and Society* 21 (4): 395–407.

PART II

Accountability

Holding Police Abuse to Account: The Challenge of Institutional Legitimacy, a Chilean Case Study

Michelle D. Bonner

In 2011, student and labor protests were abundant in Chile. On August 25 of that year 16-year-old Manuel Gutiérrez went with his brother, Gerson, and friend Giuseppe, to watch one protest that was taking place near their house in the Santiago neighborhood of Macul. While they observed from a footbridge, two Carabinero police officers fired lead bullets in their direction. The bullets ricocheted off the walls and one went into Manuel's chest. He died less than two hours later in hospital. A fellow bystander, Carlos Burgos, was shot in the arm but survived.

Unlike in most Latin American countries, the police in Chile do not have the reputation of being violent or corrupt. Indeed the Carabineros, the country's primary national police force, has consistently been one of the institutions in which citizens have the most confidence, often ranking higher than the Catholic Church in public opinion polls. For example, in 2008, 63% of Chileans had confidence in the Carabineros compared to 47% in the Catholic Church, 31% in the government, and 17% in the judiciary (CEP 2015). Yet as the chapters in this book illustrate, police

M. D. Bonner (✉)
University of Victoria, Victoria, BC, Canada

© The Author(s) 2018
M. D. Bonner et al. (eds.), *Police Abuse in Contemporary Democracies*,
https://doi.org/10.1007/978-3-319-72883-4_5

113

abuse, even homicide, occurs in all countries. Police abuse is defined in this chapter as it is in the introduction: "police actions that may or may not be 'illegal' but severely limit selective citizens' rights." Ideally, in a democracy, police abuse is reduced through holding those responsible to account.

But what do we mean by accountability and, by extension, what is its purpose in democracy? While political scientists have studied this question extensively, how do the roles they identify for accountability in democracy apply in distinct ways in cases of police abuse? Through a close examination of accountability in the case of Manuel Gutiérrez, I argue that, in practice, a key function of accountability, as it pertains to police abuse, is to reinforce the institution's legitimacy. The goal of legitimacy may or may not include changes in police or political practices that might better support equality of the rule of law and prevent repetition. Thus, if political science is to better integrate reduced police abuse into concepts of democratic accountability, stronger attention must be paid to establishing limits on the prioritization of legitimacy over the goals of equality and non-repetition.

Democratic Accountability, Legitimacy and the Police

Accountability is a fundamental feature of all definitions of democracy and is widely studied in political science as a central component of the rule of law. It refers to a system of oversight that provides two key functions: answerability and enforcement (Schedler 1999). Answerability involves public *transparency* regarding the actions and omissions of those with public power and the results of those actions and omissions. It also includes the requirement for those actors thought to have been involved in wrongdoing to provide an explanation or *justification* for their actions or omissions (Schedler 1999, p. 14; March and Olsen 1995). Enforcement necessitates that a body vested with legal authority *punish* those found to have committed a wrongdoing (Schedler 1999; Mainwaring 2003).

Accountability can be political (e.g., resignations, loss of elections, official inquiry). In a minimal definition of democracy, political leaders are simply held accountable by elections at which time they have to answer for what they have done, not done, or plan to do, and may be sanctioned by an electoral loss. Broader, liberal definitions of democracy include state actors being held accountable by other branches of the state, such as the judiciary. Political leaders are also held accountable for the actions and inactions of those civil servants, in our case the police, under their responsibility. Indeed it is often assumed in political science studies of accountability that police follow political orders. Thus, political leaders may lose elections or be asked to resign based on the actions of police.

Accountability is also legal. Indeed this is where accountability most strongly dovetails with the concept of the rule of law. Democratic rule of law establishes rules over the use of (coercive) power and relations between people and groups ideally agreed upon by the majority and applied to all citizens equally (Maravall and Przeworski 2003, p. 13; Holmes 2003, p. 19; Fukuyama 2015, p. 12). The judiciary then becomes a key actor of accountability and, as a consequence, this institution is well studied in political science. However, in many cases, it is in fact the police who make the initial decision as to whether to apply or not apply the law, provides justifications for their choice, and pursue initial punishments (e.g., arrest). As Francis Fukuyama notes "even the most legitimate democracies require police power to enforce the law" (2015, p. 13). When police are themselves suspected of wrongdoing, they may police themselves (through investigations by internal affairs departments), be policed by another police force or oversight body, or the judiciary may become involved, or all three. In this sense, ideally, police actions are bounded by the rule of law.

The purpose of accountability and the rule of law in a democracy is threefold; it provides equality, predictability, and legitimacy (Schedler 1999; Maravall and Przeworski 2003; Holmes 2003; O'Donnell 1999; Fukuyama 2015).

Equality. Accountability and the rule of law in the ideal liberal democracy are meant to ensure that the rules apply to all citizens equally, no matter how much or how little power an individual or group possesses. It thus directly challenges the inequality in citizenship produced by police abuse discussed in Chapters 2–4. Ideally, accountability involves placing limits on political and state power that in turn serve to support the protection of civil, political, social, and human rights to varying degrees depending on the definition of democracy one is using (Sklansky 2008). For those most vulnerable to potential abuses of political or police power, the purpose of this aspect of accountability is also to ensure non-repetition.

Predictability. The rule of law establishes rules and procedures for governance that allow citizens the autonomy to act or not act with reasonable certainty regarding the consequences (Maravall and Przeworski 2003, p. 2). Yet, as Stephen Holmes notes, "no state, however liberal or democratic, treats all citizens equally before the law" (2003, p. 21) and thus the law can be very predictable for the powerful and well-off (whose support leaders need to govern) and "maddeningly erratic for the less well-off" (2003, p. 22). Moreover, as Mainwaring (2003) and Fukuyama (2015) point out, the balance between accountability and effective governance is always a challenge. Greater accountability may provide more predictability for more people (and thus greater equality) but may decrease effective governance. Thus, legal interpretation and justification become very important.

This is particularly true in the case of alleged police wrongdoing. Police have the legitimate right to use violence against citizens. They are often issued with and trained to use guns and other lethal weapons. They have a high degree of discretion when using violence, thus, for the police, a context of legal predictability would logically require significant leniency in authorities' acceptance of police justifications. Here we start to see how the purpose of accountability as it relates to equality begins to conflict with the inclusion of the goal of predictability. The question then becomes whose legal predictability is more important, that of the police or those affected by police abuse? Returning to Holmes's (2003, p. 22) point, political leaders need the support of the police in order to govern, thus it follows that legal predictability for the police would be a political priority in democracies.

Legitimacy. Finally, and most important in the analysis that follows, accountability in democracy serves the purpose of reaffirming the legitimacy of the institutions and actors of governance. Drawing on Machiavelli, Stephen Holmes argues that the judicial system and rule of law help to dampen class antagonism and give the support of the poor to the regime needed to build armies (2003, p. 32). From this perspective, the more the law is equally and predictably applied across classes, the greater the legitimacy gained by political leaders and democratic institutions such as the police. It is citizens' direct experience with the police, and hence police practices, that affects institutional legitimacy. In this line of argument, it is in the interest of the police, like political leaders, to protect citizen rights, apply the law consistently, and use minimal levels of violence (Beetham 1991).

Yet legitimacy can equally be derived from the *perception* of democratic accountability based on justifications that convince the intended audience because they are familiar or consistent with existing beliefs (Beetham 1991, p. 11; Tankebe 2010; March and Olsen 1995). Effective political, police, and media narratives can construct acceptable authoritative justifications that provide the public appearance of equal and predictable accountability, reinforcing democratic legitimacy, while doing little to ensure non-repetition. That is, the stories we tell about accountability are as important as the institutions and laws established to govern it. Indeed these stories can shape how we use these laws and institutions and whether or not steps are taken to reform or alter their practices or functions. Elsewhere, I have referred to this as discursive accountability (Bonner 2014). Dominant public discourses or narratives define an act as wrongdoing or not, justify the reasons, identify who is responsible, and select the appropriate punishment or remedy, all from an often wide range of options.

In sum, if the goal is to reduce police abuse in democracy then, ideally, the priority of accountability would be to ensure equality and this, in turn, would determine the laws that define predictability for police actions and provide the basis upon which their legitimacy is derived. However, if police abuse is not a concern and the primary goal of accountability is legitimacy then equality may be sacrificed in favor of establishing a public *perception* of police legitimacy. That is, the dominant goals of accountability and the relative importance of police abuse within it, determine the contours of the practice of democratic accountability and citizens' lived experience of policing.

METHODOLOGY

In what follows I look at the stories told about accountability in the case of the police shooting of Manuel Gutiérrez. The study is based on the analysis of all newspaper articles published in Chile's leading two national newspapers, *El Mercurio* and *La Tercera*, for the first three weeks following Gutiérrez's death (August 26–September 16, 2011, a total of 54 articles). These media were chosen for their recognized agenda-setting function and influence on political and public discourse in Chile (Léon-Dermota 2003; Lagos 2009). Then, through keyword searches in these and other online Chilean media, I analyzed 16 follow-up stories on the unfolding of accountability over the next four years. In all these articles, I identified how interviewees and the media publication itself framed or justified accountability (what type of accountability was needed and why) and how these mechanisms of accountability unfolded in practice. The objective is to analyze the dominant discourses that frame discussions of police accountability and legitimacy and their consequences. While an analysis of the role of the media in producing these discourses is interesting and I have examined this elsewhere (Bonner 2013, 2014, in press), this chapter centers on an examination of the dominant discourses themselves.

The Gutiérrez case was chosen for a number of important reasons. First, it involved a death of a civilian perpetrated by a police officer. This is obviously one of the most extreme acts of violence a police officer can take and is the most likely to receive high levels of public and political scrutiny. As one scholar and legal reformer interviewed in Chile explained: "the majority of the [Chilean] population [...] believes that there should be order and are ready to tolerate what I would call low-intensity human rights abuses; not torture, disappearances, or imprisonment without trial, but that the police hit people on the streets with truncheons, yes. That the police throw tear gas without much justification, yes."[1] Thus, a death is more likely to be considered a "high-intensity" human rights abuse.

Second, while Gutiérrez was from an economically poor family and lived in a *población* (shantytown), he could not be dismissed in public discourse as "deserving" what happened. The articles made clear that he had not been involved in causing "disorder" or violence by protesting, actions commonly used in Chile to justify police abuse (Bonner 2014, Chapter 8). Rather the news articles described him as an electronics student who aspired to be an evangelical pastor and the first professional in his family. He attended church with his grandmother three times a week, sang in the church choir, and had just returned from church prior to going to watch the protest. A 2015 book on the incident, written by a journalist, proclaimed: "We are all Manuel Gutiérrez" (Tamayo Grez 2015).

Third, Gutiérrez's death was the most extreme act of police abuse in a list of many such public complaints during protests that year. This contributed to the issue of police abuse becoming more prominent in public debates than it had been since the return of democracy in 1990. For example, this was the first year that Chile's Diego Portales University's annual Human Rights Report dedicated a full chapter to "police violence." In sum, if police were to be held accountable for wrongdoing in the homicide of a civilian, this would be a likely case. Finally, since the death occurred in 2011, enough time has elapsed to follow the completion of judicial accountability, which ended with a Supreme Court ruling in 2015.

In what follows I present three key narratives found in the newspaper articles analyzed. I define narratives as the stories, or sequences of events, which political actors (state, civil society, and media) tell to make sense of events (Schram and Neisser 1997; Roe 1994; March and Olsen 1995). The manner in which the stories are told or constructed will reveal a certain perspective. Dominant narratives are those repeated most often and taken by many people to be simply "the truth." These are also generally the narratives used by those with the most power such as the president, members of the government, or chief of police, or those used most frequently in the agenda-setting media. Counternarratives are those stories that offer a contrasting account to the dominant one (Schram and Neisser 1997; Roe 1994; March and Olsen 1995).

The first narrative found in the articles is that of "successful accountability," which dominated for the first three weeks after Gutiérrez's death (August 26–September 16, 2011). The second is the dominant narratives and counternarratives around "diminished accountability" that emerged during the unfolding of justice from November 2011 to December 2015. Finally, the last section examines the "lost counternarratives," scattered throughout all the articles, on alternative forms of accountability not pursued.

Successful Accountability

The death of Manuel Gutiérrez occurred at a difficult time for the Carabineros and the Chilean government, in general. Police response to ongoing student and labor protests had been garnering increasing public criticism as cases such as mass arbitrary arrests, beatings in police vehicles, and sexual abuse in police stations, came to public light. Indeed, for the first time in decades, public confidence in the Carabineros plummeted from 65% in 2009 to 50% in 2011 (CEP 2015). Consequently, it was important from a public relations perspective, if not for democracy, to show that the police were accountable to democratic procedures and institutions. As Director General of the Carabineros, Eduardo Gordon stated on August 30, 2011: "I want to reiterate, to our community, that they keep believing in their Carabineros, keep having confidence in your Carabineros."[2]

Indeed, in the first three weeks after Gutiérrez's death, it did appear that democratic institutions of accountability were functioning as they should. While there were some significant errors, even the Gutiérrez family said they were confident in Chilean justice and initially kept their distance from social movement activists and political leaders who offered their support.[3]

Almost immediately after the shooting, the public prosecutor's office initiated an investigation with the Investigative Police's (PDI, Chile's only other police force) Homicide Brigade and the Legal Medical Service (SML). This was an important act of legal accountability, as the initial official response of the Carabineros was that they would not be pursuing an internal investigation because Carabineros were not involved.[4] The Carabineros argued that the bullet most likely came from gangs or pro-testers who were in the neighborhood causing violence at the time. This was a theory supported by National Renovation (then the governing political party) congress member Alberto Cardemil and repeated often in articles in the conservative *El Mercurio* newspaper. It was perhaps the pressure of the public prosecutor's investigation that led the Carabineros' Internal Affairs department to pursue some form of investigation, which resulted in a confession by one of their officers on the afternoon of August 29 that he had fired a weapon in the area (retracting his previous denial). This confession was followed by an announcement that evening by the public prosecutors that physical proof had been found linking the officer, Second Sergeant Miguel Millacura, to the death.

Both the government and the Gutiérrez family filed legal action against those responsible for the death of Manuel on August 30.[5] Millacura was charged for the death of Manuel Gutiérrez and the injury of Carlos Burgos and sent to prison while the case continued to be inves-tigated.[6] As is the procedure in Chile with cases of police officers causing wrongdoing against civilians (and for which there is concrete evidence), the case was transferred from civilian to military court. On the night of August 30, Military Prosecutor Paola Jofré assumed responsibility for the investigation and began taking testimonies.[7] Charges were eventually laid against Sub-lieutenant Claudia Iglesias for covering up the alleged crime.[8] Like Millacura, Iglesias had initially denied that police officers had fired shots in the area.

Political accountability was equally swift. As soon as Millacura admit-ted his wrongdoing, he was asked to resign along with four of his col-leagues who were working in the same area that night. By August 31, nine officers had been dismissed or asked to resign, including Sergio Gajardo Oelckers, General of the Second Metropolitan Area, for initially denying Carabinero involvement and rejecting an internal investigation.[9] There were some early rumours reported that Director General Eduardo Gordon, the head of the Carabineros, would be asked to resign but this did not occur until September 2 and was then framed by him and the mass media as a response to his health condition and allegations he interfered in the investigation into his son's car accident in 2010 (allegations he denied).[10]

Finally, public apologies, a form of answerability, were provided by Director General Gordon and the accused sergeant, Millacura. In his apology, Gordon carefully reasserted institutional legitimacy, while condemning individual acts of wrongdoing. For example, he states: "Particular cases are not institutional policies, we Carabineros are never going to permit people to act outside the legal boundaries within which we build our profession [...] To those who have thought to rely on this dignified uniform – that we wear with honor – to commit any action contrary to what corresponds, please do not hurt us any more, we do not deserve to be harmed."[11] Millacura apologized to the family stating: "I had no intention to kill him. [...] I didn't know who shot him."[12] In the first case, wrongdoing is individualized and in the second intention is denied.

The vast bulk of the news coverage on this story occurred in the first two weeks after the event. For a few days, it was front-page news and *El Merucrio* even dedicated a section to "The Crisis in the Police." Most Chileans learned about accountability for police abuse in this case during this time period and it appeared to reinforce the goals of equality, legitimacy, and legal predictability. In the next section, I follow the unfolding of accountability over the next few years. These news stories and the dominant narratives they emphasize did not receive the same degree of public attention due to the time elapsed and the limiting of most these news stories to small "factual" follow-up articles, rather than more contextualized stories.

DIMINISHED ACCOUNTABILITY

By 2012, Carabineros had regained their traditional rank in public opinion polls as one of the institutions in which Chileans have the most confidence (CEP 2015). Public (or at least media) attention on the Gutiérrez case dwindled. Yet small and periodic articles reveal an unraveling of accountability grounded and justified in legal reasoning. In what unfolds we see how justifications, and the legitimacy of police use of violence, place important limits on broader understandings of police accountability.

The unraveling arguably began November 17, 2011. After two and a half months in jail, the military court unanimously agreed to release Millacura while the investigation continued.[13] While Millacura's lawyer, Víctor Neira, argued that poor due process in military courts had meant Millacura had already spent too long in jail (UDP 2012, p. 305), the reversal of the initial decision was a symbolic shift. The family, and their supporters, rejected the decision as a form of "impunity."[14] Their opposition continued into the new year when on January 25, 2012, the family (and protest supporters) presented a letter to then President Sebastián Piñera, which called for: Millacura to go to jail; the resignation of the Minister of the Interior Rodrigo Hinzpeter; and, a "profound reform of military justice" (discussed more in the next section).[15]

In February 2012, Carabineros confirmed that three of the nine police officials who had been dismissed in August, were still in active service but had been transferred to different police stations. At this point, the confidence of the family in the Chilean justice system began to waiver. Gerson Gutiérrez, Manuel's brother who was with him when he was shot, said that Carabineros appeared to be treated differently than other citizens, "because we don't have money and because we are poor people we have been made fun of."[16] That is, the equality goal of accountability was not being upheld. The Minister of the Interior, Hinzpeter, asked for a report on the situation from the Carabineros. A press release from the Carabineros explained that the sanctions had never been "firm." The officers had been given "temporary removal" and after further investigation, they decided that for two of the officers the wrongdoing was not grounds for dismissal and the other was on maternity leave and a final decision would be made after the trial.[17] Legal predictability for police was reasserted. In 2015, journalist Tania Tamayo Grez discovered, through a freedom of information request, that in the end only Millacura was permanently dismissed from the Carabineros (2015, Chapter 25).

It took almost three years for the military court to issue their sentence. Given the evidence produced in the investigation, the family's lawyer, Washington Lizana, stated that the minimum sentence for

Millacura was five years and a day.[18] On May 12, 2014, the military court in Santiago sentenced Millacura to three years and a day of probation for "unnecessary violence resulting in death" in the case of Manuel Gutiérrez.[19] Claudio Iglesias was absolved of "cover-up."[20] The family immediately announced they would appeal the decision.[21] Despite these criticisms, in May 2015, the Military Appeals Court decided to further reduce Millacura's sentence to 400 days probation for the death of Gutiérrez and 61 days for the injury of Carlos Burgos. The punishment included a ban from holding public positions or offices for the period of the sentence. In the Appeals Court, the designation of both crimes was also reduced from "unnecessary violence" to "partial crime" (*causidelito*) because, it was decided, Millacura did not intend to kill or harm the two people in question as he did not fire directly at them.[22] Amnesty International rejected this decision.[23] The sentence also changed the family's confidence in the judiciary. Manuel's sister stated in response: "We are clearer now that justice will not come and we don't have hope that it will come."[24]

The family appealed the decision to the Supreme Court (where the judges were comprised of four civilians and one military). On December 15, 2015, the Supreme Court rejected the appeal and reaffirmed the previous court's decision that Millacura did not shoot directly at Gutiérrez and Burgos with the intention of killing and harming them.[25] The action was deemed "imprudent" but not "intentional." In response, on December 18, 2015, the National Institute for Human Rights (INDH) issued a complaint to the Supreme Court calling for the sentence to be overturned and for Millacura to be sentenced to five years and a day for the death of Gutiérrez and 61 days for the shooting and injury of Burgos.[26]

In sum, in the first three weeks after the death of Manuel Gutiérrez, it appeared that accountability for wrongdoing would be pursued. Yet the accountability was carefully limited to individual police officers who were dismissed, asked to resign, or charged with a crime. As media attention declined (and thus the image of the police and governance institutions were less vulnerable) the punishments for those individuals deemed involved were slowly reduced using technical and legal language that protect the right granted to police to use violence against citizens, even if lethal, as long as there is a legally acceptable justification. Thus, accountability to ensure police legitimacy and legal predictability for police was favored over its role in equality. In the final section, I explore some threads in the media stories that reveal counternarratives of accountability that were neglected in favor of definitions that prioritized judicialization and dismissals.

LOST COUNTERNARRATIVES

Certainly, the manner in which state officials, namely the police, judiciary, and the Piñera government, managed discursive accountability in the case of Manuel Gutiérrez succeeded in reaffirming the legitimacy of the police forces without limiting the ability of the police to continue to use high levels of violence in the future. As mentioned, by 2012, confidence in the police had returned to its usual high levels (CEP 2015). In this sense, the definition of accountability applied in this case reaffirmed the legitimacy of the rule of law and the general public's *perception* of predictability and equality, but not necessarily the goal of non-repetition. Two key counternarratives on accountability—a broader definition of accountability and a reform of the military courts—are found scattered throughout the news articles.

The first narrative that is discussed as a minor part of news stories and then ultimately rejected by governing state officials was the argument that the definition of accountability that needed to be applied in the case of Manuel Gutiérrez should be broader. In particular, it should include an examination of the responsibility of the police institution as a whole (including its procedures) and corresponding political responsibilities. This discussion began August 29, once the public prosecutor's investigation found evidence that Carabineros were involved and Millacura confessed to firing his weapon in the area.

In these counternarratives, the primary issue was police procedures that contributed to Gutiérrez's death, not simply the individual officer's actions. From this perspective, the officer's actions were taken within a context that facilitated, if not encouraged, such choices. While the police leadership stressed that Millacura's actions violated police procedures,[27] the counternarratives emphasized that police abuse (albeit until then not lethal) was notably common in the management of protests that year.[28] According to Boris Paredes, the lawyer working with Congress Member Hugo Gutiérrez (Communist Party), the incidents that led to Manuel Gutiérrez's death "do not constitute, in our judgment, isolated situations, rather they are concentrated and coordinated repressive acts."[29]

Indeed, 36-year-old Millacura had 18 years experience as a Carabinero and had been trained in GOPE (police special forces that are responsible for managing protests).[30] The weapon used by Millacura was a 9 mm UZI submachine gun and the public prosecutor's investigation team examined 500 such UZIs available to officers to use in the zone where the incidents occurred.[31] While the investigators note that Millacura incorrectly completed the paperwork to sign-out the gun (making it unclear which gun he used), the counternarratives concerned the guns themselves. Socialist Senator, Alejandro Navarro submitted a request to the Inter-American Human Rights Commission asking that it call on the State of Chile to stop using war weapons against its own citizens and call for police to visibly wear their identification at all times.[32]

Without explicitly making the link, *La Tercera* published articles on August 30 and 31 situating Gutiérrez's death in a list of other cases of police abuse such as the police killings of Jaime Mendoza Collio (age 24) on August 12, 2011, Matías Catrileo Quezada (22) in January 2008, Cristián Castillo (15) on September 11, 2005, and 14 people in Alto Hospicio in October 2001, all of which led to minimal charges for the officers involved.[33]

Student leaders and Socialist Senator Alejandro Navarro are quoted as placing Manuel Gutiérrez's death within a larger political context, described by Navarro as one in which "all Chile has been witness to the abuse of power by Carabineros who have used disproportionate force during marches and protests by children and young students, and the decided support they have received from the Minister of the Interior in each action."[34] Raising similar issues of political responsibility, one news article reports that an unidentified source claimed that Gajardo had received an order from a superior (implied in the article to be from the political executive) on the Friday of Manuel Gutiérrez's death to "dissipate any doubts that Carabineros had been involved in this case."[35] This counternarrative implies that not only should police procedures be questioned but political leaders need to be held accountable for encouraging, if not leading, police actions.

Yet, the judicialization of accountability placed limits on pursuing institutional and political accountability. The family's lawyer, Washington Lizana, stated that "We would have liked to have advanced more in regards to other penal responsibilities that occurred within the Carabineros, particularly those related to institutional cover-up of events. But unfortunately, they won't accept from us any more charges [*diligencias*]. The Military Prosecutor is concentrating on the perpetrator and the circumstances around this event and is not going to widen the investigation."[36] Indeed, Millacura was not the only officer who fired his gun in the area that night. Patricio Bravo fired his standard issued Taurus revolver and he, like Millacura, cleaned his weapon with cotton and alcohol afterward and replaced the bullets (Tamayo Grez 2015, Chapter 24).[37] However, since Bravo's bullets did not kill or injure anyone, no charges were laid.

Moreover, government officials rejected demands by student leaders, other social movement organizations, some political leaders, and eventually the Gutiérrez family, for the resignation of Minister of the Interior Rodrigo Hinzpeter (whose Ministry is politically responsible for the Carabineros). Government officials defended the Minister's actions arguing that he acted as he should have and that it is up to the Public Ministry (public prosecutors) to investigate.[38] A spokesperson for the government argued that the opposition was simply politicizing the event by claiming there was political responsibility; the events, he argued, were "beyond the job of any minister" and the Minister of the Interior fulfilled his role "with absolute diligence and the requirements of law."[39]

Indeed, if the law pertains only to the firing of the weapon causing death, with the primary purpose of providing accountability to reaffirm institutional legitimacy, then the government's assessment of accountability is correct. However, if accountability includes the social and political context within which the officer's choice was made and thus emphasizes the goals of equality and non-repetition, then the government's assessment of accountability is inaccurate. In this manner, the importance of one's definition of accountability is highlighted.

The government and police never took responsibility for the incidents as acts requiring institutional or procedural reforms. However, the ongoing critiques of the Carabineros' actions against protesters in 2011, their lack of transparency regarding their protocols for managing protests, and the decline in public confidence in the police (as seen in polls) contributed to some small but important changes within the institution, made at their own initiative.

In 2011, Carabineros created their own Department of Human Rights, which aims to train officers in the importance of respecting citizens' human rights. As the head of the department, Coronel Rodney L. Weber Orellana, explained, "human rights have been present in all our programs for more than 80 years" but the social and political climate of 2011 called on them to "modernize."[40] They chose to work with the International Red Cross to establish human rights training programs for their officers. Of course, training programs only change practices if, when officers are on the job, they can use the training. Consistent with this goal, the police's Department of Human Rights rewrote their police procedures for managing protests.

In August 2014, for the first time ever, Carabineros made their protest policing protocols publicly available.[41] While this transparency is an important part of accountability, Chile's National Institute of Human Rights notes that the protocols themselves appear at first glance to place significant limits on police action but when examined closely are vague enough to permit the continuation of police abuse in practice. In one of many examples, they note that the protocols state that officers' use of and choice of force must receive prior approval by Carabineros. INDH explains that this permits wide discretion on the part of the police force. Instead, according to human rights standards, INDH holds that police actions should be constrained by the law, not Carabinero approval (INDH 2015, p. 25). Thus, again, these institutional changes, while important, are consistent with a restricted definition of accountability that contributes to reinforcing legitimacy but limits constraints on repetition.

The second counternarrative found scattered among these articles includes demands for the reform of the military courts, in particular, that they should no longer be used to try cases involving civilians. The Gutiérrez family, Congress Member Hugo Gutiérrez, and Amnesty International, are all quoted in news articles as calling for the end of military justice that, in Hugo Gutiérrez's words "is a permanent source of impunity."[42] On May 27, 2015, Amnesty International explains, in reaction to the Military Appeals Court's reduction in Millacura's sentence, that the Chilean government "should not only advance soon in legal reform of military jurisdiction, but also ensure that all cases of human rights, including those involving the use of excessive force by members of the police, should be duly investigated and judged by ordinary courts."[43]

Traditionally in Chile, cases of wrongdoing involving Carabineros, in which there is clear evidence, go to military court. In November 2005, the Inter-American Human Rights court decided in the Palamara case that the Carabineros should be removed from these courts because there are problems with access, transparency, and due process that affect the democratic rights of the accused and victims (UDP 2012, p. 289). Since 2005, Chilean governments have made some attempts to reform military justice. However, the only substantive change was Law 20.477 published in December 2010, which excluded civilians who perpetrated a crime against the police or military from trial in military courts (although there are significant restrictions on when this can apply) (UDP 2012, p. 291). Cases of Carabinero wrongdoing against a civilian continue to fall under the jurisdiction of military courts. Since 2011, the case of Manuel Gutiérrez has served as an emblematic example, used by some media and human rights organizations in their advocacy for military justice reform, but no further changes have been achieved (UDP 2012).[44]

In sum, these counternarratives, given little attention in the agenda-setting news media and articulated by people and institutions with less power than the government, police, or judiciary, emphasize the equality and non-repetition goals of accountability. Yet the counternarratives are rejected in state officials' dominant narratives that focus on definitions of accountability that reinforce government and police legitimacy as well as legal predictability for police.

CONCLUSION

The case of Manuel Gutiérrez encourages us to rethink the definition and purpose of accountability in democracy. If we define accountability in merely legal terms and with the primary objective of providing police legal predictability and reaffirming state (and police) legitimacy, then the Gutiérrez case is an example of successful accountability. Of course, even using this limited definition of accountability, it could be argued, as do some of the counternarratives, that reforming military justice would improve legal accountability. This is a valid and important criticism. However, accountability in civilian courts would still be individualized, contingent upon police justifications, and likely favor police legal predictability.

In contrast, if the goal of accountability is equality and non-repetition, then it becomes important that the political and social context within which the officer made the decision to bring and use a UZI submachine gun at a protest, be considered. As some counternarratives argue, this political and social context matters and will determine the likelihood of non-repetition more than individual accountability. Indeed, police abuse has continued since August 25, 2011 (INDH 2015; CECT 2012, 2013; UDP 2015). For example, in May 2015, student protester Rodrigo Áviles was hit by a Carabinero water cannon and received a severe head injury that nearly caused his death. Again, the Carabineros denied responsibility until TV video footage proved otherwise.[45] Thus, police abuse challenges political science studies of accountability to more critically consider the implications for democracy of prioritizing some goals over others. While institutional legitimacy and legal predictability for police are important for governance, clearer limits are needed on its pursuit so as to not compromise other goals of democratic accountability, notably equality and non-repetition.

NOTES

1. Anonymous. Author interview. Santiago de Chile. June 30, 2009.
2. González, Andrea. "Las frases que marcaron el discurso del general director de Carabineros." *La Tercera*, August 30, 2011.
3. *La Tercera*. "La Hermana del menor baleado en Macul: No buscamos responsibilidades políticas." August 26, 2011.
4. Vergara, Rodrigo. "Manuel Gutiérrez falleció de un disparo durante la madrugada de ayer: Investigación maneja dos hipótesis sobre mortal baleo a joven en Macul." *El Mercurio*, August 27, 2011, p. C12.
5. *El Mercurio*. "Hermano de la victim fatal y confesión de Millacura: 'Demuestra que lo que yo vi era verdad; demuestra que no estaba mintiendo'." August 30, 2011, p. C7.
6. *La Tercera*. "Ex suboficial Millacura cambió su testimonio ante fiscal military y dijo que disparó 'en diagonal'." August 20, 2011.
7. Vergara, R., T. Costas, and M. J. Soler. "Segunda declaración del ex sargento: Millacra cambia su version y reconoce disparo directo." *El Mercurio*, August 31, 2011, p. C9.
8. EMOL. "Caso Manuel Gutiérrez: Tribunal Militar cierra etapa de sumario y familia analiza acciones civiles." March 25, 2013. http://www.emol. com/noticias/nacional/2013/03/25/590186/caso-manuel-gut ierrez-tribunal-militar-cierra-etapa-de-sumario-y-familia-analiza-ac ciones-civiles.html (last accessed July 7, 2016).
9. *El Mercurio*. "Baleado en Macul: Muerto en disturbios: Fiscale pide registro de cenral de Carabineros." August 28, 2011, p. C16.
10. Lezaeta, Pedro, Mario Gálvez, and Rienzi Franco. "Ayer, en la Moneda, la comunicó primero al ministro Hinzpeter y luego al Presidente Piñera: El jueves en la noche, Gordon tomó decision de presenter su reuncia."

El Mercurio, September 3, 2011, p. C8; Ferraro, L., and P. Carrera. "Carabineros: Piñera nombra director a oficial que apoyó a general Gordon." *La Tercera*, September 9, 2011.

11. González, Andrea. "Las frases que marcaron el discurso del general director de Carabineros." *La Tercera*, August 30, 2011.

12. González, Andrea. "Padre de menor baleado agradece disculpas de Millacura: 'Me parece bien que tenga arrepentimiento'." *La Tercera*, September 2, 2011.

13. *La Tercera*. "Corte Marcial deja en libertad a ex carabinero acusado de disparar a Manuel Gutiérrez." November 17, 2011.

14. EMOL. "Piden revocar fallo que otorgó libertad a ex sargento por muerte de estudiante." November 21, 2011. http://www.emol.com/noticias/nacional/2011/11/21/513727/piden-revocar-decision-de-otorgar-libertad-a-ex-sargento-por-muerte-de-estudiante.html (last accessed July 7, 2016).

15. *La Tercera*. "Familia de menor baleado en Macul exige que cabo Millacura permanezca en prisión." January 25, 2012.

16. EMOL. "Familia de Manuel Gutiérrez: Carabineros se burla porque somos gente pobre." February 13, 2012. http://www.emol.com/noticias/nacional/2012/02/13/526062/hermano-de-manuel-gutierrez-carabineros-se-burla-porque-somos-pobres.html (last accessed July 7, 2016).

17. Ibid.

18. García Jiménez, Bernardita. "Justicia Militar otra vez en la mira: critican sentencia de tres años de libertad vigilada para carabinero que asesinó a Manuel Gutiérrez." *El Mostrador*, May 12, 2014. http://www.elmostrador.cl/noticias/pais/2014/05/12/justicia-militar-otra-vez-en-la-mira-critican-sentencia-de-tres-anos-de-libertad-vigilada-para-carabinero-que-asesino-a-manuel-gutierrez/ (last accessed July 7, 2016).

19. Ibid.

20. Ibid.

21. EMOL. "Condenan a tres años de libertad vigilada a carabinero que dio muerte a joven en Macul." May 12, 2014. http://www.emol.com/noticias/nacional/2014/05/12/659737/condenan-a-tres-anos-de-libertad-vigilada-a-carabinero-que-dio-muerte-a-joven-en-macul.html (last accessed July 7, 2016).

22. EMOL. "Amnestía Internacional rechaza rebaja de condena de carabinero en caso Manuel Gutiérrez." May 27, 2015. http://www.emol.com/noticias/nacional/2015/05/27/718891/amnistia-rechaza-rebaja-de-condena-de-carabinero-en-caso-manuel-gutierrez.html (last accessed July 7, 2016); López, Andrés, and Angélica Baeza. "Muerte de Manuel Gutiérrez: Corte Marcial rebaja pena a ex sargento de carabineros."

La Tercera, May 20, 2015. http://www.latercera.com/noticia/nacional/2015/05/680-630559-9-muerte-de-manuel-gutierrez-corte-marcial-rebaja-pena-a-ex-sargento-de.shtml (last accessed July 7, 2016).

23. EMOL. "Amnestía Internacional rechaza rebaja de condena de carabinero en caso Manuel Gutiérrez." May 27, 2015. http://www.emol.com/noticias/nacional/2015/05/27/718891/amnistia-rechaza-rebaja-de-condena-de-carabinero-en-caso-manuel-gutierrez.html (last accessed July 7, 2016).

24. EMOL. "Familia de Manuel Gutiérrez concreta recurso para revertir baja de pena a ex carabinero." May 25, 2015. http://www.emol.com/noticias/nacional/2015/05/25/718473/recurso-de-casacion-en-caso-manuel-gutierrez.html (last accessed July 7, 2015).

25. Soychile. "La Corte Suprema confirmó el condena contra el carabinero que mató a Manuel Gutiérrez." December 15, 2015. http://www.soychile.cl/Santiago/Sociedad/2015/12/15/364023/La-Corte-Suprema-confirmo-la-condena-contra-el-carabinero-que-mato-a-Manuel-Gutierrez.aspx (last accessed July 7, 2016).

26. INDH. "INDH presenta recurso de queja ante Corte Suprema por caso de Manuel Gutiérrez." December 18, 2015. http://www.indh.cl/indh-presenta-recurso-de-queja-ante-corte-suprema-por-caso-de-manuel-gutierrez (last accessed July 7, 2016).

27. González, Andrea. "Las frases que marcaron el discurso del general director de Carabineros." *La Tercera*, August 30, 2011.

28. *La Tercera*. "Diputado Gutiérrez pide ministro en visita para indagar actuar de Carabineros en manfiestaciones." August 30, 2011.

29. Ibid.

30. Vergara, R., T. Costas, and M. J. Soler. "Segunda declaración del ex sargento: Millacura cambia su version y reconoce disparo directo." *El Mercurio*, August 31, 2011, p. C9.

31. Vergara, R., M. J. Soler, and T. Costas. "Las marcas encontradas en el proyectil de 9 mm fueron claves para establecer el origen del tiro: La bala que mató al estudiante salió de la UZI del sargento Millacura." *El Mercurio*, August 30, 2011, p. C7.

32. *La Tercera*. "Navarro: 'Los estudiantes no pueden ser reprimidos con armamentos de guerra'." August 29, 2011.

33. Labrín, S., J. Ramírez, and M. Vega. "Gobierno pide renuncia de general de Carabineros por muerte de joven." *La Tercera*, August 30, 2011; Carrera, Patricio. "Gordon pide perdón por muerte de menor en peor crisis policial desde Alto Hospicio." *La Tercera*, August 31, 2011.

34. *La Tercera*. "Navarro: 'Los estudiantes no pueden ser reprimidos con armamentos de guerra'." August 29, 2011.

35. Gálvez, Mario, and Pedro Lezaeta. "Ya suman nueve las exoneraciones por la muerte del estudiante Manuel Gutiérrez: General Gordon pide

perdón y ordena que dos jefes y un oficial abandonen la institución." *El Mercurio*, August 31, 2011, p. C9.

36. EMOL. "Caso Manuel Gutiérrez: Tribunal Militar cierra etapa de sumario y familia analiza acciones civiles." March 25, 2013. http://www.emol. com/noticias/nacional/2013/03/25/590186/caso-manuel-gutierrez-tribunal-militar-cierra-etapa-de-sumario-y-familia-analiza-acciones-civiles.html (last accessed July 7, 2016).

37. Vergara, Rodrigo. "Declaración de ex oficial por muerte de Manuel Gutiérrez en Macul: Teniente revela que otro carabinero también disparó su arma y lo ocultó." *El Mercurio*, September 14, 2011, p. C8.

38. *La Tercera*. "Gobierno descarta existencia de responsabilidades políticas en caso de Carabinero acusado de balear a adolescente en Macul." August 30, 2011.

39. Ibid.

40. Author interview with Coronel Rodney L. Weber Orellana, Head of the Department of Human Rights, Carabinero de Chile. Santiago de Chile. July 8, 2015.

41. EMOL. "Carabineros transparenta sus protocolos para el mantenimiento del orden en manifestaciones." August 15, 2014. http://www.emol. com/noticias/nacional/2014/08/15/675192/carabineros-transparenta-sus-protocolos-para-el-mantenimiento-del-orden-en-manifestaciones. html (last accessed July 13, 2016).

42. García Jiménez, Bernardita. "Justicia Militar otra vez en la mira: critican sentencia de tres años de libertad vigilada para carabinero que asesinó a Manuel Gutiérrez." *El Mostrador*, May 12, 2014. http://www.elmostrador.cl/noticias/pais/2014/05/12/justicia-militar-otra-vez-en-la-mira-critican-sentencia-de-tres-anos-de-libertad-vigilada-para-carabinero-que-asesino-a-manuel-gutierrez/ (last accessed July 7, 2016).

43. EMOL. "Amnestía Internacional rechaza rebaja de condena de carabinero en caso Manuel Gutiérrez." May 27, 2015. http://www.emol.com/noticias/nacional/2015/05/27/718891/amnistia-rechaza-rebaja-de-condena-de-carabinero-en-caso-manuel-gutierrez.html (last accessed July 7, 2016).

44. Castillo, Gonzalo. "Reforma a la Justicia Militar: uno de los pendientes del Gobierno." *DiarioUChile*, June 12, 2015. http://radio.uchile. cl/2015/06/12/reforma-a-la-justicia-militar-uno-de-los-pendientes-del-gobierno/ (last accessed July 13, 2016).

45. EMOL. "Estudiante que sufrió lesión en la cabeza durante protesta en Valparaíso sigue grave." May 21, 2015. http://www.emol.com/noticias/nacional/2015/05/21/717987/estudiante-que-sufrio-lesion-en-la-cabeza-durante-protesta-en-valparaiso-sigue-grave.html (last accessed July 22, 2016); BioBio Chile. "Video confirma que chorro que carro

lanzaaguas de Carabineros provocó caída de Rodrigo Áviles." May 28, 2015. http://www.biobiochile.cl/noticias/2015/05/28/nuevo-video-confirma-responsabilidad-de-carabineros-en-caida-de-rodrigo-aviles.shtml (last accessed July 22, 2016).

References

Beetham, David. 1991. *The Legitimation of Power*. Atlantic Highlands, NJ: Humanities Press.

Bonner, Michelle D. 2013. "The Politics of Police Image in Chile." *Journal of Latin American Studies* 45 (4): 669–94.

Bonner, Michelle D. 2014. *Policing Protest in Argentina and Chile*. Boulder, CO: Lynne Rienner.

Bonner, Michelle D. in press. "Media and Punitive Populism in Argentina and Chile." *Bulletin of Latin American Research*.

Centro de Estudios Públicos (CEP). 2015. "Encuesta CEP y confianza en Carabineros." Powerpoint prepared for the author by Ricardo González T., Coordinator of the Public Opinion Area. July 22.

Comisión Ética contra la Tortura (CECT). 2012. *La tortura es el miedo a las ideas de los otros: Informe de derechos humanos 2012*. Santiago de Chile: Quimantú.

Comisión Ética contra la Tortura (CECT). 2013. *En la senda de la memoria, los derechos y la justicia: Informe de derechos humanos 2013*. Santiago de Chile: Quimantú.

Fukuyama, Francis. 2015. "Why Is Democracy Performing So Poorly?" *Journal of Democracy* 26 (1): 11–20.

Holmes, Stephen. 2003. "Lineages of the Rule of Law." In *Democracy and the Rule of Law*, edited by José María Maravall and Adam Przeworski, 19–61. New York: Cambridge University Press.

Instituto Nacional de Derechos Humans (INDH). 2015. *Informe Annual 2014*. Programa de Derechos Humanos, Función Policial y Orden Público. www.indh.cl (last accessed July 21, 2016).

Lagos, Claudia, ed. 2009. *El Diario de Agustín*. Santiago: LOM.

Léon-Dermota, Ken. 2003. *And Well Tied Down: Chile's Press Under Democracy*. Westport, CN: Praeger.

Mainwaring, Scott. 2003. "Introduction: Democratic Accountability in Latin America." In *Democratic Accountability in Latin America*, edited by Scott Mainwaring and Christopher Welna, 3–33. New York: Oxford University Press.

Maravall, José María, and Adam Przeworski. 2003. "Introduction." In *Democracy and the Rule of Law*, edited by José María Maravall and Adam Przeworski, 1–16. New York: Cambridge University Press.

March, James G., and Johan P. Olsen. 1995. *Democratic Governance*. New York: Free Press.

O'Donnell, Guillermo. 1999. "Polyarchies and the (Un)Rule of Law." In *The (Un)Rule of Law and the Underprivileged in Latin America*, edited by Juan E. Méndez, Paulo Sérgio Pinheiro, and Guillermo O'Donnell. Notre Dame, IN: University of Notre Dame.

Roe, Emery. 1994. *Narrative Policy Analysis: Theory and Practice*. Durham and London: Duke University Press.

Schedler, Andreas. 1999. "Conceptualizing Accountability." In *The Self-Restraining State: Power and Accountability in New Democracies*, edited by Andreas Schedler, Larry Diamond, and Marc F. Plattner, 13–28. Boulder: Lynne Rienner.

Schram, Sanford F., and Philip T. Neisser. 1997. "Introduction." In *Tales of the State: Narrative in Contemporary U.S. Politics and Public Policy*, edited by Sanford F. Schram and Philip T. Neisser, 1–14. Lanham, Boulder, New York, Oxford: Rowman & Littlefield.

Sklansky, David Alan. 2008. *Democracy and the Police*. Stanford, CA: Stanford University Press.

Tamayo Grez, Tania. 2015. *Todos Somos Manuel Gutiérrez: Vida y muerte de un mártir de la democracia*. B Chile: Santiago de Chile.

Tankebe, Justice. 2010. "Public Confidence in the Police: Testing the Effects of Public Experiences of Police Corruption in Ghana." *British Journal of Criminology* 50 (2): 296–319.

Universidad Diego Portales (UDP). 2012. *Informe Anual Sobre Derechos Humanos en Chile 2012*. Santiago de Chile: Ediciones Universidad Diego Portales.

Universidad Diego Portales (UDP), Centre for Human Rights. 2015. *Informe anual sobre derechos humanos en Chile 2015*. Santiago de Chile: Ediciones Univeridad DiegoPortales.

CHAPTER 6

Police Abuse and Democratic Accountability: Agonistic Surveillance of the Administrative State

Rosa Squillacote and Leonard Feldman

Introduction: Agonistic Surveillance, Police Reform, and the Administrative State

Since the 2014 deaths of Michael Brown in Ferguson, Missouri, and Eric Garner in Staten Island, New York, police abuse of civilians and the need for police reform have been rightfully at the forefront of American political culture. We define police abuse as both *misconduct* (using policies in a discriminatory or unwarranted way) and *biased practice* (standard policing practice that—as a policy—targets communities and individuals based on their identity rather than criminal activity). In other words, police abuse, as the introduction to this volume asserts, is not only limited to the violence of state authorities that violates clearly established legal norms, but also includes the coercive practices that become contested by

R. Squillacote
Department of Political Science, The Graduate Center,
City University of New York, New York, NY, USA

L. Feldman (✉)
Department of Political Science, Hunter College and the Graduate Center,
City University of New York, New York, NY, USA

© The Author(s) 2018   135
M. D. Bonner et al. (eds.), *Police Abuse in Contemporary Democracies*,
https://doi.org/10.1007/978-3-319-72883-4_6

those subject to them (Bonner et al., Chapter 1). Police abuse, therefore, includes actions such as the killing of Eric Garner, who was choked to death during a routine stop, and policies such as stop-and-frisk, which are targeted almost exclusively at low-income neighborhoods of color. It thus shapes selective citizens' experience of democracy.

In response, police reform projects often call for greater police accountability. While the political science literature on democracy generally focuses its attention on judicial forms of accountability with little regard to its application to police abuse (Bonner et al., Chapter 1; Bonner, Chapter 5), we put the reduction of police abuse at the center of our analysis of accountability. In furtherance of the project of police reforms that might reduce police abuse, we draw on political theory to examine the role of police as administrative agents, and suggest that robust police reform must take seriously (a) the potential for democratic accountability within administrative agencies and (b) practices of agonistic surveillance by nonstate actors.

If institutions shape the political identity of citizens, then current police practices create less democratic experiences, causing individuals to be less willing to participate in traditional democratic activities such as voting (Lerman and Weaver 2014). While political science studies of democracy have been slow to recognize the importance of police abuse, recent public attention to the issue in the United States—particularly the murder of civilians—has brought out a renewed sense of democratic engagement on the part of the public. Mass protests and calls for reform have provided outlets for citizens "signaling" the need for new administrative policies and decision-making. In addition, street protests against police violence have played a significant role in triggering investigations by the Department of Justice into systemic civil rights abuses by police departments in Ferguson, Baltimore, Cincinnati, and elsewhere. These democratic actions are important, and indicate one method of public accountability for the police as an administrative agency. However, these actions often lead to calls for traditional methods of police reform that we argue are ineffective. In particular, we argue that police body cameras are an insufficient reform proposal: because police are administrative agents, civilians will never have direct control over the regulations, application, and enforcement of police body cameras. Practices of civilian surveillance such as Cop Watch should be encouraged as a democratic police reform mechanism in and of itself[1] and as a more effective way of practicing civilian oversight over the police.

POLICE POWER, THE POLICE, AND THE ADMINISTRATIVE STATE

Police powers are a common law articulation of the fundamental right of governments to rule. Police powers are understood as the ability to make laws to protect and regulate the "health, safety, morals, and general welfare" of a society. The Supreme Court has read the protection of states' traditional police powers in the Constitution's 10th Amendment.[2] The exercise of police powers is typically carried out through administrative agencies. In particular, the police power is what grants states the ability to make criminal laws and to create police departments as administrative agencies to enforce those laws. Police themselves are administrative agents empowered under executive authority to ensure the safety of the population.

For some, the police power may create a democratic crisis since administrative agencies are not electorally accountable to the public, and yet make many of the decisions and policies that impact our daily lives. In particular, the increasing use of administrative agencies to carry out punitive state actions illustrates the very real threat of insulated, unaccountable administrative agencies. Police are not the only part of the administrative state; Beckett and Murakawa (2012) demonstrate how administrative agencies across the board have recently been infused with an increasingly punitive logic. (Just two examples are incarceration for civil debt and immigration detention.) Yet, this "shadow carceral state" does not reflect an expansion of punishment into a new realm of administrative agencies; rather, it is an expansion of the reliance on punishment within an already-existing administrative framework. The use of administrative governance to regulate the "welfare" and "morals" of the population isn't new territory, but rather a fact of American governance that is as foundational as the Constitution. What is new is the increasingly punitive trend of these regulations. While this trend is reflected in many administrative regulations, its most visible indication is in our increased reliance on police departments.[3]

The experience of the administrative state can be deeply unsettling for a culture with a shared commitment to democratic rule. As Mark Greif writes, "part of the reason police seem at present unreformable is that they have no intelligible place in the philosophy of democracy" (Grief 2014). The unintelligibility of police reform might be related to a deeper disconnect: Markus Dubber (2005, p. 1) notes that police are associated with heteronomy; the law with autonomy—these separate logics may be one reason why it is hard to regulate police powers through a traditional (constitutional and legislative) legal framework. Policing is not a form of "self-government" but a form of "other-government." "Other-government" is not, of course, confined to the institutions and agents we understand in the contemporary world as police—what Ranciere calls the "petty police" (1999, p. 28). Rather, "other-government" is constitutive of a wider, older understanding of police—what Greif describes as "the administrative state management of population and territory" (Grief 2014). In this articulation, police as administrative agencies represent "other-government" and are beyond the scope of democratic accountability.

However, the concern over the democratic limitations of administrative agencies is misplaced. Edward Rubin argues that our concept of democracy is a relic from an older era, preceding the rise of the administrative state. Shot through with "social nostalgia," our preoccupation with democracy disables us from thinking through the practices of responsiveness in what he terms an "interactive republic" (Rubin 2005, pp. 132–134). Rubin urges us to accept the administrative state, instead of mourning the loss of democracy, and to use the tools and methods of accountability that are built into the administrative state through the practice he calls "signaling." Signaling refers to contact between citizens and government agents, and government agents' responsiveness to citizen input in policy making (Rubin 2005, p. 133). In a different vein, Posner and Vermeule (2010) argue that the administrative state, filled inevitably with legal grey holes and black holes, makes judicial or legislative oversight a chimera. The only effective mechanism of accountability is not legal but political—democratic elections as a referendum on the executive branch in its entirety.

So we begin with a banality that is not sufficiently recognized: the police are a bureaucratic organization. They are part of the administrative state. They exercise wide discretion like other actors of the administrative state, yet unlike other administrative agents, they are authorized to employ physical violence, up to and including deadly force. Thus, the question of democratic accountability is all the more urgent. Given this urgency, Rubin's recognition of what is genuinely new and different in the logic of administrative power is important, but his dismissal of "the myth of self-government" as a discursive relic seems inapt; it misses the ways in which competing political logics and practices intersect and combine (Rubin 2005, p. 125). Posner and Vermeule's move to nest the legal grey and black holes of administrative discretion within the terrain of democratic electoral mechanisms represents an important step in this regard. But their version of democratic accountability does not itself reflect the transformation of the modern executive: they retain a very old, formal model of accountability (elections) when the forms of power they describe require, and have led to, new forms of oversight and accountability. We agree with Posner and Vermeule that legal, juridical mechanisms of accountability are weak, but in shifting the focus from the legal to the political, Posner and Vermeule suffer from an exceedingly limited conceptualization of democratic politics. Rather than dismiss democracy as a rhetorical remnant of a bygone era, or truncate it to a narrowly electoral mechanism of accountability, we argue that the administrative state *is* a democratic state.

Administrative agencies are not inherently undemocratic and should not be presumed to be less democratically legitimate than institutions more closely aligned with the formal processes of representative democracy. There are a number of ways to ensure public accountability of government agents: voting and elections are just one among many. As can be seen with *Citizens United*, the Electoral College, closed primaries, and voter restriction laws, the power of elections can be severely curtailed by a democratic state. Other avenues of administrative accountability include due process protections, such as hearings with recourse to judicial proceedings; public notice and comment over the change in administrative policies; formal intra-institutional complaints; and informal contact with administering agencies.

When asking ourselves how we can hold the administrative state accountable, we must broaden the scope of democratic "signaling": how can the people provide feedback to the administrative government actors? We argue that the recognition of police as administrative agents opens new avenues of reform—such as institutional oversight including independent review boards and Department of Justice monitoring. In particular, it is our contention that the best hope for police reform lies in shifting our understanding of police from "other-government" to "self-government" specifically through civilian surveillance of police practices.

Traditional Models of Accountability in Democratic Theory

Courts and Constitutionalism

In contemporary political and legal theory, the approach we will call liberal constitutionalism places courts in a central position in monitoring and constraining the actions of other state agents. While theorists such as David Dyzenhaus (2008) view the rule of law as a collaborative project requiring the active support of all branches of government, judges retain a special role. Their job is to assert a thick, substantive conception of the rule of law when faced with challenges to discretionary and potentially illegal administrative procedures, rules, practices, and decisions of legislatures and executives. Liberal constitutionalism is a theory of the role of constitutional courts in restraining oppressive majorities that legislatively violate individual rights, and a theory of the role of courts in restraining overreaching executives who violate individual rights in wartime and other (asserted) exigent circumstances.

While some liberal constitutionalists may justify this role of judicial oversight in terms of the enforcement of certain natural or pre-political rights by a branch of government most insulated from politics, others justify it in more explicitly democratic terms: In one view, judicial review and constitutionalism more generally are a form of "self-binding" by democracies to protect against subsequent violations of an earlier democratic will (Holmes 1993, p. 236). Another approach, developed by John Hart Ely and others out of the famous *Carolene Products* footnote,[4] situates judicial review and constitutionalism as a mechanism to remedy the democratic process itself when democratic majorities violate the preconditions of democratic decision-making by attacking the rights of minorities.

The central role of the courts as guardians of individual rights and political process in the face of majority rule and executive overreach has been contested by the empirical literature. Rebutting the notion of judicial review as a counter-majoritarian force in democratic politics, Robert Dahl famously argued that the Supreme Court is more often a part of the ruling coalition in American politics and rarely moves too far out of step with the governing bloc and dominant public opinion (Dahl 1957). Lacking its own enforcement power, concerned about preserving its own tenuous legitimacy, and deferential when it comes to "political questions," the Court in practice fails to live up to the heroic image of liberal constitutionalism (Law 2009, p. 730). The normatively oriented theorists of liberal constitutionalism are hardly ignorant of these issues. David Cole (2003), for instance, recognizes the frequently deferential orientation of the courts when faced with administrative actions justified as responses to national security emergencies. His argument is that (a) the Court does more than any other branch or institution to protect basic rights and (b) even if the Court is deferential during an emergency, it has, historically, moved to constrain emergency powers after the crisis has passed and thereby also established limits on what government actors can do when the next emergency comes around.

The empirical critics of the liberal constitutional view appear to have the upper hand when we consider the relationship between the federal courts and those particular administrative agents that can and do use deadly force—police. The Supreme Court's criminal procedure jurisprudence and individual civil litigation have been the primary route through which the courts have articulated the outer boundaries of constitutional police action. Yet, the Warren Court's extension of criminal procedure protections has been slowly eroded away, and what protections still exist are hard to enforce (Weisselberg 2008). Likewise, courts set the limits of reasonable force and thereby render police abuse accountable to the law, but this form of accountability has also been increasingly eroded. Criminal prosecutions are exceptionally rare, even with innovations such as independent prosecutors. The Supreme Court's reasonable force jurisprudence, developed in the context of private civil rights tort litigation, has been largely deferential to police officers. The Court has developed an "objective reasonableness" test for distinguishing between reasonable and excessive force, a test which privileges the perspective of a "reasonable officer" at the scene, and prohibits the judgment of hindsight. Thus, an officer can make a perceptual mistake—believing that a suspect was armed when he was in fact unarmed, for instance—and still be deemed reasonable. Furthermore, the Court has expanded the doctrine of "qualified immunity"[5] to protect officers from litigation. Under the Court's logic, if the law covering the use of force was not completely clear at the time of the officer's actions, the officer is entitled to immunity and the Court has expanded the circumstances under which it deems this doctrine to apply (Feldman 2017). Even if the courts were more assertive in defending the rights of victims of police violence, one of the weaknesses of placing courts at the center of accountability is the individualized nature of responsibility (Harmon 2012a). A second problem, particularly with the use of private civil litigation, is that municipalities may be all too willing to absorb the costs of civil judgments against their police officers and departments without putting any pressure on them to change practices (Newman 2015). These challenges echo those raised by Bonner in the case of Chile (Chapter 5 of this volume).

Deliberative Democratic Fora

A second approach within contemporary political theory makes legislative bodies and deliberative publics central to the project of accountability. In this approach, accountability is primarily political, not legal. This approach has diverse roots and diverse expressions: Roman republicanism, Rousseauian popular sovereignty, and Habermasian deliberative democracy all emphasize the centrality of law-making assemblies. In contrast to the liberal vision of the rights-bearing individual who is protected by an independent judiciary, this democratic vision places the citizenry (and/or their representatives) in a more active role.

In one version, the deliberative bodies within the state that make decisions (strong publics) should be accountable to the "weak publics" of civil society. Elaborating how this dynamic is supposed to function according to Habermas's *Between Facts and Norms*, Nancy Fraser writes, "Theorizing law as the proper vehicle for translating communicative into administrative power, the work distinguished an 'official,' democratic circulation of power, in which weak publics influence strong publics, which in turn control administrative state apparatuses from an 'unofficial,' undemocratic one, in which private social powers and entrenched bureaucratic interests control law-makers and manipulate public opinion" (Fraser 2007, pp. 13–14). Indeed, a key virtue of the deliberative approach, following Habermas, is that it does not situate accountability exclusively in deliberative bodies with decision-making power but rather sees processes of debate, evaluation, and judgment as involving both the "subjectless modes of communication" of public opinion and decision-making bodies (Habermas 2000, p. 248). Most recently, deliberative democracy has developed this idea in terms of "deliberative systems." Focusing on the macro-level systemic processes allows us to see how different sites of political activity (legislatures, social movements, universities, administrative agencies) constitute "nodes" in a deliberative system (Mansbridge 2012).

Another version of deliberative democracy has focused more on micro-level processes and practices of communication between citizens. This includes quasi-experimental work setting up "deliberative polls" of citizenry and reforms such as participatory budgeting that bring small-scale face-to-face deliberation by citizens into the decision-making apparatus of governments (Fishkin 2009). Archon Fung, in particular, has examined the role of citizen deliberation in the context of policing. Fung describes how the Chicago Police Department instituted as part of its community policing initiative in the 1990s a series of regular meetings between police officers and neighborhood residents, which Fung views optimistically as "autonomous in the sense that they set and implement, through deliberative processes, specific ends and means toward broad public aims such as school improvement and public safety" (Fung 2003, p. 113). But Fung's account of these deliberative fora also reveals their limitations: While Fung alerts us to the domination of educated and wealthy citizens in these deliberative fora, another limitation is implicit in the very structure of the meetings:

> Police and residents begin by using a "brainstorming" process to generate a comprehensive list of crime and safety problems in their neighborhood. They then agree to focus on two or three listed items as priority issues, then pool information and perspectives to develop analyses of these problems. (Fung 2003, p. 118)

Devoted to a collaborative process in which residents and police identify and prioritize the *key threats to public safety* in the community, it appears as though police misconduct and violence were completely off of the agenda of these meetings.

The Chicago experiments of the 1990s are echoed in more recent efforts to create deliberative spaces for dialogue between citizens, particularly in lower income communities of color, and police officials. This time, the turn to deliberation is motivated by the emergence of the Black Lives Matter movement,[6] and so police abuse is explicitly on the agenda. Nevertheless—although this is not the framework articulated by Black Lives Matter—many of these new deliberative fora manifest some of the same weaknesses as their earlier community policing versions. Rather than serve as opportunities for citizens to deliberate about police department policies and practices, they become framed as dialogic encounters *between* citizens and state agents with the goal of "building trust" (TrustandJustice.org).

Sklansky also expresses the concern that a reliance on deliberative democracy "tends to focus attention on the cultural underpinnings of democracy at the expense of the institutional structures of decision making" (2008, p. 69). By emphasizing the need to reach consensus, this model "directs attention away from the possibilities that some arguments are incoherent, that some political positions are unworthy of respect, and that some systems should be overthrown" (Sklansky 2008, p. 69). Simply bringing more voices into conversations about police abuse is insufficient if those conversations do not have the express goal of ending abuse through implementing institutional policy changes.

Without a doubt, deliberative democratic approaches are useful for clarifying some of the dynamics of the politicization of police violence. While racialized police abuse has been a long-standing issue of concern for African-American communities, it has largely existed outside of the wider national political agenda. Black Lives Matter protests have succeeded in bringing police abuse to the attention of white citizens by forcing it onto the agenda of the national media. The broader public debates conducted on cable television and online social media about the causes and consequences of police violence are a part of the process of developing a culture of accountability within a deliberative system. But the attempt to fold the institutionalization of democratic accountability of police into the framework of deliberative fora in which police officials and community members engage in reasoned argument oriented toward consensus about "appropriate" or "effective" policing practice risks reinscribing as opposed to challenging the prevailing power relations: the hierarchical relationship between police officers, with their powers of surveillance and violence, and the citizenry, understood as a subjected population, subordinated both by virtue of the police claim to legitimate violence and to administrative expertise.

The trust-building focus of deliberative fora involving police and community members connects to the wider and inadequately defined concept of "community policing," a frequent refrain in current police reform efforts. The idea is that marginalized communities should have more power in determining policing/criminal justice policy. Yet Broken Windows (also called Zero Tolerance) policing is a policy born out of community concerns. It was first introduced in New York City as a response from both business and low-income communities who were concerned about growing visible social disorder and crime (Vitale 2008). The logic of this model is that a broken window puts a community at risk for further criminal harm.

Following Sklansky, we view the community policing rubric as counterproductive in promoting greater democratic accountability of the police. As Sklansky writes, "community policing, no matter how it is defined, should not be understood or defended as a way to make the police more answerable to 'the public.' This way of thinking ignores what the pluralists rightly stressed: the heterogeneity of interests in any community—particularly in a modern, urban community" (2008, p. 117). One of the problems with constructing "community" is that by totalizing a group of diverse and disagreeing individuals, we risk erasing our diversity and difference. The heterogeneity of "communities" makes simple calls for community policing at risk of implementation that continues to protect those with relatively more power (e.g., small business owners). Without a robust and complicated understanding of contradictions within "community," calls for police reform as community policing will be of limited practical value.

New York City: The Limits of Traditional Reform

The 2013 New York City Mayoral election provides one local example of the limits of traditional democratic action. During the Democratic primaries, Bill de Blasio trailed behind political favorite Christine Quinn. Late in the primaries, he came out more strongly against common policing strategies, in particular, stop-and-frisk. His promise to "end stop-and-frisk" was one of the reasons he won the Democratic nomination (Edwards-Levy 2013). Joe Lhota, his Republican opposition in the main election, ran an attack ad about de Blasio's "soft on crime" attitude—a position that was a spectacular failure in the polls and ultimately the election ("Can't Go Back" 2013). After winning the mayoral race, de Blasio appointed a new Police Commissioner—William Bratton. Bratton, the architect of Broken Windows policing in New York, was a disappointment to advocates, yet many were willing to wait and see if the shifting political climate expressed through the election would be enough to create significant policy changes within the New York City Police Department (NYPD). Bratton did order a dramatic reduction in the number of stop-and-frisks; however, this reduction was accompanied by an *increase* in the use of misdemeanor level arrests (Police Reform Organizing Project 2015). Democratic action focusing on the need for police reform resulted in a mere shift from one punitive police encounter to another.

Another local example of the limitations of traditional reform strategies is the 2013 Community Safety Act (CSA)—legislation championed by a New York City-based advocacy coalition called Communities United for Police Reform. The first part of the CSA included legislation that would reiterate constitutional protections against discrimination and expand those protections to new classes of people; the second part required the creation of a new city agency in the form of an Inspector General's office (CSA 2013). The first part of this law is functionally inadequate in that it merely reasserts existing law and constitutional rights. The reassertion of protections against discrimination and privacy violations implicitly acknowledges that already-existing legal frameworks are inadequate and unenforceable, and yet no new mechanisms for enforcement are suggested.

The creation of a new administrative office at least recognizes that a central component of police reform is an administrative oversight. However, because the New York City Charter places the NYPD as an administrative agency under the executive's purview, the new office lacks any enforcement powers (NYC Charter 2004). The new Inspector General (IG) is empowered merely to issue reports and make recommendations. While reports filed by the IG provide useful resources to advocates, there is little evidence that these reports have had a significant impact on policing practices (Paybarah 2015). In 2016, the IG's office issued a report condemning Broken Windows policing, finding "no empirical evidence demonstrating a clear and direct link between an increase in summons and misdemeanor arrest activity and a related drop in felony crime" and "no evidence to suggest that crime control can be directly attributed to quality-of-life summonses and misdemeanor arrests" (OIG-NYPD 2016, p. 3). While it is certainly rhetorically significant that a city agency denounced Broken Windows policing, this finding has no force for the NYPD's regular practice. In fact, according to the Court Monitoring Project of the Police Reform Organizing Project (PROP), discussed in greater detail below, the daily practice of policing in New York City continues the harmful Broken Windows policy (through fines and tickets rather than stop-and-frisk) that leads to cases of police misconduct.

DEMOCRATIC ACCOUNTABILITY WITHIN THE ADMINISTRATIVE STATE

The administrative structure of police leads us to the conclusion that traditional routes of reform alone will be ineffective. Certainly, legislation and the courts have a significant role to play in protecting democratic rights. But these fora are insufficient by themselves. The promise of police reform must come from an institutional understanding of police as administrative agents, and an opening up of what methods are possible for democratic accountability. Police are one of many administrative agencies, and reform measures will be more successful if we understand them in this way. The culture within police departments clearly has contributed to the toleration of police abuse and misconduct. Yet, culture itself is created through institutional mechanisms, such as training, quota requirements, early warning systems for high-risk police officers, data reporting (or the lack thereof), and in particular, leadership from police chief executives. Administrative policy changes must be a fundamental part of police reform goals. Here, we examine two alternative police reform programs: federal investigations and civilian oversight boards.

Federal Oversight

Understanding the limits of courts as a primary locus of accountability does not mean abandoning the norms and institutions of legality. Rachel Harmon, in her discussion of the limits of constitutional law as a method of ensuring police accountability and reform, argues that we move "beyond the conventional paradigm to recognize the significance of other institutions and sources of law in regulating the police" (Harmon 2012a, p. 764). While constitutional rights are effective at establishing the limits of acceptable behavior, because the police are an administrative agency they require more incentives, directives, regulations, and checks than constitutional provisions allow (Harmon 2012a). Harmon argues for greater federal oversight—in particular through data collection—over local police departments as central to effective reform (Harmon 2012b). The information provided by data collection is necessary for voters to make informed decisions about how to direct their elected officials to govern the police. It is also necessary to hold the police accountable as an administrative agency. That police departments—such as the NYPD—have routinely failed to comply with information requests is a sign of insufficient political will as well as a failure on the part of reform advocates (who rarely make reporting requirements their primary goals) to understand the police as an administrative agency.

Another method of achieving this oversight is through Department of Justice investigations. The Department of Justice selects only a small number of police departments where police violence has already become politicized (either by protest movements or by political leaders) for investigation and eventual reform. One study documented 38 police departments subject to formal investigation by the Justice Department with 19 of those cases resulting in a settlement agreement between 2000 and 2013 (Rushin 2014, p. 3226). Not only to investigate misconduct, the goal is also to shape police department policies more broadly: the DOJ hopes to establish benchmark policies to be emulated by non-investigated departments (Chanin 2011; Department of Justice 2001).

Civilian Review Boards

Civilian Review Boards (CRBs) were an early reform attempt to engage with the police as administrative agencies by relying on citizens' democratic participation in new oversight agencies. These review boards were first advocated for in the 1920s and 1930s; however, police misconduct in that era was understood primarily as a result of political corruption. More popular reform efforts sought to remove the police from political influence, which "translated into a strong bias against any citizen input into policing" (Walker 2001, p. 21). Later, reform initiatives from the 1960s—motivated by increased protests against racist and abusive police practices, and by a growing concern over the need for democratic control over government agencies—again sought community control of the police. In the 1990s, CRBs were revitalized and they are now a common presence throughout the country. However, their effectiveness continues to be limited by significant pushback from police departments and police unions (Walker 2001).

The need for CRBs to have a role in shaping the *policy* of departments is paramount. In New York City, for example, a former head of the Civilian Complaint Review Board (CCRB) found that the agency could not create meaningful change in police conduct because of its inability to inform police department policy. That in large part was due to the lack of NYPD cooperation with the CCRB (Livingston 2004). The need for buy-in from police departments is essential; this is largely because, as noted above, review boards alone are insufficient to guarantee long-lasting police reform. The administrative agency itself—the department—must be committed to reform. Thus, one of the chief problems of effective civilian review procedures is "the difficulty of establishing a review mechanism which will be acceptable to both the community and the professionals involved" (Hudson 1971, p. 538).

In short, Civilian Review Boards are a promising opportunity for reform advocates; however, these review boards must work with invested executive leadership and be given sufficient resources and institutional capacity to effect policy changes. Fundamentally, they contribute to police reform by establishing a norm of civilian monitoring over the police. This monitoring is fundamental because "it is a basic principle of democratic society that citizens control and direct government agencies" (Walker 2001, p. 180). In this way, having civilian oversight of police departments is part of a larger shift in the status of citizenship in an administrative state—a shift from "supplicants to rights-bearing citizens" (Hudson 1971, p. 516). In the next section, we turn to another important form of civilian monitoring of police that remains in an external, agonistic relationship to the administrative actors being surveilled.

Extra-Institutional Agonistic Surveillance

A crucial factor in democratic police reform is the presence of noninstitutional civilian oversight. Police abuse has become a subject of national attention largely because of civilian recordings of violence committed by police officers. This is a method of reform based on the community surveillance of the police that relies primarily on the individual action: what we call agonistic surveillance.

The history of civilians informally surveilling government actors is old. In one collection of essays by police officers, printed in 1873, this was the advice given to a new officer: "your acts will at all times be subject to the observation and the animadversion of the public" (Potere 2012, p. 274). The 1960s and 1970s saw a resurgence of this tactic as a coordinated political strategy: "Cop Watch" as we think of it today began with the Black Panthers, who organized groups of civilians to post street watches in California specifically to monitor police conduct. The 1960s also saw the beginning of a "decentralizing television" movement, using civilian news recordings for organizing around contentious political issues. "Guerilla television" was used as a means of spreading political information from the ground: "distinguishing themselves from network reporters who stood loftily above the crowd, video guerrillas proudly announced they were shooting from *within* the crowd, subjective and involved" (Boyle 1992, p. 71). The subjectivity of guerrilla television was a crucial part of its political claim of reasserting power from within traditionally powerless communities. The tradition of agonistic surveillance continues today and for the same reasons: a concern about police abuse and a need to articulate political identity through sharing on-the-ground news. In so doing, "citizen journalism" has the effect of setting a new political agenda within the media, and of creating a new space for political subjectivity to be articulated (Antony and Thomas 2010).

Civilian monitoring of police practices extends to the courtroom, where those subjected to Broken Windows policing end up. In New York City, the Police Reform Organizing Project's (PROP) Court Monitoring Project provides the kind of data collection most helpful to advocates: By simply sitting in public courtrooms and recording details about typical criminal cases, PROP demonstrates that racist and harmful police practices continue unabated.[7] As PROP's work indicates, the fervor of organized police reform in the last several years in New York City has not created the kind of fundamental restructuring of the police that is needed.

In keeping up with new technologies of the police, citizen journalism is a kind of "sousveillance," or surveillance-from-below (Mann and Ferenbok 2013), as a response to growing state surveillance, such as public CCTVs, meta-data collection by the NSA and DHS, and the use of police officers on the street to keep watch over individuals not suspected of having committed a crime (Brito 2013). This sousveillance—what we call agonistic surveillance—is not an administrative reform. Rather it is a response to the failure of traditional legal and political mechanisms to achieve reform within an administrative system.

Because recent reform efforts have not resulted in significant policy changes, vigilant civilian surveillance of police remains an essential part of the police reform movement. The most prominent form this surveillance takes is through Cop Watch—a national movement rooted in local organizers training people who live in communities where police misconduct is prevalent to film the police. By sending regular patrols out in "hot spot" areas,[8] Cop Watchers hope to protect and empower individuals and communities impacted by police violence.

Agonistic Surveillance and Community

Groups such as Cop Watch and the Police Reform Organizing Project initiate practices of agonistic surveillance central to democratic accountability. Nevertheless, social movements are vulnerable to criticism that they are in fact anti-democratic—that they constitute a tiny minority of the public, whose views diverge from mainstream opinion and who do not represent "the community." This is precisely the criticism levied against PROP by outgoing police commissioner Bratton in a 2016 television interview:

> Has anybody actually taken a good look at who these people are, these self-appointed activists who claim to represent the community? ... I wish that instead of always investigating us, the police, go investigate some of them. We've got one character Robert Gangi who claims to head some kind of activist group that sits in the courtroom all month long and counts how many minorities come through versus whites... Who is Robert Gangi, who does he represent, is he appointed by anybody...? (Inside City Hall 2016)

Bratton's critique, like the proposals for "community policing" reforms discussed above, rely on anti-pluralistic and ultimately hegemonic conceptions of "the community." Furthermore, Bratton relies on the narrow concept of *electoral representation* to delegitimate social movement surveillance activism.

Recent approaches to democratic theory have attempted to complicate a unitary conception of the citizenry, in favor of an approach that emphasizes the multiple channels of influence and mechanisms of participation. For instance, Pierre Rosanvallon reconceptualizes practices of democratic accountability in a way that avoids invoking an implicitly unitary conception of popular sovereignty, of the people. As Rosanvallon writes in *Democratic Legitimacy* about the problem with the prevailing democratic theory, even a thinker such as Habermas "remains within the confines of a monist vision of popular sovereignty. He merely shifts the locus of that sovereignty from a concrete social body to a diffuse space of communication" (2011, p. 8). By contrast, in *Counter-Democracy* (2012), Rosanvallon offers us a critical re-description of democracy in terms of the civic practices of surveillance, prevention, and judgment. Surveillance itself takes on different forms and is performed by various social actors: the vigilance of a watchful citizenry, the act of denunciation—uncovering and condemning injustice, and practices of expert evaluation such as quantitative performance measurement and benchmarking. Social movement watchdogs are central to the project of democratic surveillance. Seen from this perspective, the claim that citizen monitors of courtrooms and police actions are not "representative" of "the community" is neither true nor false—it simply misses the point of social movement watchdog activity, which is to make the practices of the administrative state visible to the broader public.

Democratic theorists need to move beyond the institutions of elective representation to consider, more broadly, what Rosanvallon calls "the organization of distrust." (Rosanvallon 2012, p. 5) This conceptualization of democratic surveillance brings into focus a plethora of democratic actors that are not as well-conceptualized as the electorate. Social movement organizations operate as "watchdogs" within their area of focus and concern. The internet, for Rosanvallon (2012, p. 70), is similarly best understood not as a medium of democratic deliberation but as "the *realized* expression of these powers... of vigilance, denunciation and evaluation."

Cop Watch as Agonistic Surveillance

Cop Watch embodies the democratic principles of agonistic surveillance in a strategic political movement by relying on the plurality and subjectivity of individual recordings of police conduct, creating a sort of subjective mass media database of accountability. The logic of Cop Watch is fundamentally democratic: if "we the people" are to be subjected to constant surveillance by the police, "we the people" can create our own surveillance mechanisms. Cop Watch organizations in New York City and across the country have taken the tools of the administrative state (regulation by means of surveillance and data collection) and turned them on their head. For example, the NYC Cop Watch website takes a hold of the NYPD's "See Something, Say Something" campaign encouraging civilians to spy on one another in the name of anti-terrorism and uses this phrase to encourage civilians to report police misconduct: "See Something? Say Something. If you've witnessed discriminatory or unjust policing, report it." (Peoplesjustice.org) By allowing any individual to film the police and record instances of abuse and harassment, Cop Watch has set the current political agenda squarely on the need for police reform.

Jocelyn Simonson, in her excellent summary of Cop Watch programs, finds that Cop Watch does three things: deters police misconduct; bears witness to police brutality (by collecting information); and asserts political subjectivity (Simonson 2016). Cop Watchers hope to deter incidents of brutality, arbitrary arrests, or police harassment. Proving the effect of deterrence is notoriously difficult; however, social science research has found that police act differently when they know they are being recorded, and that being forced to engage in conversation may limit the impact of implicit biases (Simonson 2016, p. 413).

The deterrent effect of Cop Watch is one reason why police departments are sometimes hostile to the practice. In Sandhu and Haggerty's study of police perspectives on being recorded by civilians, for example, several officers indicated a concern about "camera shy" police officers who may hesitate to act decisively in a critical moment because of fear of misrepresentation (2017, p. 82). It should be noted that this study did not provide any anecdotes of hesitancy preventing a necessary arrest, but did discuss delays in engaging suspicious individuals that had "racial overtones." In one instance, a city officer failed to approach a black man acting suspiciously on a corner because of the presence of CCTV cameras as well as a group of young people with cell phone cameras. The officer waited for the man to leave the area before approaching him (Sandhu and Haggerty 2017, p. 86).

Part of the mission of Cop Watch organizations is to spread a "culture of Cop Watch," encouraging random members of the public to film encounters with the police. It is from this culture that political discourse has been forced to acknowledge the scope of police violence against civilians. The filming of the deaths of Eric Garner, Philando Castile, and countless others has raised substantial public concern over police abuse, a concern that Black Lives Matter has translated into pushing for substantive policy solutions, such as their Campaign Zero and Movement for Black Lives platform.[9] Although an indirect effect, the filming of police killings has also helped to spur wider data collection efforts by journalists—such as the Guardian's project The Counted, the website Fatal Encounters, and others. Similarly, the Department of Justice's Bureau of Justice Statistics announced a redesign of their record-keeping of arrest-related deaths on August 4, 2016, one day before the two-year anniversary of Michael Brown's death (Federal Register 2016).

Citizen participation in government accountability is at the heart of Cop Watch's democratic nature. Perhaps the most important political impact of Cop Watch is its adversarial nature—by "promoting public participation," it permits a new kind of political subjectivity as citizens (Simonson 2016, p. 394). This agonistic political engagement is a direct response to the new "custodial citizenship"—Americans increasingly experience government through punitive carceral mechanisms, which can "lead custodial citizens to withdraw from civic society and political life, at great cost to their communities" (Lerman and Weaver 2014, p. 56). Cop Watch offers a new kind of political engagement reflecting both custodial citizenship (where the primary experience of the state is through carceral institutions) and administrative citizenship (where "signaling" is the primary method through which individuals provide governing feedback to policy makers). The administrative/carceral state creates a new identity of citizenship, one that experiences all-encompassing regulation and monitoring and punishment. This citizenship is not that of the passive victim subject to the whims of an arbitrary state, however. It is a citizenship based on the promise of service, safety, and rights. It is a citizenship that requires a new culture of civic engagement, based on personal encounters and agonistic values. Cop Watch "combines public participation and accountability in one practice"; in so doing, it allows civilians to make themselves the *subjects* rather than the *objects* of surveillance (Simonson 2016, p. 396).

Police Body Cameras

This last impact of Cop Watch—providing an expression of democratic subjectivity and citizenship—is one reason why police body cameras are a poor substitute for Cop Watch. While police body cameras *may* function to expose instances of excessive force, they do not provide the same experience of democratic participation as citizens filming police. The use of body cameras denies civilians the ability to act as subjects, keeping them instead as objects of state action. Therefore, we urge caution before turning to an additional layer of police surveillance to address the problem of police violence. The substitution of body cameras for Cop Watch poses a threat to the democratic principles of Cop Watch by removing the role of civilians in ensuring accountability, and continues the policy of keeping police outside the realm of democratic engagement with civilians.

Considerations on police use of body cameras must first address whether these cameras are effective in achieving the three goals of Cop Watch: reduction in police violence; deterrence against police misconduct and harassment; and, protection of democratic political subjectivity. One study of body cameras worn by police officers in Rialto, California found that these cameras did result in a reduction of use-of-force and a reduction in citizens' complaints (Barak et al. 2014). In San Diego, the adoption of body cameras resulted in a reduction in public complaints, but an increase in use of force (Winkley 2015). For some, this means that body cameras must be implemented in conjunction with "sound policies and procedures to govern their use" and requirements that police officers abide by these policies (Balko 2016). The use of body camera raises other adjacent concerns, such as privacy and due process rights for those being filmed.

So body cameras alone are not sufficient—they must come with new internal policies and both internal and external mechanisms to ensure the police officers follow these policies. Yet, this last requirement is at the heart of our understanding of police as administrative agents. What mechanisms allow for democratic accountability in ensuring police use body cameras correctly? Already we have public reports of police officers' cameras "breaking" during incidents of use of force (Smith 2016; Wing 2015).

Additionally, the administration of body cameras would expand the state's surveillance power; a concern that police reform advocates must take seriously. Already law enforcement officials collect massive amounts of information on civilians, whether or not these individuals have been convicted of a crime. Individuals who are arrested have their fingerprints (and in some cases eye scans) recorded, and those records are maintained—even if charges are dropped or the individual is found not guilty (Moynihan 2012; Snow 2010). Because New York City has such high level of arrests, this means that the NYPD maintains ever-growing records of the population. New York City's Domain Awareness System, "which syncs the city's 3,000 closed circuit camera feeds in Lower Manhattan, Midtown, and near bridges and tunnels with arrest records, 911 calls, license plate recognition technology, and even radiation detectors," is another highly sophisticated program that captures information about civilians constantly (Robbins 2012). This program, already an example of the potential for unchecked administrative agencies to act as surveillance state actors, is also a public–private partnership with Microsoft, which licenses the program out to other cities, giving New York City 30% of its profits (Coscarelli 2012; Morrison 2016). Recently, the NYPD expanded its Domain Awareness System in collaboration with Vigilant Solutions, a company that holds billions of records from across the country garnered from license plate readers (Currier 2016; Joseph 2016; Levin 2016); While there is nothing illegal about these arrangements, they suggest the need for evermore vigilant civilian oversight of the relationship between state surveillance and private profits.

We have an opportunity to be vigilant with the implementation of body cameras. In addition to concerns over their efficacy, body cameras raise serious questions about financial interests of this program. Taser International, which "controls about three-quarters of the body camera business in the United States," is an eager advocate of body camera technology for police departments (Gelles 2016). These contracts can be highly lucrative: the Dallas police department signed a contract with Taser for $3.7 million (Weise 2016). It is not surprising that advocates, such as the Stop LAPD Spying Coalition (2015), are concerned about "conflicts of interests [and] the lack of substantive community input and debate" on these deals. Body cameras may be a useful tool for police reform, but it is one that advocates should watch closely.

Cop Watch is not just a question of the efficiency of preventing police abuses, nor are body cameras problematic just because of their ability to expand the surveillance state in conjunction with questionable financial relationships. It is more fundamentally a question of the exercise of democratic citizenship. Cop Watch entails a *power transfer* from the state to citizens. It allows individuals to express democratic citizenship, to actively participate in the conditions of governance. This, in turn, allows citizens the ability to shape the conversation, to present their viewpoint—literally. The use of video footage in various criminal legal frameworks—whether their use as evidence in criminal trials, or their use in taping confessions—does not yield an objective accounting of events. Rather, research suggests that video used as evidence is perceived in accordance with the perspective of the "subject" of the footage—we identify with the person behind the camera; the object of filmed footage becomes the object of our eye as well. One study of police body cameras found that these videos "remain susceptible to bias" while simultaneously leading people "to become more convinced that they are right" (Sommers 2016, p. 1350). This is particularly true when one takes into consideration that when cameras reproduce the point of view of the police officers, viewers are more likely to find the video favorable to the police (Lassiter et al. 2007; Williams et al. 2016).

CONCLUSION

The perspective of Cop Watch videos is that of agonistic citizenship— one that forefronts the adversarial articulation of rights. The question of whether the police can be a democratic institution is not just a question about the internal dynamics or the policy choices of police departments. It is a question of where civilians can engage the police institution as democratic subjects. For administrative agencies, democratic engagement requires more than relying on courts or legislative reforms—the focus of most political sciences studies of democracy. For an administrative agency with the power to inflict deadly harm—a power that is frequently used—democratic engagement is even more crucial. Cop Watch expresses this democratic engagement through the practice of agonistic citizenship, therefore acting as a more robust accountability mechanism than police body cameras. In this way, Cop Watch is Rancierian democratic action. For Ranciere (2014, p. 85), the fundamental political question of democracy is "that of the competence of the incompetent, of the capacity of anybody at all to judge the relations between individuals and collectivity, present and future." The logic of governing by drawing lots is at the core of democracy—the possibility that anyone, regardless of external qualification, is competent to govern. The Cop Watch program is this logic applied to our contemporary society. Who polices the police? The people do, and we do so without permission but by voluntary individual actions asserting competence and equality.

Notes

1. As well as a protected First Amendment constitutional right.
2. For example, *Jacobson v Massachusetts* 197 U.S. 11 (1905), in which the Court found that individuals may be compelled to undergo vaccinations as part of the state's lawful exercise of its police powers. The 10th Amendment reads: "The powers not delegated to the United States by the Constitution, nor prohibited by it to the States, are reserved to the States respectively, or to the people."
3. For example, there are more police offices in New York City public schools than guidance counselors (Rankin 2016).
4. *Carolene Products*, 304 U.S. 144 (1934) held that the Supreme Court should review Congressional action with a presumption of constitutionality; that the Court should not intervene in legislative decisions unless those decisions are arbitrary or unreasonable. In Footnote Four, the Court gave itself an exception to this rule, stating that a "more searching judicial scrutiny" may be required if legislation targets "discrete and insular minorities" or targets rights guaranteed by the Bill of Rights. In effect, this footnote established the basis for strict scrutiny review and later 14th Amendment jurisprudence. For further discussion, see Shapiro (2009).

5. "Qualified immunity" is a doctrine that protects individual state actors from lawsuits unless that the actor violated a clearly established statutory or constitutional right. For more, see *Pearson v. Callahan* 494 F. 3d 891 (2009) and *Harlow v. Fitzgerald* 457 U.S. 800 (1982).
6. The Black Lives Matter movement began in 2013, and was originally organized by Alicia Garza, Patrisse Cullors, and Opal Tometi. The movement began as a response to George Zimmerman's acquittal in the death of Trayvon Martin, and has become increasingly focused on police violence and abuse (https://blacklivesmatter.com/about/herstory/).
7. Over a two-year period of monitoring, PROP has found that 91% of defendants were people of color. In the four month period of its last report, 96% of individuals arrested were released after arraignment. No Equal and Exact Justice: A PROP Court Monitoring Report (2016).
8. One example is the annual Cop Watch team, organized by FIERCE, sent to the post-Pride celebrations in the West Village; these celebrations are typically populated by low-income queer youth of color, and often incur a disproportionate police presence (Fiercenyc.org [last accessed November 22, 2017]).
9. The Black Lives Matter movement, focused on police abuse, launched these two campaigns. Campaign Zero issues policy recommendations based on the substantive research into various aspects of policing. The Movement For Black Lives is a broader policy platform, where ending police abuse is one recommendation among others, such as a broader criminal justice reform platform, reparation/economic investment programs, and others (https://www.joincampaignzero.org/ [last accessed November 22, 2017]; https://policy.m4bl.org/ [last accessed November 22, 2017]).

References

Antony, Mary, and Ryan Thomas. 2010. "'This is Citizen Journalism at Its Finest': YouTube and The Public Sphere in the Oscar Grant Shooting Incident." *New Media & Society* 12 (8): 1280–96.

Balko, Radley. 2016. "Once Again, Body Cameras Are Only as Good as the Policies That Come with Them." *The Washington Post*, May 25. https://www.washingtonpost.com/news/the-watch/wp/2016/05/25/once-again-body-cameras-are-only-as-good-as-the-policies-that-come-with-them/ (last accessed November 22, 2017).

Barak, Ariel, William A. Farrar, and Alex Sutherland. 2014. "The Effect of Police Body-Worn Cameras on Use of Force and Citizens' Complaints Against the Police: A Randomized Controlled Trial." *Journal of Quantitative Criminology* 31 (3): 509–35. http://dx.doi.org/10.1007/s10940-014-9236-3 (last accessed November 22, 2017).

Beckett, Katherine, and Naomi Murakawa. 2012. "Mapping the Shadow Carceral State: Toward an Institutionally Capacious Approach to Punishment." *Theoretical Criminology* 16 (2): 221–44.

Boyle, Deirdre. 1992. "From Portapak to Camcorder: A Brief History of Guerilla Television." *Journal of Film & Video* 44 (1/2): 67–79. http://www.jstor.org/stable/20687964 (last accessed November 22, 2017).

Brito, Jerry. 2013. "Sousveillance Turns the Tables on the Surveillance State." *Reason.com*, November 18. http://reason.com/archives/2013/11/18/sousveillance-turns-the-tables-on-the-su (last accessed November 22, 2017).

Campaign Zero website. http://www.joincampaignzero.org (last accessed November 22, 2017).

Chanin, Joshua. 2011. "Negotiated Justice? The Legal, Administrative and Policy Implications of 'Pattern or Practice' Police Misconduct Reform," PhD Diss. American University. https://www.ncjrs.gov/pdffiles1/nij/grants/237957.pdf (last accessed November 22, 2017).

Cole, David. 2003. "Judging the Next Emergency." *Michigan Law Review* 101 (8): 2565–95. http://scholarship.law.georgetown.edu/facpub/69 (last accessed November 22, 2017).

Community Safety Act. 2013. Communities United for Police Reform. http://changethenypd.org/community-safety-act (last accessed November 22, 2017).

Cop Watch NYC website. http://www.copwatchnyc.org.

Coscarelli, Joe. 2012. "The NYPD's Domain Awareness System Is Watching You." *New York Magazine*, August 9. http://nymag.com/daily/intelligencer/2012/08/nypd-domain-awareness-system-microsoft-is-watching-you.html (last accessed November 22, 2017).

Currier, Cora. 2016. "A Walking Tour of New York's Massive Surveillance Network." *The Intercept*, September 24. https://theintercept.com/2016/09/24/a-walking-tour-of-new-yorks-massive-surveillance-network/ (last accessed November 22, 2017).

Dahl, Robert. 1957. "Decision-Making in a Democracy: The Supreme Court as a National Policy-Maker." *Journal of Public Law* 6 (2): 279–95.

Dubber, Markus Dirk. 2005. *The Police Power: Patriarchy and the Foundations of American Government.* New York: Columbia University Press.

Dyzenhaus, David. 2008. "Schmitt V. Dicey: Are States of Emergency Inside or Outside the Legal Order?" *Cardozo Law Review* 27: 2005–41. https://papers.ssrn.com/sol3/papers.cfm?abstract_id=1244562 (last accessed November 22, 2017).

Edwards-Levy, Ariel. 2013. "Bill De Blasio Leads New York City's Democratic Mayoral Primary." *Huffington Post*, August 13. http://www.huffingtonpost.com/2013/08/13/bill-de-blasio-poll_n_3750084.html (last accessed November 22, 2017).

Fatal Encounters website. http://www.fatalencounters.org/ (last accessed November 22, 2017).

Feldman, Leonard. 2017. "Police Violence and the Legal Temporalities of Immunity." *Theory & Event* 20 (2): 329–50.

Fishkin, James. 2009. *When the People Speak*. New York: Oxford University Press.

Fraser, Nancy. 2007. "Transationalizing the Public Sphere." *Theory, Culture and Society* 24 (4): 7–30.

Fung, Archon, and Wright, Erik eds. 2003. *Deepening Democracy*. New York: Verso.

Gelles, David. 2016. "Taser International Dominates the Police Body Camera Market." *New York Times*, July 12. https://www.nytimes.com/2016/07/13/business/taser-international-dominates-the-police-body-camera-market.html (last accessed November 22, 2017).

Grief, Mark. 2014. "Seeing through Police." *N+1* 22 (Spring). https://nplusonemag.com/issue-22/police/seeing-through-police/ (last accessed November 22, 2017).

Habermas, Jurgen. 2000. *The Inclusion of the Other*. Cambridge, MA: MIT Press.

Harlow v. Fitzgerald. 1982. 457 U.S. 800.

Harmon, Rachel. 2012a. "The Problem of Policing." *Michigan Law Review* 110 (5): 761–817. https://papers.ssrn.com/sol3/papers.cfm?abstract_id=1957702 (last accessed November 22, 2017).

Harmon, Rachel. 2012b. "Why Do We (Still) Lack Data on Policing?" *Marquette Law Review* 96 (4): 1119–46. http://scholarship.law.marquette.edu/mulr/vol96/iss4/8/ (last accessed November 22, 2017).

Holmes, Stephen. 1993. *Passions and Constraint: On the Theory of Liberal Democracy*. Chicago: University of Chicago Press.

Hudson, James. 1971. "Police Review Boards and Police Accountability." *Law and Contemporary Problems* 36 (Fall): 515–38. http://scholarship.law.duke.edu/lcp/vol36/iss4/6 (last accessed November 22, 2017).

Inside City Hall. 2016. "Bratton, Incoming Police Commissioner O'Neill Discuss the NYPD and Policing." *NY1 Online*, Thursday, August 4. http://www.ny1.com/nyc/all-boroughs/city-hall-newsmakers/2016/08/4/ny1-online–bratton–incoming-police-commissioner-o-neill-discuss-the-nypd-and-policing.html (last accessed November 22, 2017).

Jacobson v Massachusetts. 1905. 197 U.S. 11.

Joseph, George. 2016. "Racial Disparities in Police 'Stingray' Surveillance, Mapped." *CityLab*, October 18. http://www.citylab.com/crime/2016/10/racial-disparities-in-police-stingray-surveillance-mapped/502715/ (last accessed November 22, 2017).

Lassiter, Daniel, Shari Seidman Diamond, Heather C. Schmidt, and Jennifer K. Elek. 2007. "Evaluating Videotaped Confessions Expertise Provides No Defense Against the Camera-Perspective Effect." *Association for Psychological*

Science 18 (3): 224–26. http://journals.sagepub.com/doi/full/10.1111/j.1467-9280.2007.01879.x (last accessed November 22, 2017).

Law, David. 2009. "A Theory of Judicial Power and Judicial Review." *Georgetown Law Journal* 97: 723–801. https://papers.ssrn.com/sol3/papers.cfm?abstract_id=1112613 (last accessed November 22, 2017).

Lerman, Amy E., and Vesla M. Weaver. 2014. *Arresting Citizenship: The Democratic Consequences of American Crime Control*. Chicago: University of Chicago Press.

Levin, Same. 2016. "Half of US Adults are Recorded in Police Facial Recognition Databases, Study Says." *The Guardian*, October 18. https://www.theguardian.com/world/2016/oct/18/police-facial-recognition-database-surveillance-profiling (last accessed November 22, 2017).

Lhota, Joe. 2013. "Can't Go Back." October 18. *Youtube*. https://www.youtube.com/watch?v=mGVDSr0-PFY (last accessed November 22, 2017).

Livingston, Debra. 2004. "The Unfulfilled Promise of Citizen Review." *Ohio State Journal of Criminal Law* 1: 653–69. https://kb.osu.edu/dspace/bitstream/handle/1811/72771/OSJCL_V1N2_653.pdf?sequence=1 (last accessed November 22, 2017).

Mann, Steve, and Joseph Ferenbok. 2013. "New Media and the Power Politics of Sousveillance in a Surveillance-Dominated World." *Surveillance & Society* 11 (1/2): 18–34.

Mansbridge, Jane, and John Parkinson, eds. 2012. *Deliberative Systems: Deliberative Democracy at the Large Scale*. New York: Cambridge University Press.

Morrison, Rebekah. 2016. "New York's Domain Awareness System: Every Citizen under Surveillance, Coming to a City Near You." *North Carolina Journal of Law and Technology*. Blog. February 23. http://ncjolt.org/new-yorks-domain-awareness-system-every-citizen-under-surveillance-coming-to-a-city-near-you/ (last accessed November 22, 2017).

Moynihan, Colin. 2012. "Some Who Decline an Optional Iris Photo Are Kept Longer in Jail, Critics Say." *New York Times*, February 12. http://www.nytimes.com/2012/02/13/nyregion/new-objections-to-nypds-iris-photographing-program.html (last accessed November 22, 2017).

National Initiative for Building Community Trust and Justice website. https://trustandjustice.org/ (last accessed November 22, 2017).

Newman, Zach. 2015. ""Hands Up, Don't Shoot": Policing, Fatal Force, and Equal Protection in the Age of Colorblindness." *Hastings Constitutional Law Quarterly* 43 (1): 117–60. http://hastingsconlawquarterly.org/archives/V43/I1/Newman_Final.pdf (last accessed November 22, 2017).

NYC Charter. 2004 July. Ch 18 sec 431. http://www.nyc.gov/html/records/pdf/section%201133_citycharter.pdf.

Office of the Inspector General of the NYPD (OIG-NYPD). 2016. An Analysis of Qualify of Life Summonses. New York. http://www1.nyc.gov/assets/oign-ypd/downloads/pdf/Quality-of-Life-Report-2010–2015.pdf (last accessed November 22, 2017).

Paybarah, Azi. 2015. "Inspector General, A Year In, on Measuring Police Oversight." *Politico*, May 28. http://www.politico.com/states/new-york/city-hall/story/2015/05/inspector-general-a-year-in-on-measuring-police-oversight-022499 (last accessed November 22, 2017).

Pearson v. Callahan. 2009. 555 U.S. 223.

Police Reform Organizing Project. 2015. Nearly 2,000,000 Per Year: Punitive Interactions Between the NYPD and New Yorkers. http://www.policereform-organizingproject.org/prop-reports/ (last accessed November 22, 2017).

Posner, Eric, and Adrian Vermeule. 2010. *The Executive Unbound: After the Madisonian Republic*. New York: Oxford University Press.

Potere, Michael. 2012. "Who Will Watch the Watchmen? Citizens Recording Police Conduct." *Northwestern Law Review* 106 (1): 273–316. http://scholarlycommons.law.northwestern.edu/nulr/vol106/iss1/6/ (last accessed November 22, 2017).

Ranciere, Jacques. 1999. *Disagreement*. Minneapolis: University of Minnesota Press.

Ranciere, Jacques. 2014. *Hatred of Democracy*. New York: Verso.

Rankin, Kenrya. 2016. "STUDY: Nation's Largest Public Schools Have More Police Than Counselors." *Colorlines*, March 29. http://www.colorlines.com/articles/study-nations-largest-public-schools-have-more-police-counselors (last accessed November 22, 2017).

Robbins, Christopher. 2012. "Photos: Inside the NYPD's New 'Domain Awareness' Surveillance HQ." *Gothamist*, August 8. http://gothamist.com/2012/08/08/photos_the_nypds_new_ultimate_domai.php#photo-1 (last accessed November 22, 2017).

Rosanvallon, Pierre. 2011. *Democratic Legitimacy: Impartiality, Reflexivity, Proximity*. Princeton: Princeton University Press.

Rosanvallon, Pierre. 2012. *Counter Democracy: Politics in an Age of Distrust*. New York: Cambridge University Press.

Rubin, Edward. 2005. *Beyond Camelot: Rethinking Politics and Law for the Modern State*. Princeton: Princeton University Press.

Rushin, Stephen. 2014. "Federal Enforcement of Police Reform." *Fordham Law Review* 82: 3189–247. https://papers.ssrn.com/sol3/papers.cfm?abstract_id=2414682 (last accessed November 22, 2017).

Sandhu, Ajay, and Kevin Haggerty. 2017. "Policing on Camera." *Theoretical Criminology* 21 (1): 78–95.

Shapiro, Ian. 2009. *The State of Democratic Theory*. Princeton: Princeton University Press.

Simonson, Jocelyn. 2016. "Copwatching." *California Law Review* 104 (2): 391–445. https://papers.ssrn.com/sol3/papers.cfm?abstract_id=2571470 (last accessed November 22, 2017).

Sklansky, David Alan. 2008. *Democracy and the Police.* Stanford, CA: Stanford University Press.

Smith, Mitch. 2016. "Body Camera Failed to Record Chicago Police Shooting of Black Teenager." *New York Times,* August 1. https://www.nytimes.com/2016/08/02/us/body-camera-failed-to-record-chicago-police-shooting-of-black-teenager.html (last accessed November 22, 2017).

Snow, Mary. 2010. "Eye Scans Will Help Keep Better Track of Suspects, NYPD Says." *CNN,* November 17. http://www.cnn.com/2010/US/11/17/new.york.iris.scanners/ (last accessed November 22, 2017).

Sommers, Roseanna. 2016. "Will Putting Cameras on Police Reduce Polarization?" *Yale Law Journal* 125 (5): 1304–62. http://www.yalelawjournal.org/note/will-putting-cameras-on-police-reduce-polarization (last accessed November 22, 2017).

Stop LADP Spying Coalition. 2015. "Body-Worn Cameras: An Empty Reform to Expand the Surveillance State." https://stoplapdspying.org/wp-content/uploads/2015/04/Stop-LAPD-Spying-Coalition-Report-on-Use-of-Body-Cameras-by-Law-Enforcement-April-2015.pdf (last accessed November 22, 2017).

The Guardian. 2016. "The Counted." *The Guardian.* https://www.theguardian.com/us-news/series/counted-us-police-killings (last accessed November 22, 2017).

U.S. Department of Justice. 2001, January. Principles for Promoting Police Integrity: Examples of Promoting Police Practices and Policies. https://www.ncjrs.gov/pdffiles1/ojp/186189.pdf (last accessed November 22, 2017).

U.S. Federal Register. 2016, August 4. Arrest Related Death Programs. 81 FR 51489. https://www.federalregister.gov/articles/2016/08/04/2016-18484/agency-information-collection-activities-proposed-collection-comments-requested-new-collection#furinf (last accessed November 22, 2017).

United States v. Carolene Products. 1934. 304 U.S. 144.

Vitale, Alex. 2008. *City of Disorder: How the Quality of Life Campaign Transformed New York State Politics.* New York: New York University Press.

Walker, Samuel. 2001. *Police Accountability: The Role of Civilian Oversight.* Wadsworth Group.

Weise, Karen. 2016. "Will a Camera on Every Cop Make Everyone Safer? Taser Thinks So." *Bloomberg News,* July 12. https://www.bloomberg.com/news/articles/2016-07-12/will-a-camera-on-every-cop-make-everyone-safer-taser-thinks-so (last accessed November 22, 2017).

Weisselberg, Charles. 2008. "Mourning Miranda." *California Law Review* 96 (6): 1519–602. https://papers.ssrn.com/sol3/papers.cfm?abstract_id=1095620 (last accessed November 22, 2017).

Williams, Timothy, James Thomas, Samuel Jacoby, and Damien Cave. 2016. "Police Body Cameras: What Do You See?" *New York Times*, April 1. https://www.nytimes.com/interactive/2016/04/01/us/police-bodyc-am-video.html (last accessed November 22, 2017).

Wing, Nick. 2015. "Here's How Police Could End up Making Body Cameras Mostly Useless." *Huffington Post*, October 10. http://www.huffingtonpost.com/entry/police-body-camera-policy_us_5605a721e4b0dd8503079683.

Winkley, Lyndsay. 2015. "Year of SDPD Body Cameras Yields Surprises." *The San Diego Union-Tribune*, November 8, 2015. http://www.sandiegounion-tribune.com/sdut-sdpd-body-cameras-use-of-force-complaints-2015sep08-htmlstory.html (last accessed November 22, 2017).

CHAPTER 7

Protest and Police Abuse: Racial Limits on Perceived Accountability

Christian Davenport, Rose McDermott and David Armstrong

Many view the mass response to the brutal repressive action of Police Chief Eugene "Bull" Connor and the Birmingham police against the American Civil Rights movement during 1963 as crucial for understanding the end of repression undertaken against black activists (Williams 2005). Unified in their perception of egregious police behavior in response to protest, blacks as well as whites in the North and South quickly moved to stop the actions (i.e., the uses of fire hoses, dogs, and nightsticks) and also the government actors (i.e., police) that were associated with them.

C. Davenport (✉)
Department of Political Science, University of Michigan,
Ann Arbor, MI, USA

R. McDermott
Department of Political Science, Brown University,
Providence, RI, USA

D. Armstrong
Department of Political Science, University of Western Ontario,
London, ON, Canada

© The Author(s) 2018
M. D. Bonner et al. (eds.), *Police Abuse in Contemporary Democracies*,
https://doi.org/10.1007/978-3-319-72883-4_7

While these events are readily recalled now, however, only the astute historian remembers the lack of mass response to the activities of Police Chief Laurie Pritchett and the Albany police department during 1961 and 1963 when they were confronted with similar tactics from the same organizations. In this case, as African Americans attempted to protest, Pritchett simply arrested everyone. There were no hoses, no dogs, and no nightsticks used. Unlike the situation in Birmingham, in the case of Albany, opinions of the contentious events were mixed. For example, blacks in the South and North were largely unsupportive of the police response to the protesters; whites in the South were generally supportive, viewing police action as acceptable; and, whites in the North viewed the actions as unfortunate but still within the jurisdiction of local political authorities.

The political science literature on democracy assumes that police repression of protests, like other state wrongdoing, will be held accountable through established liberal democratic institutions of political and legal accountability (Bonner et al., Chapter 1; Bonner, Chapter 5; Squillacote and Feldman, Chapter 6). Yet public perception matters a great deal to that which is considered police abuse and that which is not. The variation among observers in the second case, mentioned above, is crucial for understanding why repression was allowed to continue. Without similar responses across bystanders, there was no organization of the outraged, no mass mobilization, no hindrance of veto players who might stand in the way of reform/change and no broad call/demand for political accountability. As the introduction to this volume notes, shared notions of wrongdoing constitute an essential prerequisite for accountability in democratic systems. Without some shared understanding of what occurred, it becomes difficult if not impossible to make actors who violate civil rights fully accountable for their actions. Thus a study of police abuse, such as this one, highlights the limitations of institutional political science studies of accountability and encourages us to reconceptualize this important aspect of democracy.

The situations described above are far from exceptional or confined to a period in US history. Indeed, one immediately thinks of the uneven mass response to the policing of the anti-Vietnam war protests or to the more recent "Occupy" movement (also see Dupuis-Déri, Chapter 4). Also in these cases, the police's treatment of challengers prompted the public to adopt different positions—some favorable to change and supportive of those protesting political authorities, some favorable to the protection of the status quo (i.e., the police). Examples of such situations abound beyond the United States. In the end, as the case of the "Arab Spring" shows, mass response to protest policing can make the difference between revolution and regime change or political stability and continued authoritarianism. That is, it matters to democracy; it can mark the distinction between acceptable and unacceptable violence and thus whether or not police abuse is held to account.

Despite the role of bystanders in the outcome of dissident–state interactions, very little is known about how citizens respond and when they decide to intervene. Previous research tends to focus on responses to either dissent and dissidents (e.g., Opp and Muller 1986; Opp and Roehl 1990; Opp and Gern 1993) or to repression and the actions of political authorities (e.g., Davis 2007; Gibson 2008), while missing the critical interaction between the two. Additionally, previous scholarship tends to ignore the identity of observers and their relation to protesters. Specifically, drawing on recent work (e.g., Davenport et al. 2011), we argue that *who* engages in dissent and repression matters a great deal with regard to how their behavior influences public opinion about their actions as well as attributions of blame and responsibility. Moreover, drawing on the literature on "coalitional affiliation" (e.g., Smith and Holmes 2003; Stults and Baumer 2007; Taylor 1998; Weitzer and Tuch 2005) we maintain that, in the case of the United States, the race of protesters, as well as that of those policing and observing, independently influences spectators in decisive ways regardless of the content of the conflict. In short, we maintain that the race of political opponents, as well as observers and respondents, cues certain general beliefs regarding coercion and these, in turn, influence opinions such as the willingness to blame the different actors. Blame is important to understand for it lies at the core of "moral outrage" (providing the target of derision [e.g., Hess and Martin 2006]) and it seems at the core of "framing" (providing the target of mobilization [e.g., Benford and Snow 2000]). Such attributions also remain key to notions of discursive accountability, whereby police are trained, or come to know, which actions will violate universal norms so that they may get into trouble and suffer consequences from violating them (Bonner 2014, Chapter 2).

Using a nationally representative sample of (423) American citizens in 2011 stratified by race, we conducted an embedded experiment to examine how the race of the police, protesters, and respondent affected attitudes toward dissent and protest policing. The results are quite interesting and support our claim that identity influences how people view dissident–state interactions. From this study, we find that when both protesters and police are the same race, African Americans are less likely to blame protesters than whites. When respondents are black, they are less likely to blame protesters when protesters are black and police are white, whereas when respondents are white they are less likely to blame police when protesters are black and police are white. Each race places less blame on their own group, tends to hold the "other" responsible for the greater violation of norms; in this way, each ethnicity tends to hold the "other" more accountable for whatever goes wrong as a consequence of protest or escalation.

To present our research, the chapter begins with a review of the extant literature on protest, policing, and public perceptions. A discussion of our own theoretical argument about the influence of race follows, after which we outline our experiment and present the results. The paper concludes with some discussion of the broader implications of the research.

PROTEST, POLICING, AND PERCEPTION: WHAT WE KNOW

Traditionally, researchers concerned with protest, protest policing, and state repression have investigated what prompts each type of behavior. Attention on protest as a dependent variable is normally the domain of sociologists with a focus on the United States (e.g., McAdam 1982; Earl and Soule 2006; Soule and Davenport 2009), while attention to protest policing or repression as a dependent variable generally falls under the domain of political scientists who focus on the United States and other countries (e.g., Poe and Tate 1994; Davenport 1995; Francisco 1996; Moore 2000; Conrad and Moore 2010, as well as Dupuis-Déri in this volume).[1] While comparatively less attention has been given to the aftereffects of dissident or state action beyond their immediate effects on each other, some work in this area has led to important advances. For example, some studies address media coverage where researchers try to figure out how much of what challengers and governments do ends up being captured by the news media—generally with a focus on newspapers (e.g., Davenport 2010).[2] Drawing on earlier discussions of Gamson (1979) as well as Piven and Cloward (1977), there has also been some work on how dissent influences public policy (e.g., Giugni 1998; McAdam and Su 2002; Soule and King 2006). Here, the interest lies with understanding how well contentious claim-making advances a particular cause (i.e., how effective or "successful" it is).[3]

Directly related to our topic, researchers have expressed interest in what impact political dissent (e.g., Opp and Roehl 1990; Opp and Gern 1993) or state repression (e.g., Davis 2007; Gibson 2008) have on mass opinion. This is important because the activity undertaken by political challengers and government officials tends to be seen as only partially directed against each other. In fact, scholars from different theoretical and methodological orientations maintain that *the influence of political dissent and state repression on an observing audience constitutes the most important aftereffect to be considered in analyzing such confrontations.* Indeed, the narratives that emerge from contentious events can profoundly influence future notions of what is acceptable and what is not, as well as of who should be held accountable for what transgressions and how. Such narratives help structure norms and condition police and judicial concepts of accountability within democratic structures, which help define who has power and influence in the system. Moreover, such events and consequences (or lack thereof) help formulate norms and set boundaries of acceptable behavior. Consequently, researchers of the American civil rights movement (CRM) repeatedly discuss the importance of the CRM in prompting police violence in the South to compel Northern outrage, disappointment, and intervention (e.g., McAdam 1982). In a similar vein, comparative politics and international relations researchers and policymakers often discuss the importance of winning the "hearts and minds" of the citizenry during counterinsurgency efforts to weaken support for the rebels (e.g., Mason and Krane 1989; Petraeus 2006).

While interested in protest or repressive activity individually considered, we maintain that researchers are actually studying how specific dissident–state interactions influence mass opinion *jointly*. Such a point is not generally acknowledged, however, in a largely divided literature.

On the one hand, researchers (predominately in sociology) emphasize behavioral challenges like protests while considering protest policing/repression. For example, Opp and Gern (1993) seek to understand what led individuals to participate in the East German "revolution" of 1989 as an example of a large-scale protest. To examine this topic, Opp and Gern considered individual perceptions of both macro and micro factors which they (and the literature) thought were important, including the overall political situation (e.g., the liberalization of Europe and degrees of discontent with the provision of public goods), one's personal network (i.e., whether they encourage or discourage collective action), the existence of opposition groups trying to mobilize people (noting if someone was a member) and, most importantly for the current study, the expectation of state repression (which was presumed to be ubiquitous within an authoritarian government and less important than the other factors identified above). Opp and Gern (1993) assess their argument with public opinion data from 1300 people in the city of Leipzig, which at the time was considered the "vanguard of the struggle" (Opp and Gern 1993, p. 663). From this investigation, results show that what mattered most was individuals' personal networks.

While important, this work reveals limitations with the general approach that seem relevant for our analysis. For example, Opp and Gern (1993) examine attitudes in 1990, after the East German Revolution, without considering how contentious interactions, whether dissident behavior or government responses, influence mass opinion prior to these events. The researchers identify self-reported experiences with repression (in the past), their severity, as expectations of government action that subjects had back in 1989. This does not, however, consider how the person came to be repressed, what connection they had to those engaged in behavioral challenges, who may have been tied to repression, nor who was believed to be at fault for what takes place when challengers and governments confront one another. To address these issues the authors would need to consider specifically what challengers and governments did as they responded to one another. Additionally, Opp and Gern's study assumed that all dissent was "good" and supported, and that all repression was "bad" and not supported. The authors identified no interactions between dissent and repression that would influence public opinion one way or the other. Again, this issue would involve getting at the dynamic interaction between challengers and governments.

On the other hand, researchers (predominately in political science) have emphasized repressive behavior such as arrests and political banning largely in the context of some form of behavioral challenge. For example, Davis and Silver (2004) study mass opinion about repressive action in the United States after the terrorist attacks on September 11, 2001. Specifically, they examine a civil liberties "tradeoff" approach where they suggest that individuals generally support civil liberties (i.e., less repression) unless they feel themselves threatened, in which case they support personal security (i.e., greater repression). The power of this relationship is conditional on trust in the government: that is, a willingness to make oneself vulnerable to those in political authority in the belief that they will not take advantage. To investigate this argument, Davis and Silver evaluate responses to a national survey carried out shortly after the 9/11 attack. Results generally support their argument.

While interesting and insightful, this study shows limitations as it relates to the subject of our research. First, there is no explicit consideration of what governments did to establish political order—generally conceived, leaving the sheer diversity and intensity of actions unexplored. This is important because Davis and Silver appear to argue that the specifics of government action matter. Second, the study generally ignores what specific challengers (i.e., Al Qaeda) did in the United States and what the authorities did in response to their actions. This is important because public opinion is likely influenced by the degree of "tit for tat" between two political actors. Challengers that engage in far more protests, even violent, than the authorities employ protest policing will likely be viewed differently than challengers that engage in less, or in nonviolent protests than the authorities employ protest policing. This is important because Davis and Silver appear to argue that the relationship between the two types of action should influence opinion. Rather than black box 9/11 and post-9/11 protest policing to assess individual threat perception, Davis and Silver needed to identify and examine relevant challenger and government behavior explicitly.

Of course, such a criticism should not be leveled against these authors alone. This type of research generally pays no attention to contention over, or relative success of the "war on terror" by, for example, evaluating a specific repressive action such as the Patriot Act or torture at Guantanamo Bay. These issues matter. We object to the assumption that one's opinion of conflict can be constructed in an abstract manner without probing the specific interaction between particular government and challenger activities. We disagree with this and develop this argument below.

Toward a New Understanding of Mass Responses to Political Contention

Consistent with research done previously, we argue that individuals have opinions about what political challengers and governments do to one another. Indeed, we go somewhat further to argue that it is only through the *joint* consideration of both protests and protest policing that one can understand people's opinions about dissent and repression, as we explore below. Deviating still further, we also argue that mass attitudes are influenced by the particularities of what takes place during specific interactions between challengers and governments, as well as by who those actors are, in terms that their identity appears as relevant to the observer.

Our claims seem largely consistent with existing approaches. Even though not explicitly identified, the basic unit of analysis across studies in this area is the interaction between governments and those citizens challenging them. Thus, in the Opp and Gern (1993) work described above, individuals came together to overthrow an authoritarian government as the police attempted to protect political authorities in the city of Leipzig; in the Davis and Silver (2004) research, ordinary citizens gathered to advance a particular cause as government agents throughout the United States regulated their activity through restrictions on civil and political liberty in the aftermath of a terrorist attack.

Actors are important to identify but so are their actions. With a focus on the dynamics between protests and protest policing,[4] challengers engage in particular types of activity (e.g., strikes, boycotts, sit ins, and demonstrations) in their attempt to collectively and overtly put forward a claim and show support for such efforts. Political authorities, in turn, engage in particular types of responses to these activities (e.g., just showing up, using pepper spray, or beating challengers) as they attempt to constrain, intimidate, and eliminate said efforts.

Conceived in this manner, different elements in the interaction between challengers and governments have been the focus of much attention, including the claims that behavioral challengers put forward, the claims most likely to prompt police response, or the tactics challengers use to advance their interests and the ways in which authorities respond to different challenges (e.g., Tilly 1978; McAdam 1988; Earl et al. 2003; Soule and Davenport 2009; Davenport et al. 2011). There are some areas less well explored, however, which we believe are crucial for this research agenda. Following up on the insights of newer work (e.g., Davenport et al. 2011), we argue that in evaluating dissident–state interactions it is important not only to pay attention to the factors identified above but also to identify who is engaging in challenging the authorities, who takes part in the government response, and who evaluates the interaction (e.g., Davis and Silver 2004).

We argue that the identity of participants and observers is crucial because it affects the opinions and attitudes of observers, as this information signals "coalitional affiliation" (Kurzban et al. 2001). Identity is especially important because it can provide a readily accessible heuristic basis upon which to decide whether a particular person is "with you or against you," informing witnesses about who is right and who is wrong based solely on assessments of similarity (Abdelal et al. 2006).[5]

We acknowledge that our interest in race emerges from our reading of American history and the consistent relevance of this topic within the specific context of challenger–state interactions that have taken place therein (e.g., Franklin and Starr 1967; McAdam 1982; Bonilla-Silva 2001; Cunningham 2004; Davenport et al. 2011). While the original work on coalitional affiliation (Kurzban et al. 2001) was designed to show how the perceptual influence of race would be "erased" when purposely crossed with coalitional cleavages independent of race, it nonetheless remains a fact that in the United States, race serves as a powerful, if often inaccurate, proxy for all kinds of personal and professional affiliations. Indeed, in many respects race has been identified as one of the most salient aspects of life in the United States. Racial disparities have instigated state-sponsored government coercion to maintain various social, economic, and political contexts, as they have sparked mass activism against these institutional orders. Examples begin with slavery and resistance to it, and run through various waves of post-slavery restrictions such as Jim Crow, civil rights activism, and black nationalism, followed by various efforts to address distinct social, economic, and political forms of discrimination such as police brutality that persist up to the present.[6]

At the same time, despite the salience of black activism and government action relevant to such behavior, researchers are generally skeptical that empirical investigations can find statistically significant effects from self-reporting alone. Over time, it has been noted, the willingness of Americans to openly discuss issues of race and racism has diminished. We are supposedly in an age of "new racism" or "post racialism" where explicit reference to racial topics has diminished. Skepticism that emerges from important experimental work by Kurzban et al. (2001) demonstrates that the effects of race on perception can be eliminated in less than an hour once race is crossed with coalitional status as noted above.[7] It is thus unclear whether our standard methods for detection will prove sufficient as people tend to hide any perceived racial or ethnic biases.

Despite these historical and psychological caveats, we believe that race is salient in large part because it provides a useful signal of coalitional status along categories such as class, political affiliation, and social standing (e.g., Fiske and Taylor 1984). Generally, people want to spend as little time and energy as necessary to figure out uncertain events and experiences. Given this fact, individuals may disproportionately lean on quick cues such as race to make decisions about which side to join, or which side is correct, thereby obviating the need to render independent and costly judgments regarding what happened, who is right, and what should be done. It is important to note that these processes happen quickly and automatically, in an unconscious manner, as categorization serves people quite well to quickly assess and understand the world around them.[8] For example, this is how people identify and separate out things to eat from those that are poisonous, or that they distinguish potential predators from nonthreatening members of the animal kingdom. Yet most people remain wholly unaware that these processes are taking place and they will likely not even know that they remain susceptible to such biases.

Rapid assessments thus serve two important purposes: (1) they allow individuals to quickly make sense of uncertain events (i.e., what to think regarding a dissident–state standoff, or confrontation); and, equally as important, (2) they provide motivation for future actions. If a fight broadens, observers want to know whose side to join. Fence sitters may want to join the winning coalition, but they also want to join one that will have them as a member. Race, like sex, serves as a powerful signal of coalitional status. Yet, race is precisely that: a quick and easy signal of the more important psychological goal of figuring out where you belong, and which group is most likely to represent your interests and not harm you.

Along these lines, we suggest that the race of police and protesters as well as the race of respondents (i.e., the observers of challenger–government interactions) will affect the attitudes observers have toward those engaged in contentious behavior and their interaction with other relevant actors. Race provides a quick and clear signal of coalitional status that makes individuals see those who are racially similar as *less* to blame and those who are racially different as *more* to blame, regarding contentious interactions. We test for every possibility in our experimental examination.

Blame

In line with the discussion above, if race does not matter, then our expectations concerning blame (i.e., who is responsible for the relevant action) are fairly straightforward given the way the experiment was structured (discussed further below). Under this circumstance, protesters should receive more blame than police regardless of the race of the

Table 7.1 Protester, police, and observer identity combinations

Alternative scenarios	Protester	Police	Observer
1	White	White	White
2	White	White	Black
3	White	Black	White
4	White	Black	Black
5	Black	Black	Black
6	Black	Black	White
7	Black	White	Black
8	Black	White	White

protester, police, or observer. That is, none of the combinations revealed in the Table 7.1 should matter.

If, however, race does matter, then results will be somewhat different across the various combinations identified above.

Our starting point is one that we believe most would find uncontroversial. African Americans have had a much different experience with authorities in general, and police in particular, than have whites. This experience is important for our research because decades of disproportionate tension-filled interactions with authorities (especially the principal agents of coercion—the police) lead us to maintain that an African American observer would be more sympathetic to protesters in general and less likely to blame them for the conflict than white observers, considering the same combination of protester and police race (i.e., scenarios 2, 4, 5, and 7 in Table 7.1 vs scenarios 1, 3, 6, and 8, respectively). Having been the historic underdog, forced to rely upon institutions outside the existing political system to advance their causes, this group should be more favorable to challengers. Perceiving a lack of accountability within the political system, African Americans would be more likely to envision behavioral challenges and challengers as providing some mechanism for addressing their substantive problems and view them more positively. Whites, on the other hand, have historically been the victors and thus should be more likely to support institutions that maintain and perpetuate the status quo. This provides the following set of expectations:

$$P(Prot|Pr = W, Po = W, Ob = B) < P(Prot|Pr = W, Po = W, Ob = W)$$
$$P(Prot|Pr = B, Po = B, Ob = B) < P(Prot|Pr = B, Po = B, Ob = W)$$
$$P(Prot|Pr = B, Po = W, Ob = B) < P(Prot|Pr = B, Po = W, Ob = W)$$
$$P(Prot|Pr = W, Po = B, Ob = B) < P(Prot|Pr = W, Po = B, Ob = W),$$

where "*Pr*" refers to protester race {W = white, B = Black}, "*Po*" refers to the police race, "*Ob*" refers to the race of the observer and $P(Prot|...)$ indicates the probability that protesters are blamed given the stated conditions. Reversing the inequality signs, we could derive the same set of expectations about the probability that the police are blamed for the incident.

According to our argument, when dissident–state interactions involve participants from different racial or ethnic groups (i.e., heterogenous dyads such as when the protesters are white and police are black or when the protesters are black and police are white), we expect African Americans to side with whomever shares their ethnicity. For example, in scenario 7 African Americans will be more likely to place blame on the police as they share an identity with the protesters. Differing from the situation described above, however, in scenario 4 blacks will place blame on protesters as they share an identity with the police. However, given the historically uneasy relationship between African Americans and the police, the effect here (i.e., the extent to which protesters are more likely to bear the brunt of the blame) will be diminished somewhat. Thus, we expect:

$$P(Prot|Pr = B, Po = W, Ob = B) < P(Prot|Pr = W, Po = B, Ob = B).$$

Co-ethnic sympathies should also result in changes from the baseline situation (i.e., the homogeneous dyads) in the expected way. For example:

$$P(Prot|Pr = B, Po = W, Ob = B) < P(Prot|Pr = W, Po = W, Ob = B).$$

$$P(Prot|Pr = B, Po = W, Ob = B) < P(Prot|Pr = B, Po = B, Ob = B).$$

We expect the same mechanism to work for white observers. Thus, in scenario 3 whites will place blame on the police as they share an identity with the protesters. Differing from the situation described above, however, in scenario 8 whites will be more likely to place blame on protesters as they share an identity with the police producing the following expectation:

$$P(Prot|Pr = B, Po = W, Ob = W) > P(Prot|Pr = W, Po = B, Ob = W).$$

Again, co-ethnic sympathies imply deviations from the baseline for white observers as well:

$$P(Prot|Pr = W, Po = B, Ob = W) < P(Prot|Pr = W, Po = W, Ob = W).$$

$$P(Prot|Pr = W, Po = B, Ob = W) < P(Prot|Pr = B, Po = B, Ob = W).$$

Expectations for blaming the police are not just the reverse of the expectations above. In both cases (for white and black observers), we expect heterogeneous dyads with co-ethnic police (i.e., where the observer and police are both white or black) will be less likely to be blamed than heterogeneous dyads with co-ethnic protesters (i.e., where the observer and protesters are both white or black). In other words, blacks and whites are more likely to side with the police when the police share their race than when protesters share their race. We also expect that observers viewing heterogeneous dyads with co-ethnic police should be less likely to blame police than those viewing homogeneous dyads.

It is worth noting that in the above expectations, it remains an open question as to the difference between respondents viewing heterogeneous dyads with co-ethnic police and those viewing homogeneous dyads. In other words, it is not clear if race shifts and trumps an observer's sense of who is responsible for escalation. If there is some kind of absolute sense of responsibility, race should not matter, but if race helps actually define responsibility, then it might override designations of responsibility that might differ if race is held constant between protesters and police. In the provided scenario (again described below), the blame lies unambiguously with the protesters (i.e., they escalate the situation). Thus, following our argument, when race is removed as a criterion for adjudication (i.e., in homogeneous dyads), the probability that protesters get blamed should be high. Will it be higher for heterogeneous dyads with co-ethnic protesters? This is really a question of whether animosity attaches to the judgment. One possibility is that when judgments based on coalitional thinking corroborate the facts (i.e., when white respondents view black protesters and white police), respondents feel free to ascribe blame where it lies (i.e., with the protesters). Another possibility is that viewing racially heterogeneous dyads leads respondents to be more likely to ascribe blame to the non-co-ethnic party. That is, white respondents viewing black protesters and white police might be even more likely to blame protesters than when viewing homogeneous dyads. While our theoretical perspective does not provide leverage on this question, we discuss the patterns that result from this question below.

DATA AND DESIGN

To test these possible relationships within a representative population survey sample, we undertook an embedded experimental design (Kuklinski et al. 1997). Using Time-Sharing Experiments in Social

Table 7.2   Race of respondents by experimental treatment

Experimental treatment		Number of respondents	
Protesters	Police	White	Black
Black	Black	58 (87)	45 (15)
Black	White	57 (84)	41 (14)
White	Black	60 (101)	57 (17)
White	White	53 (87)	52 (15)

Main entries are raw counts; weighted counts are in parentheses. On average, the weighted counts induce a proportion of African Americans approximately equal to 0.17. The US Census Bureau (see http://quickfacts.census.gov/qfd/states/00000.html) identifies the proportion of African Americas (among all Whites and African Americans) as roughly 0.14

Science (TESS),[9] 423 people were examined. These subjects were approximately equally distributed across four experimental conditions (noted in Table 7.2). The sample was stratified by race, such that roughly equal proportions of blacks and whites were in each category in order to provide a fair test of our hypotheses and not suffer from insufficient numbers (other descriptive measures for the remaining variables in the study are available in Appendix A).

To administer our experiment, we presented subjects with a hypothetical protest scenario in which the race of the participants was systematically manipulated (Appendix B). Specifically, we altered the race of the police and the protesters in a between-subjects experimental design. We employed a two by two cell design where the race of police and protesters were either black or white. Each subject was asked to read a scenario that revolved around a protest in response to the death of a young woman at the hands of an uninsured motorist and then asked the person to answer a sequence of Likert-style response questions (Appendix C). In these questions, we asked subjects for their opinions about the police and the protesters' actions as well as their attitudes toward the issue at hand (i.e., mandatory car insurance—not discussed in this paper). In addition, respondents also answered some basic demographic questions as well as questions regarding racial attitudes and political ideology in order to control for any external potential biases.

The scenario we presented, which was based on an actual event we extracted from a newspaper, mimicked the kind of article that subjects might find/read in a local newspaper or online media report. We held all other aspects of the protest itself constant in order to control independently for the relative importance of the race of participants.[10]

As designed, the experiment allows us to examine the effect of the race of protesters and police on responses to the questions of perceived responsibility for the confrontation. In our analysis, we sought to model subjects' responses to the following question: Which group do you find most responsible for escalating the conflict in this scenario? This question interrogated individual variance in response to the experimental scenario. It is measured on a seven-point scale ranging from one (indicating protester responsibility for question one) to seven (indicating police responsibility for question one).

Why focus on blame? Essentially, we do this for two reasons.

First, blame is central to the idea of backfire and moral outrage, which is the principal manner in which repression leads to resistance within the population (e.g., Barkan 1984, 2001; Jasper and Poulsen 1995; Hess and Martin 2006). We argue that for a repressive event to backfire, two factors must be present. First, an audience must perceive the event to be unjust. Violent repression of a social movement advancing claims widely perceived to be legitimate is one example of a situation that some people will perceive as unjust, particularly in a civil rights scenario (Della Porta and Reiter 1998, p. 18; Wisler and Giugni 1999). Second, information about the event or situation needs to be communicated effectively to receptive audiences that are substantial enough that authorities must take their outrage into consideration. In the case of the Rodney King beating, television broadcasts of a videotape recorded by observer George Holliday were crucial in leading to backfire; there had been many far more serious beatings by Los Angeles police officers and police officers from other agencies that were not widely known and, therefore, generated little or no public outrage.

While the evaluation of the repressive event is the element most often discussed in the literature, the identification of the relevant actor or perpetrator is as important. Without this information, it is unclear against whom individuals should be outraged and against whom counteraction would be mobilized.

Second, blame is essential to what is commonly labeled "framing" (e.g., Goffman 1974; Benford and Snow 2000). Framing largely involves the process of locating, perceiving, identifying, and labeling situations in a manner that allows actors (e.g., social movements) to *diagnostically* ascertain what problems exist as well as who is responsible for them, to

Table 7.3 Conditional distributions of responses

Experimental treatment		Responsibility for escalation		
Protesters	Police	Protesters	Both	Police
Black	White	58	31	9
		(0.592)	(0.316)	(0.092)
White	Black	70	28	21
		(0.588)	(0.235)	(0.176)
White	White	65	31	6
		(0.637)	(0.304)	(0.059)
Black	Black	66	31	5
		(0.647)	(0.304)	(0.049)
Total		259	121	41

Note Main entries are weighted counts, row percentages in parentheses

prognostically put forward actions that would resolve the issues identified and *motivationally* activate individuals to participate in designated activities. Blame is essential here because if there is no party responsible for the problem of interest, then the targeting is vague, mobilization hindered, and accountability limited.

To facilitate interpretation of the models estimated below, we collapse the first three categories into a single value and the last three categories into a single value, generating a three-category variable. The midpoint represents the perception that both groups were responsible for escalation.[11] Table 7.3 presents the frequencies and conditional counts of the two questions of interest. We discuss variation in these values below, but a cursory glance seems to bear out at least some of our expectations. Respondents viewing homogeneous dyads are more likely to blame protesters and less likely to blame police.

When modeling the responses above, we include control variables, namely age (in years), gender, education (four categories: <HS, HS, Some College, BA/S or Higher), and partisanship (Democrat, Independent and Republican).[12] We also include the race of the respondent (white or black) in our model specifications. These are fairly standard in the relevant literature.

To model the responses, multinomial logistic regression is used. We recognize that ordinal logistic regression is often used for variables like these, but a Clarke test (Clarke 2007) of the two different specifications (ordered vs multinomial) identified the MNL as statistically superior ($p <$ 0.05) in the case of our responsibility measure. This is evidence that the parallel regressions assumption implicit in the ordinal regression model does not hold.

Given that our expectations relate to homogeneous versus the two different types of heterogeneous dyads, we use a three-category operationalization of the experimental treatment. Dyads (protester–police) are coded as homogeneous (i.e., black police–black protester and white police–white protester), black police–white protester and white police–black protester.[13] We use the following model specification for the question on responsibility:

$$Pr(Y = m | X) = \frac{e^{XB_m}}{\sum_j e^{XB_j}}$$

where X includes age, gender, three non-reference categories of education (High School, Some College, College Degree+, <High School is the reference), two non-reference categories of partisanship (Independent and Republican, Democrat is the reference), black–white dyad, white–black dyad, and respondent race. As our argument suggests that the effect of the experimental treatment will vary by the race of respondents, we include interactions of the relevant variables in the model.[14] All control variables are included additively and models were estimated in R 2.14.2 (R Core Development Team 2012) with the multinom function from the nnet package (Venables and Ripley 2002). We employed a sampling weight to ensure a nationally representative sample along important demographic characteristics.

RESULTS

Table 7.4 presents the results of our models concerning blame and responsibility in the first two columns. The individual coefficients give the difference in the log-odds of being in the identified category versus being in the reference category ("Protesters" in this case). From the results, we see that age is the only control variable to reach statistical significance (at the 0.05 level). The variables of interest (i.e., respondent race, protester race, and police race) are included multiplicatively, which presents a little difficulty as two- and three-way interactions are hard to conceptualize under any set of circumstances, more so in a nonlinear

Table 7.4 Multinomial logistic regression results

| | Responsibility | |
	Both	Police
Intercept	0.064	−2.346*
	(0.555)	(0.937)
Black respondent	1.035*	1.331
	(0.460)	(0.743)
Black–White (protester–police)	0.061	0.348
	(0.309)	(0.603)
White–Black (protester–police)	−0.100	1.582*
	(0.312)	(0.475)
Partisanship: Independent	0.550	0.268
	(0.338)	(0.546)
Partisanship: Democrat	0.617*	0.811
	(0.278)	(0.449)
Age	−0.019*	−0.011
	(0.007)	(0.011)
Gender (female)	0.089	−0.301
	(0.235)	(0.358)
Education: HS	−0.864*	−0.231
	(0.415)	(0.630)
Education: Some college	−0.479	0.101
	(0.407)	(0.627)
Education: BA/S or higher	−0.296	−0.347
	(0.405)	(0.665)
Black respondent × Black–White	0.304	1.067
	(0.854)	(1.135)
Black respondent × White–Black	−1.048	−1.857
	(0.776)	(1.038)
N	423	
log(Likelihood)	−341.876 (26)	
PRE (ePRE)	0.129 (0.103)	

*$p < 0.05$ (two-tailed)

model like the multinomial logistic regressions presented in Table 7.4. Fortunately, the variables involved in the interactions are all categorical with few categories, which allows for the exploration of all possible combinations making the task somewhat more reasonable. To make the results as clear as possible, we present direct evaluations of our expectations, rather than relying on coefficients, specifically those on interactions, to convey the substantive and statistical significance of the results. Thus, it is not necessary to attempt to evaluate the implications of the interactions simply by looking at the model coefficients.

Table 7.5 Difference in predicted probability between white and black observers

	Dyad (protester–police)	Black observer	White observer	Δ	p-value
Blame protesters	Homogeneous	0.380	0.638	**−0.258***	0.006
	Black–White	0.266	0.612	**−0.346***	0.015
	White–Black	0.593	0.568	0.025	0.409
Blame police	Homogeneous	0.103	0.044	**0.059**	0.107
	Black–White	0.252	0.062	**0.190**	0.198
	White–Black	0.128	0.174	−0.046	0.230

Entries are based on simulated predicted probabilities of blaming police and protesters holding other variables constant at central values. Bolded differences are those consistent with our expectations

*$p < 0.05$, one-sided

As suggested above, the coefficients themselves do little to aid in evaluating the extent to which the expectations derived from coalitional theory are borne out by the data. Table 7.5 presents the numerical results directly relevant to evaluating our first set of expectations that white observers are generally more likely to blame protesters than black observers (regardless of the particularities of the situation under consideration [i.e., the race of those involved]). We simulate predicted probabilities (in a manner similar to King et al. 2000), and provide one-sided *p*-values (i.e., the probability of finding a difference as big as we did [in the indicated direction] if the null hypothesis of no difference is true).[15]

The results here are largely consistent with our expectations. The difference between black and white observers is significant and in the expected direction for homogeneous dyads (e.g., scenarios 2 and 5 in Table 7.1). When protesters and police are of the same ethnicity, African Americans are less likely than whites to blame protesters for the conflict. The differences for the probability of blaming the police have similar patterns to those identified above, but the differences here are not statistically significant, suggesting that there is no difference between blacks and whites regarding their propensity to blame police when protesters and police are of the same race.

The coalitional theory described earlier suggests that observers should be more sympathetic to co-ethnics than to others when viewing heterogeneous dyads. This leads to a set of expectations about differences in the probability of blaming diverse actors for the conflict. These probabilities are in Table 7.6.

Table 7.6 Probability of protester blame

	Dyads (protester–police)			Δ	p-value
	Black–White	White–Black	Homogeneous		
Black observers	0.264	0.592		−0.328*	0.031
	0.264		0.381	−0.117	0.211
White observers	0.614	0.567		0.048	0.264
		0.567	0.638	−0.071	0.166

Entries under "Black–White," "White–Black," and "Homogeneous" are predicted probabilities of blaming dyads holding other variables constant (see fn 14 for values). The dyad designation refers to protester–police races. Bolded differences are those consistent with our expectation

*p < 0.05, one-sided

Concerning protester blame, the differences in predicted probabilities between blacks and whites are perfectly consistent with our results, though only one is significantly different from zero at conventional levels of statistical significance. For black observers, the probability of blaming protesters when viewing black protesters and white police (scenario 7) is much smaller (at statistically significant levels) than when viewing white protesters and black police (scenario 4). In the former situation (black observers, black protesters, and white police), black co-ethnics are likely perceived as the victim of hostile government agents and thus less likely to receive blame whereas in the latter situation (black observers, white protesters, and black police) affinity with black police diminishes the general orientation to support those challenging authority, increasing protester blame. Interestingly, white observers are found to not allocate blame any differently across diverse ethnic combinations.

As discussed above, a similar set of expectations emerge regarding the probability of blaming police. Here, we expected observers viewing heterogeneous dyads to be less likely to blame co-ethnic police. This expectation should hold when the comparison is made with heterogeneous dyads with co-ethnic protesters as well as with homogeneous dyads. Table 7.7 provides results to evaluate these expectations.

When this is done, we find that considering the two different heterogeneous dyads, our expectations are partially borne out by the data. The expected difference (though similar in magnitude for both black and white observers) is only statistically significant for white observers. We thus find that when observers are white, they tend to be less likely to blame police when protesters are black and police are white relative to

Table 7.7 Probability of police blame

	Dyads			Δ	p-value
	Black–White	White–Black	Homogeneous		
Black observers	0.255	0.128		**0.127**	0.147
		0.128	0.105	0.023	0.415
White observers	0.063	0.176		**−0.113***	0.007
	0.063		0.044	0.018	0.282

Entries under "Black–White," "White–Black," and "Homogeneous" are predicted probabilities of blaming dyads holding other variables constant (see fn 14 for values). The dyad designation refers to protester–police races. Bolded differences are those consistent with our expectation
*$p < 0.05$, one-sided

when protesters are white and police are black. There seems to be no significant difference (either substantive or statistical) for the comparison between heterogeneous dyads with co-ethnic police and homogeneous dyads.

In the discussion above, we left as an open question what happens regarding the likelihood of blaming protesters when observers view heterogeneous dyads with co-ethnic police versus when they view homogeneous dyads. Considering the possibilities, two rival expectations emerge and our theory does not provide much guidance in adjudicating between them. Since protesters are unambiguously to blame for the conflict according to the experimental treatment that everyone read, those viewing homogeneous dyads (where race is taken out of consideration) should, rightly, have a high probability of blaming protesters. When similar people view heterogeneous dyads with co-ethnic police, however, do they impose what might be seen as an extra penalty on protesters because they are facing the observer's non-co-ethnics? Coalitional theory suggests that when race is held constant, people can blame the protesters easily. The question then becomes how much of an additional penalty is extracted on protesters when observers view a situation where the police share their race and protesters do not? That is what we have sought to parse both by holding the responsibility constant across conditions where the protesters are responsible, and for varying race of participants across conditions.

The empirical evidence here is interesting. For black respondents, the probability of blaming protesters is 0.2 higher when viewing white protesters and black police than when viewing homogeneous dyads (i.e., where protesters and police are either both black or both white). While not significant at conventional levels, a p-value of 0.087 indicates with a bigger sample, there may be an interesting effect there. On the other hand, the same cannot be said for white observers. They are marginally less likely to blame black protesters facing white police than protesters facing co-ethnic police. This difference, however, is both substantively small (0.07) and not statistically significant ($p = 0.157$).

Alternatively, whether extra benefits accrue to co-ethnic police in heterogeneous dyads is also at issue. The idea is that observers may be less likely to blame co-ethnic police facing non-co-ethnic protesters than they are when the same type of observer views homogeneous dyads. We find no evidence in the data for this phenomenon. For both black and white observers, the effect of interest is both substantively small and not statistically significant. This is not surprising since the probability of blaming police is already low.

CONCLUSION

In our attempt to better understand how citizens respond to dissident–state interactions, we have described some of the mechanisms underlying the emergence and evaluation of one form of political conflict—protest and protest policing. In so doing, we have examined one specific characteristic, race, that has been historically important in the United States context, and investigated how it may affect citizen perceptions of what transpires following challenger–government confrontation and who is to be held accountable.

Racial asymmetries, we have found, affect observers' perceptions of blame and responsibility. When protesters and police are of the same race, African Americans are much less likely to blame protesters compared to whites. When the protesters and police are of different races, findings vary. For example, blacks are less likely to blame protesters when protesters are black and police are white. In turn, whites are less likely to blame police when police are white and protesters are black.

This research significantly advances previous work by systematically exploring the interaction of race with perceptions of social movement and police activity (i.e., contentious politics). Our results highlight some potentially critical factors involved in how contentious interactions may escalate into larger confrontations as individuals perceiving one party as being responsible for a conflict may choose to take action (i.e., instigating a lawsuit, circulating a petition or initiating protest behavior). Our research has implications for how individuals perceive problems of order, choose to act politically in support of their beliefs, make decisions about which political attitudes to champion and the ways to do so, and assess the legitimacy of participants' actions, as well as for who they hold accountable for disruptions and escalations, and for how willing they are to sacrifice the civil rights of others to ensure public order.

Additionally, our work has implications for how scholars might study challenger–state interactions as well. While this study was focused on the importance of race during a specific challenger–government interaction, future work might examine other aspects of identity (i.e., sex, class, religion, ideology as well as combinations of characteristics such as race and sex or ideology and class). To put this another way, our study identified one type of coalition that may be at play as a heuristic in evaluating the responsibility of challengers and governments when a confrontation takes place. Perhaps other factors matter as the topic of intersectionality would lead us to conclude. Researchers might also explore the impact of who instigates the conflict (i.e., protesters, police, or ambiguous), the substantive subject of dispute (i.e., health care, war/international security, civil liberties, racism, sexism, wages, educational reform, and economic inequality), the means used (i.e., rocks, explosives, and guns), the influence of the specific locale (i.e., where interactions take place), and the earlier history of interactions between specific groups or police regarding dissident–state interactions. Any of these factors might influence perceptions of blame as discussed here and in the literature on contentious politics. As researchers and ordinary citizens attempt to understand why some challenger–government interactions prompt subsequent outrage and participation in protests while others prompt mass support for governments and subsequent anti-mobilization behavior, this line of inquiry is crucial for advancing knowledge and promoting freedom.

Indeed, accountability in democratic systems, we maintain, must rest on shared notions of responsibility. Most political science studies assume the law represents societies' shared understanding of right and wrong. However, the case of police abuse, especially in the management of protests, reveals that the public's attribution of responsibility is decidedly more ambiguous. Here we find that public perception and whether or not it provokes moral outrage is important to the determination of wrongdoing and the use of liberal democratic institutions of accountability. If there are racial boundaries to such shared notions of accountability for police action or protest action, then attribution for blame becomes skewed, and public calls demanding accountability will largely lose or win in ways that are contingent on race. If shared notions of moral outrage are precluded by the race of participants, it makes the administration of equal justice impossible to achieve. This sits as one of the biggest topics left unaddressed by the existing literature.

NOTES

1. Despite the fact that researchers interested in one type of contentious behavior tend to ignore the other (e.g., Lichbach 1992), the two literatures draw on similar explanatory factors: political democracy; economic development; and tactical responses to opponents.
2. Others address coverage in NGO reports (e.g., Davenport and Ball 2002).
3. There has been no similar field of research conducted on the outcomes of state repression—again, beyond its success in vanquishing behavioral challengers.
4. Some work on insurgency and counterinsurgency seems comparable in that in this case citizen opinions about prior challenger–state interactions influence whether they "join" the challengers (either participating directly in the organization and/or assisting them with resources as well as safe havens), join the state (identifying the challengers in their midst and/or those supportive of them), or they do nothing (attempting to pick no side). Similar to Opp and Gern (1993), citizen opinion concerns a willingness to side with challengers.
5. Although, in this case, we examine the effects of racial similarity on subsequent judgments and evaluations, we expect that a similar process would work with all significant existential identifications, such as sex, age, religion, or even external identifications such as occupation and class. Note that this has nothing to do with what actually happens when challengers and governments interact.
6. It seems that the recent revelation that there is a largely antiblack and latino stop-and-frisk policy being practiced by New York police is setting the stage for another confrontation (for discussion see: http://www.nyclu.org/issues/racial-justice/stop-and-frisk-practices [last accessed November 18, 2017]).
7. Think of Sunday Night Football: This number one ranked program does not show any racial disparity in viewership although blacks and whites show no other overlap in their top ten television shows. But team membership can trump racial disregard; similarly, those who are romantically involved with another race fail to show typical prejudice toward racial outgroups (Phelps and Thomas 2003).

8. In many respects, newer research on implicit bias also supports this point.
9. See http://www.tessexperiments.org/ (last accessed November 18, 2017).
10. Within subsequent research we plan to vary other components.
11. We do not have expectations about what happens in the middle category on either measure. We don't see this as particularly problematic as we can still examine the difference between the two extreme categories, which should follow the expectations set out above.
12. The partisanship variable was also originally a seven-point variable, but was recoded so partisan categories included pure partisans and leaners. Only "true" independents remain in the "Independent" category.
13. We could have coded the variable as having two categories—heterogeneous and homogeneous, but given the understanding that there may be clear differences between the black–white and white–black protester–police dyads (especially when they interact with respondent race), we thought this was more appropriate. As importantly as our theoretical expectations, we find this specification (treating both homogeneous dyads as equivalent) was not statistically worse than the specification treating them separately. This confirms our expectation that removing race as an evaluative criterion results in similar evaluations of blame regardless of the race of protesters and police.
14. We include interactions between the two non-reference category dummies for the experimental treatment and respondent race in the first model and all pairwise and three-way interactions of the two non-reference category dummies for the experimental treatment, the two non-reference category dummies for perceived responsibility and respondent race in the second model.
15. Here, we have to hold other variables in the model constant at some value. We choose the median value of age (49), the modal category for education (some college), the modal category for gender (female) and politically independent, which is not quite the median in the unweighted data, but is the median in weighted counts.

References

Abdelal, Rawi, Yoshiko Herrera, Iain Johnston, and Rose McDermott. 2006. "Identity as a Variable." *Perspectives on Politics* 4 (4): 695–711.

Barkan, Steven. 1984. "Legal Control of the Southern Civil Rights Movement." *American Sociological Review* 49 (4): 552–65.

Barkan, Elazar. 2001. *The Guilt of Nations: Restitution and Negotiating Historical Injustices.* Baltimore: Johns Hopkins University Press.

Benford, Robert D., and David A. Snow. 2000. "Framing Processes and Social Movements: An Overview and Assessment." *Annual Review of Sociology* 26 (1): 611–39.

Bonner, Michelle D. 2014. *Policing Protest in Argentina and Chile*. Boulder, CO: First Forum (Lynne Rienner).

Bonilla-Silva, Eduardo. 2001. *White Supremacy and Racism in the Post-civil Rights Era*. Boulder, CO: Lynne Rienner.

Clarke, Kevin. 2007. "A Simple Distribution-Free Test for Nonnested Hypotheses." *Political Analysis* 15 (3): 347–63.

Conrad, Courtenay R., and Will H. Moore. 2010. "What Stops the Torture?" *American Journal of Political Science* 54 (2): 459–76.

Cunningham, David. 2004. *There's Something Happening Here: The New Left, the Klan, and FBI Counterintelligence*. Berkeley: University of California Press.

Davenport, Christian. 1995. "Multi-dimensional Threat Perception and State Repression: An Inquiry into Why States Apply Negative Sanctions." *American Journal of Political Science* 39 (3): 683–713.

Davenport, Christian. 2010. *Media Bias, Perspective and State Repression: The Black Panther Party*. New York: Cambridge University Press.

Davenport, Christian, and Patrick Ball. 2002. "Views to a Kill: Exploring the Implications of Source Selection in the Case of Guatemalan State Terror, 1977–1995." *Journal of Conflict Resolution* 46 (3): 427–50.

Davenport, Christian, Sarah Soule, and David Armstrong. 2011. "Protesting While Black? The Differential Policing of American Activism, 1960 to 1990." *American Sociological Review* 76 (1): 152–78.

Davis, Darren. 2007. *Negative Liberty: Public Opinion and the Terrorist Attacks on America*. New York: Russell Sage Foundation.

Davis, Darren W., and Brian D. Silver. 2004. "Civil Liberties vs. Security: Public Opinion in the Context of the Terrorist Attacks on America." *American Journal of Political Science* 48 (1): 28–46.

Della Porta, Donatella, and Herbert Reiter. 1998. *Policing Protest: The Control of Mass Demonstrations in Western Democracies*. Minneapolis: University of Minnesota Press.

Earl, Jennifer, and Sarah A. Soule. 2006. "Seeing Blue: A Police-Centered Explanation of Protest Policing." *Mobilization* 11 (2): 145–64.

Earl, Jennifer, Sarah A. Soule, and John D. McCarthy. 2003. "Protest under Fire? Explaining the Policing of Protest." *American Sociological Review* 68 (4): 581–606.

Fiske, Susan, and Shelley Taylor. 1984. *Social Cognition*. New York: McGraw-Hill.

Francisco, Ron A. 1996. "Coercion and Protest: An Empirical Test in Two Democratic States." *American Journal of Political Science* 40 (4): 1179–204.

Franklin, John Hope, and Isidore Starr. 1967. *The Negro in 20th Century America: A Reader on the Struggle for Civil Rights*. New York: Vintage Books.

Gamson, William A. 1979. "The *Dissent* of the Governed: Alienation and Democracy in America. James D. Wright." *American Journal of Sociology* 85 (1): 187–89.

Gibson, James. 2008. "Intolerance and Political Repression in the United States: A Half Century after McCarthyism." *American Journal of Political Science* 52 (1): 96–108.

Giugni, Marco. 1998. "Was It Worth the Effort? The Outcomes and Consequences of Social Movements." *Annual Review of Sociology* 24 (1): 371–93.

Goffman, Erving. 1974. *Framing Analysis: An Essay on the Organization of Experience*. New York: Harper & Row.

Hess, David, and Brian Martin. 2006. "Repression, Backfire and the Theory of Transformative Events." *Mobilization* 11 (2): 249–67.

Jasper, James M., and Jane D. Poulsen. 1995. "Recruiting Strangers and Friends: Moral Shocks and Social Networks in Animal Rights and Anti-nuclear Protests." *Social Problems* 42 (4): 493–512.

King, Gary, Michael Tomz, and Jason Wittenberg. 2000. "Making the Most of Statistical Analyses: Improving Interpretation and Presentation." *American Journal of Political Science* 44 (2): 341–55.

Kuklinski, J., P. Sniderman, K. Knight, T. Piazza, P. Tetlock, G. Lawrence, and B. Mellers. 1997. Racial Prejudice and Attitudes Toward Affirmative Action. *American Journal of Political Science*, 402–419.

Kurzban, Robert, John Tooby, and Leda Cosmides. 2001. "Can Race Be Erased? Coalitional Computation and Social Categorization." *Proceedings of the National Academy of Sciences* 98 (26): 15387–92.

Lichbach, Mark. 1992. "Nobody Cites Nobody Else—Mathematical Models of Domestic Political-Conflict." *Defense Economics* 3 (4): 341–57.

Mason, T. David, and Dale Krane. 1989. "The Political Economy of Death Squads—Toward a Theory of the Impact of State-Sanctioned Terror." *International Studies Quarterly* 33 (2): 175–98.

McAdam, Doug. 1982. *Political Process and the Development of Black Insurgency, 1930–1970*. Chicago: University of Chicago Press.

McAdam, Doug. 1988. "Micromobilization Contexts and Recruitment to Activism." *International Social Movement Research* 1 (1): 125–54.

McAdam, Doug, and Yang Su. 2002. "The War at Home: The Impact of Anti-war Protests, 1965–1973." *American Sociological Review* 67: 696–721.

Moore, Will H. 2000. "The Repression of Dissent: A Substitution Model of Government Coercion." *Journal of Conflict Resolution* 44 (1): 107–27.

Opp, Karl-Dieter, and Christiane Gern. 1993. "Dissident Groups, Personal Networks, and Spontaneous Cooperation: The East German Revolution of 1989." *American Sociological Review* 58 (5): 659–80.

Opp, Karl-Dieter, and Edward Muller. 1986. "Rational Choice and Rebellious Collective Action." *American Political Science Review* 80 (2): 471–88.

Opp, Karl-Dieter, and Wolfgang Roehl. 1990. "Repression, Micro-mobilization, and Political Protest." *Social Forces* 69 (2): 521–47.

Petraeus, David. 2006. *The Army Counterinsurgency Manual*. Washington: US Army. http://www.fas.org/irp/doddir/army/fmi3-07-22.pdf.

Phelps, Elizabeth A., and Laura A. Thomas. 2003. "Race, Behavior, and the Brain: The Role of Neuroimaging in Understanding Complex Social Behaviors." *Political Psychology* 24 (4): 747–58.

Piven, Francis Fox, and Richard Cloward. 1977. *Poor People's Movements*. New York: Vintage Books.

Poe, Steven C., and Neal C. Tate. 1994. "Repression of Human Rights to Personal Integrity in the 1980s: A Global Analysis." *American Political Science Review* 88 (4): 853–72.

R Core Development Team. 2012. *R: A Language and Environment for Statistical Computing*. Vienna, Austria: R Foundation for Statistical Computing.

Smith, Brad W., and Malcolm D. Holmes. 2003. "Community Accountability, Minority Threat, and Police Brutality: An Examination of Civil Rights Criminal Complaints." *Criminology* 41 (4):1035–63.

Soule, Sarah, and Brayden King. 2006. "The Impact of Social Movements at Stages of the Policy Process: The Equal Rights Amendment, 1972–1982." *American Journal of Sociology* 111 (6): 1871–909.

Soule, Sarah, and Christian Davenport. 2009. "Velvet Glove, Iron Fist or Even Hand? Protest Policing in the United States, 1960–1990." *Mobilization* 14 (1): 1–22.

Stults, Brian J., and Eric P. Baumer. 2007. "Racial Context and Police Force Size: Evaluating the Empirical Validity of the Minority Threat Perspective." *American Journal of Sociology* 113 (2): 507–46.

Taylor, Marylee C. 1998. "How White Attitudes Vary with the Racial Composition of Local Populations: Numbers Count." *American Sociological Review* 63: 512–35.

Tilly, Charles. 1978. *From Mobilization to Revolution*. Reading, MA: Addison-Wesley.

Venables, William. N., and Brian D. Ripley. 2002. *Modern Applied Statistics with S* (4th edition). New York, NY: Springer.

Weitzer, Ronald, and Stephen A. Tuch. 2005. "Racially Biased Policing: Determinants of Citizen Perceptions." *Social Forces* 83 (3): 1009–30.

Williams, Julian. 2005. "Black Radio and Civil Rights: Birmingham, 1956–1963." *Journal of Radio Studies* 12 (1): 47–60.

Wisler, Dominique, and Marco Giugni. 1999. "Under the Spotlight: The Impact of Media Attention on Protest Policing." *Mobilization: An International Quarterly* 4 (2): 171–87.

PART III

Socioeconomic (In)Equality

CHAPTER 8

Supporting the "Elite" Transition in South Africa: Policing in a Violent, Neoliberal Democracy

Marlea Clarke

South Africa garnered the world's attention in August 2012 when police opened fire on striking workers at the Lonmin Platinum mine in Marikana, killing 34 and wounding 78. Some believed that this lethal use of force exposed deep problems with state policing, specifically the steady "re-militarization" of the police (Hornberger 2013), or a return to the brutality that characterized policing during the apartheid period (Bruce 2002, 2005). Others (Hart 2013; Calland 2013) quickly referred to the massacre as the "Marikana moment," a turning point in the country's history where some of the principal tensions in society and failures of the transition were exposed in one brutal incident, and compared it to other historical dividing points such as the Sharpeville massacre (1960) and the Soweto uprising (1976). Both of these tragedies increased national resistance to apartheid, and galvanized international attention and support for the liberation movement, which eventually forced the government to begin negotiations to end apartheid and transition to democratic rule.

M. Clarke (✉)
Department of Political Science, University of Victoria, Victoria, BC, Canada

© The Author(s) 2018   195
M. D. Bonner et al. (eds.), *Police Abuse in Contemporary Democracies*,
https://doi.org/10.1007/978-3-319-72883-4_8

The Marikana massacre did instigate other actions, such as the wave of strikes that swept the mining and agricultural sectors in the weeks and months that followed. However, there is little to suggest that it was a turning point. Extreme inequality, relative deprivation, and deep poverty persist in South Africa, reinforced by governing practices, neoliberal economic policies, and patterns of structural violence carried over from the apartheid period. And, as will be discussed below, despite the country's relatively peaceful transition to democracy, contemporary South Africa continues to be marked by high levels of violent crime. Much of this crime, however, is a symptom of social and economic inequalities and the legacy of apartheid rule, rather than a failure of police reform—and, as such, the crime spike does not justify the "tough on crime" approach adopted in the early 2000s. Indeed, rather than improving the crime-fighting performance and capacity of the police, the "tough on crime" approach has created an environment in which police abuse continues.

Similar to the analysis offered in this edited volume, and informed by scholarship focused on the relationship between democracy and violence in the global south (Arias and Goldstein 2010; Chatterjee 2004; North et al. 2012), this chapter views police abuse as actions that limit or restrict citizens' rights and actions aimed at agitating for socioeconomic transformation, including but not limited to the rights to protest, strike, and collectively organize. As we will see below, the policing of crime, strikes, and protests (the latter frequently focused on the demands for services in poor areas and a more equitable redistribution of wealth and assets) in South Africa have all become more violent, with successive police ministers promising to crackdown on crime and to use force to restore order (von Holdt 2013, p. 602).

This chapter argues that violence and police abuse in contemporary South Africa are not necessarily symptomatic of democratic failure (a common diagnosis in the political science literature on democratization [Bonner et al., Chapter 1]), but rather the outcome of a particular type of democratic transition. Bringing together the work of scholars on the political economy of policing and the scholarship on the political economy of South Africa's transition, this chapter echoes von Holdt's characterization of South Africa's social order as violent democracy. As he contends, violence should not be seen as an aberration. Instead, "democracy may configure power relations in such a way that violent practices are integral to them—producing a social system we may call *violent democracy*" (2013, p. 590).

Characterizing the country in such a way does not negate the fact that police reforms have taken place. As we will see, wide-reaching reforms to the police force introduced in the 1990s began to transform the brutal, racist, incompetent apartheid police force inherited by the African National Congress (ANC). However, the emphasis on legitimacy, accountability, and community-policing in these reforms was quickly set aside as violent crime began to undermine confidence in the new order. Safety and crime reduction became the top public policy concerns, and human rights oriented reforms to the police force were abandoned as they were seen to undermine the effectiveness of the police (Bruce 2002, p. 18). Further, excessive force by the police against civilians remained high, especially against striking workers and social movement actions, key features of political engagement and protest in contemporary South Africa, which are increasingly labeled as forms of "violent and unruly behavior" that hamper the economy.

This chapter is organized in the following way. The first section provides a brief historical overview of policing under apartheid in order to understand the challenges inherited by the new regime in 1994, the need for widespread reforms, and some of the ways in which the role of the police in the contemporary period bears striking resemblance to that of the police under the previous regime. The next section outlines some of the key elements of police reform under the ANC government during their first term in office. After noting some of the positive consequences of such changes, we turn to examine the effects of the government's shift to a "tough on crime" approach and related problems with police abuse. The third section examines some of the ways in which the "tough on crime" approach has spilled over into the policing of civil society protests in the context of rising socioeconomic inequality and public opposition to neoliberal economic reforms.

Police abuse should not be understood as a "policing problem" or the failure of police accountability mechanisms put in place under the African National Congress (ANC) government since 1994, as much of the work on policing tends to do (see, for example, van der Spuy 2007; de Kok and van der Spuy 2015; Bruce 2007). Instead, similar to the role of the police in the apartheid era, the aggressive use of force by the current police and private security companies serves to support government policies and reinforce the continued socioeconomic exclusion of a large percentage of society. Thus, police abuse should be understood as both a consequence and an integral aspect of the contested nature of the country's democratic transition. As other scholars have argued, the actions of the Marikana miners and the brutality of the police response can only be understood by placing them within a wider and historical context of structural violence built into the apartheid system (especially the migrant labor system), the role of the police during the apartheid period, and continued patterns of violence shaped by the post-apartheid political economy (Dixon 2015; von Holdt 2013; McMichael 2016). The chapter concludes with a call to introduce broader-based reforms, both to the police force itself and especially to policies that will address systemic poverty, inequality, and violence in South Africa. The solution to police abuse is not better training, but rather socioeconomic reforms aimed at the radical redistribution of income, wealth, and other resources.

HISTORY: POLICING AND POLICE ABUSE UNDER APARTHEID

As is well documented and needs little recounting here, the history of apartheid was a history of oppressive and inhuman police practices. Although racist and brutal policing existed before apartheid was formally adopted in 1948, police abuse escalated dramatically in the following decades. The laws and norms that governed the South African Police (SAP) under successive National Party governments gave police enormous discretionary power to use whatever force they deemed appropriate to enforce the law, keep the peace, protect property, and perhaps most importantly, maintain apartheid (Brogden and Shearing 1993). While white communities were protected from crime, black[1] communities were policed for control, not crime prevention. Overall, the SAP's primary role was enforcing apartheid and controlling the movement of black Africans. Police violence was indirect and direct. Indirectly, the SAP enforced an oppressive social, political, and legal order that controlled and shattered the lives of black South Africans (Brewer 1989; Brogden and Shearing 1993). For example, police were at the forefront of imposing the infamous Pass Laws (laws regulating and restricting the movement of black people into urban areas) alongside numerous other apartheid laws and legislation regulating black people's movements and behavior in urban areas (i.e., laws that segregated public premises and services like parks and beaches).

Direct violence was just as pervasive: the SAP was tasked with putting down all opposition to apartheid (disingenuously labeled "unrest") and often did so with excessive force. Enforcing apartheid in the face of rising opposition during the 1960s and 1970s required the use of coercive measures and brutality, from individual arrests and detentions to mass slaughters of unarmed or retreating protesters (e.g., the Sharpeville massacre in 1960[2] and the killing of hundreds of students during the Soweto uprisings in June 1976). As Brogden and Shearing argue about this period: "what sets South African policing apart from most other policing is the oppressive nature of the order promoted and the violence it has employed" (1993, p. 16).

Even with the repressive political climate, opposition to apartheid mounted throughout the 1980s: black trade unions organized strikes and other workplace actions despite the illegality of such actions, youth and student groups proliferated, and women's organizations were formed throughout the country. Resistance deepened and expanded with the formation of the United Democratic Front (UDF), an umbrella organization that brought together over 400 youth, student, church, worker, women's and other anti-apartheid and community-based organizations.

The government responded by declaring two States of Emergency, the first in 1985 and the second in 1988, both of which gave the police and military heightened powers. Security and riot police patrolled the townships, terrorizing black communities, and their organizations. Police brutality escalated: torture became a normal part of custodial and interrogative practices of the SAP, and hundreds of anti-apartheid activists were killed or injured in police custody. In order to "confuse and conceal" the racial aspect of oppression by having apartheid enforced in the townships by "the victims themselves" (Brogden and Shearing 1993), the SAP gradually hired more black officers to patrol the townships while still maintaining a racially hierarchical command structure. Black townships became such a target of police action and surveillance that by the late 1980s, the Casspir, a bright yellow armored vehicle carrying heavily armed—and increasingly black—police had become the symbol of South African policing.

In addition to brutality, five key factors characterized and shaped policing under apartheid: fragmentation; legislative context; police–military relations; politicization of crime and the related politicization of the police as an institution; and, public perceptions of the police. Police reform in the post-apartheid period needs to be understood with reference to these factors, and with regard to neoliberal economic reforms and resulting political struggles.

First, under apartheid policing took place through a large fragmented network of separate police forces, ancillary bodies, and a burgeoning private security industry. Most important in this fragmentation were regional police forces. Although the South African Police formed the largest and most dominant police force, policing during the 1970s and 1980s was carried out through numerous, geographically specific, police forces after the creation of ten new "homelands."[3] Each force was constituted under its own legislation and operated within its own jurisdiction. However, as Rauch notes, despite "nominal political independence," homeland police forces were subject to "significant control by the SAP" (2000, p. 1). One feature of these regional police forces that had long-term consequences was that homeland forces were generally made up of officers (black and white) who had been seconded to the homeland force and used the autonomy they enjoyed from central police headquarters to create networks of patronage and corruption (Rauch 2000). Further, the relatively small SAP was able to draw on members of the Police Reserve (retired SAP members), ancillary bodies such as the intelligence services' vast network of informers, and even individuals—such as employers who helped enforce pass laws and other apartheid legislation for their workforce—to carry out police work (Brogden and Shearing 1993, pp. 70–71; Brewer et al. 1988), often with relatively low levels of oversight or accountability.

These networks of public and private agencies that enhanced and supported the police increased with privatization processes[4] in the 1980s and the rapid expansion of private security, which became the largest "hidden" supplement to the police (Brogden and Shearing 1993, p. 72). Although legally separated, the private security industry had both informal and formal ties with the SAP, especially following the implementation of the Security Officers Act of 1987, which formalized and expanded their partnership. As many scholars have noted, cooperation went both ways: the SAP relied on private security companies to assist in "regular" policing, especially as police work shifted away from crime and crime prevention to political control of the townships, while the police increasingly collaborated with private security companies at the mines and other private businesses to defeat striking workers (Philip 1989; Irish 1999).

Second, as black opposition to apartheid increased, so too did the power and autonomy of the police to enforce legislation and crackdown on political opposition. Repressive new apartheid legislation gave almost unlimited power to the security policy. For example, like the Terrorism Act that proceeded it, the Internal Security Act of 1982 gave the government broad powers to ban or restrict organizations, publications, people and public gatherings, and extensive powers to detain people suspected of involvement in "terrorism and subversion" indefinitely. Police forces were at the forefront of enforcing such legislation. As others have noted, terrorism and subversion were defined so broadly that charges could be laid against school children boycotting classes or workers engaging in industrial action (Brewer et al. 1988, p. 173). The Act and other pieces of security legislation gave police almost unlimited powers to arrest and detain citizens, and provided no oversight in the treatment of their detainees.

Third, a close relationship and overlapping division of labor developed between the police and defense forces. Organizationally, the links between the SAP and the South African Defence Force (SADF) were strong and became increasingly so during the last few decades of apartheid. For example, the SADF was used to support the police in maintaining internal security and "order" in the townships, especially as resistance deepened in the 1980s (Cawthra 1993; Bruce 2002). Internal restructuring of the SADF expanded the size of the army, created reaction units (Commandos) and other smaller units to allow the SADF to quickly respond to internal "unrest," and formalized collaboration between the army and the police. Other examples of this close linkage include joint training processes for staff and officers, and the ability of SADF servicemen to complete their national service[5] in the SAP. As some scholars have put it, the army was increasingly used as a "subsidiary of the police in urban areas" (Brewer et al. 1988, p. 178).

In addition to these organizational links between the two, the SAP gradually took on a strong paramilitary character: riot control, counterinsurgency, and other forms of military training became part of the "on the job" and basic training for all police officers, while new specialist sections within the SAP, such as the Task Force on counterinsurgency, were created and supported by the SADF (Brewer et al. 1988, pp. 177–79). Even some of the most routine patrols by police forces took on the "character of military-style operations conducted from behind the barrier of wire mesh, armoured vehicles and other technology" (Brewer et al. 1988, p. 183).

Fourth, apartheid legislation and the related lack of legal channels of protest meant that virtually all political protests were criminalized,

as were most ordinary actions that could be seen to have political content. As other scholars have argued, the public disorder was progressively
defined (both in law and in practice) to include such a wide range of
activities that almost any economic, industrial, or social activity could be
defined as public disorder and the participants arrested (Brewer 1989;
Brogden and Shearing 1993). The adoption of the Internal Security
Act and other pieces of legislation during the two States of Emergency
granted the police more power and autonomy, and resulted in greater
police intrusion into all areas of life, ranging across "industrial relations,
religious services, classroom boycotts, poetry readings and township
demonstrations" (Brewer et al. 1988, p. 179).

At the same time, the police spent relatively little time focused on
ordinary crime or crime prevention, especially in black areas of the country. Even the South African Police's official historian, Marius de Witt
Dippenaar, admits that only one in ten members of the police force were
involved in crime prevention, detection, and investigation during the
apartheid period (1988, p. 374). Shaw summarizes the role of the police
under apartheid well:

> Little attempt was made by the police to reduce crime in black areas, the
> majority of police resources being concentrated in white towns and sub-
> urbs. Black people were policed for control and not crime prevention; the
> police aimed to prevent crime in white areas not by reducing it in black
> areas but by preventing the uncontrolled movement of black people, who
> were considered to be its perpetrator. Thus, the police spent an inordi-
> nate amount of resources on arresting people for apartheid administrative
> offences, such as not being in possession of a 'pass' in a white area, but
> seldom confronted criminal violence in the townships themselves. (Shaw
> 2002, p. 1)

Closely related to the politicization of crime was the politicization of the
police as an institution (Brewer 1989). The fact that there was a relationship between politics and policing was nothing unique as all political systems have such a connection. However, this relationship was more
explicit than in most with police upholding the (apartheid) policies of
the National Party (the party in power from 1948–1994) and frequently
conducting themselves in an overtly political manner. For example,
the SAP and homeland police forces sponsored or supported vigilante and conservative groups in clashes with progressive organizations,

or those linked to the UDF. Further, as several scholars have noted, the "Afrikanerization" of the SAP (Cawthra 1997) under the National Party meant that most white police officers were Afrikaans (often working class, many with limited education and skills) who strongly supported apartheid and the ruling party, and opposed any reforms that would increase public accountability of the police.

Finally, it is no surprise that public acceptance of the police among most black South Africans was extremely low. Most blacks were deeply fearful of and often deeply hostile toward the police, including black police officers from their communities. Not only did most blacks fear the police and view their role as brutal apartheid enforcers, most regarded the police as corrupt, incompetent, and uninterested or unable to deal with crime in black areas. Consequently, vigilante groups and other forms of community-based alternatives to the SAP were created to patrol the townships.

In direct contrast, and echoing the findings of Davenport, McDermott, and Armstrong in the case of United States (Chapter 7 of this volume), public approval of the police among the majority of whites remained high, and most believed that police conduct—even when brutal—was justifiable. According to Adam and Moodley, a survey among whites in the mid-1980s showed a 74% approval rating of the police and army (Adam and Moodley 1986, p. 109). However, high the white approval rating was for the police, many white neighborhoods increasingly turned to private security agencies to protect public and private property, leading to the burgeoning of the private security industry. By the late 1990s, it was estimated that there were more than four private security guards for every uniformed member of the SAP (Irish 1999, p. 3).

It was against this backdrop and in the context political reforms[6] aimed at transitioning the country to democracy that President de Klerk introduced initial reforms to the police force. Among other goals, reforms focused on police training, and aimed to depoliticize the force and increase community accountability (Rauch 2000). These goals were outlined in the SAP's 1991 Strategic Plan with specific processes, new systems, and monitoring procedures detailed in a multiparty agreement, the National Peace Accord, the same year. While these initial changes and new procedures for dealing with reported misconduct had a little immediate impact on policing, broader reforms initiated under the new post-apartheid government introduced far-reaching changes to the police service. However, as we will see, the more transformative elements of these reforms were soon set aside as high crime rates resulted in the adoption of a "tough on crime" approach and a corresponding prioritization of those reforms aimed at improving crime-fighting performance and police capacity, while reforms with a strong human rights-based approach were set aside (Bruce 2002).

DEMOCRATIC TRANSITION AND POLICE REFORMS: FROM SERVICE TO "TOUGH ON CRIME"

Apartheid officially ended in 1994 and the ANC (headed by Nelson Mandela) won a landslide victory in the country's first democratic election, winning nearly 63% of the nearly 20 million votes cast, just shy of the two-thirds majority it needed to write the new constitution with few concessions to other parties. The new Constitution, with a Bill of Rights that gives human rights clear prominence, entered into force February 3, 1997.

Police reform, a key element of transforming the public service, was one of many urgent tasks facing the new government. As noted above, the role of the police under apartheid was to maintain apartheid and control black populations, put down political opposition and keep the white government in power, and protect the white population from crime and political unrest. As Rauch notes, "this did not require traditional policing skills, and instead rewarded political loyalty and allowed large-scale abuses of power" (2000, p. 4). As such, the police force for the new democracy needed to be completely transformed into one that would protect the exercise of democratic political rights, be accountable and transparent to citizens, protect and advance human rights, and fight and prevent crime. Bringing about such massive changes to policing was no small task.

Guided by the constitution and the new legal framework, the new ANC government moved quickly to transform and restructure the police, beginning with the creation of one national police force through the amalgamation of the SAP, the ten homeland police agencies, and members of the former liberation movements. The force was renamed the South African Police Service (SAPS), and the Ministry responsible was renamed the Ministry for Safety and Security instead of the previous title, Law and Order, as one way to emphasize the importance of "protecting and servicing."

The force itself was restructured, with new management, communication and command structures put in place. A new, more rigorous system of recruitment was introduced, as was a new training curriculum. Given the history of policing, it was no surprise that accountability, improving police-community relations, and dealing with abuses of power were key imperatives of reform. Thus, alongside an array of other reforms, specific measures were taken to deal with problems of accountability, human rights violations, and corruption. Community Police Forums were created, as well as a new human rights training curriculum. A code of conduct for the police, policies regarding the use of lethal force that were in line with the Constitution, and policies and procedures aimed at preventing the use of torture were all developed and introduced (Bruce and Newham 2007, p. 20; Rauch 2000).

The transformation of policing in South Africa is often regarded as a success story. In the first few years of ANC rule, the police were effective in tackling the threat of armed insurrection posed by right-wing groups and quickly dealt with political violence in KwaZulu-Natal (Bruce 2007, p. 17). Other changes came more slowly, but compliance with new accountability processes has generally been positive, as has been the implementation of new community consultation mechanisms and procedures (Bruce 2002). Training has resulted in improved levels of professionalism and skill in conducting regular police work (Bruce 2002; Diphoorn 2016). Services have been extended to all sectors of the South African population, and improvements have been made in relations between the police and the black community. Changes in the behavior and attitudes of the police and improvements in police–community relations are evident, some of these changes directly linked to successful organizational reforms. Such basic improvements were not easy, especially given the political compromises made during the transition and budgetary constraints, both of which meant that the new SAPS would not be staffed by a completely new group of properly trained recruits. As van der Spuy reminds us, the new SAPS was saddled with around 30,000 apartheid-era "special constables" who were "scarcely literate, hardly trained and generally despised" (2007, p. 279).

Initially, reforms prioritized police legitimacy and accountability, not crime control (on this issue, see Bonner 2014; Seri and Lokaneeta, Chapter 3; Bonner, Chapter 5; Squillacote and Feldman, Chapter 6). Although high levels of crime characterized the country, crime was not seen as a pressing issue for the new government during the ANC's first term in office. According to some scholars (e.g., Shaw 2002; Diphoorn 2016), the government actively denied that crime was a problem and tried to manage crime statistics or stop their release in order to quell national fears and international concerns among tourists and investors. Such a stance was hard to maintain as public confidence in the police steadily fell alongside the public's growing preoccupation with crime (Shaw 2002; Bruce 2002).

Crime was indeed high. As Shaw notes, at the time, South Africa had the highest murder rate in the world, the highest attempted murder rate, and the highest levels of assault with force across all the developing countries surveyed in UN International Crime Victim Survey in 1998 (Shaw 2002, p. 53). The country also had (and still has) one of the highest rates of violence against women.

Although high levels of crime were not new to the country, a number of factors contributed to rates and trends, and citizen's perceptions of crime. First, white neighborhoods began experiencing higher levels of robbery and other forms of crime as apartheid barriers started to fall away. Many of these communities had largely been isolated from some types of crime during the apartheid era because crime prevention work—supported by private security companies—was focused on these communities, while the social dislocation, unemployment, and other socioeconomic conditions that create conditions conducive to crime were contained in the townships and black areas.

Second, some forms of crime, such as armed robbery and property crimes, were increasing due to a number of "push" factors—such as high levels of unemployment, poverty, the slow rate of transformation, and high levels of inequality—alongside the increased flow of guns from neighboring countries with large stocks of weapons due to recent or ongoing war and armed conflict (Shaw 2002, p. 43). Third, the brutality of some attacks, including several very violent burglaries targeting white farmers and other white property owners, shaped public views of crime. These very brutal attacks made headlines in the local and national news and contributed to popular perceptions that crime was spiraling out of control. By the 1999 national election, crime and safety had become key policy issues and the government was forced to respond.

In contrast to the broader police reforms initiated during the ANC's first term in office (1994–1999) that focused on accountability and legitimacy, reforms in the early 2000s were shaped by the government's new "tough on crime" approach. As Gordon notes (2009, p. 85) "Thabo Mbeki began his presidency with a much tougher stance on crime than his predecessor, taking aim at visible (if minor) disorder like squatting and street hawking as well as vowing new initiatives against violence."

In keeping with this approach, the emphasis swung back from "service" to "force," and reforms focused on enhancing and augmenting law enforcement as a way to address high levels of crime. For example, the National Crime Combating Strategy, drafted by the Police Service, "targeted crime fighting in 'hot spots' ... and stations with high rates of recorded crime became earmarked for support and monitoring" (van der Spuy 2007, p. 282). Steve Tshwete, the newly appointed Minister of Safety and Security, was the government's champion of this new "tough on crime" approach. After the election he traveled around the country, speaking out against crime and calling on the police to use all available means, constitutional or unconstitutional to combat crime, and referred to criminal offenders as "subhumans" (Gordon 2009, p. 85). As Shaw contends (2002, p. 87), the thrust of his message was that criminals would be treated harshly and police officers should use all the power available to them to combat crime.

Shortly after his appointment, Tshwete announced: "The criminals have obviously declared war against the South African public. ... We are ready, more than ever before, not just to send a message to the criminals out there about our intentions, but more importantly to make them feel that 'die tyd vir speletjies is nou verby' [the time for fun and games is over]. We are now poised to rise with power and vigour proportional to the enormity and vastness of the aim to be achieved" (Tshwete, as cited in Rauch 1996, p. 10).

Guided by this "zero-tolerance" approach and informed by the National Crime Combating Strategy, in early 2000 the new police commissioner, Jackie Selebi, announced a new three-year national crime combating strategy, known as "Operation Crackdown" to target crime "hot spots" and "reorganise the SAPS into units that would address their particular crime problems" (Gordon 2009, p. 257). Alongside, this was a focus on particular crimes like turf wars and related violence between taxi-drivers (informal mini-bus transport) as well as attacks on (white) farmers. Although the police sweeps of so-called hot spots and high crime areas that followed quickly resulted in large numbers of arrests, it was believed that police targeted nonnationals (leading to severe overcrowding at detention facilities where foreigners without papers were held pending deportation) as a way to meet arrest targets (Human Rights Watch 2001). Further, as Gordon (2009, p. 257) notes, human rights groups and others drew attention to the brutality of arrests and raids on certain areas and argued that police action was also used to harass squatters and intimidate political protesters.

This "tough on crime" approach derailed initial post-apartheid reforms (e.g., those aimed at increased accountability and improving community relations) and shaped police action and government policy. For example, in a 2008 speech to police officers, the Deputy Minister of Safety and Security, Susan Shabangu, explicitly instructed police officers to shoot to kill (suspected) criminals without concern for their rights. She told the audience:

> You must kill the bastards if they threaten you or the community. You must not worry about the regulations. This is my responsibility. Your responsibility is to serve and protect. I won't tolerate any pathetic excuses for you not being able to deal with crime. You have been given guns, now use them. I want no warning shots. You have one shot and it must be a kill shot ... If criminals dare to threaten the police or the livelihood or lives of innocent men, women and children, they must be killed. End of story ... the constitution says criminals must be kept safe, but I say No! I say we must protect the law-abiding people and not the criminals. (As quoted in Berger 2008)

This and other similar speeches and statements from government ministers sent a clear message to police officers, which was to set aside human rights concerns, ignore the Constitution or other safeguards and take whatever action was necessary to catch—or kill—suspected criminals. As Bruce notes, these statements and other comments from Tshwete "virtually amounted to exhortations to brutality" (2002, p. 18). The result, as Shaw (2002) and others demonstrate, was that the focus on human rights and issues of accountability that had previously guided police reform shifted to a clear concentration on combating crime and fighting criminals. As he notes, while "the two approaches are not mutually exclusive, from 1999 (and perhaps even earlier) the weight shifted decisively to crime fighting through effective law enforcement" (2002, p. 39).

SUPPORTING THE "ELITE" TRANSITION: POLICING IN A VIOLENT, NEOLIBERAL DEMOCRACY

Given the "tough on crime" approach taken in the early 2000s, perhaps it is no surprise that policing remains uneven across the country and positive changes have been offset by incompetence, corruption, systemic racism, and brutality (Steinberg 2001; Bruce 2002). While killings by police have declined since 1997, statistics compiled by the Independent Police Investigative Directorate[7] (IPID), along with other independent research, demonstrates that police abuse continues to be a serious problem (Bruce 2005; Bhana 2003; Bonner et al., Chapter 1).

Deaths as a result of police action (including killings of innocent bystanders) remain high, as do incidents of torture and assault. For example, there were 3042 deaths as a result of police action (4688 if deaths in police custody are included) in the first seven years following the establishment of the ICD (Bruce 2005, p. 144). Deaths as a result of police action each year have remained fairly steady: there were 380 deaths in 2003/2004 (Independent Complaints Directorate 2004, p. 5) decreasing only slightly to 366 in 2015/2016 (Independent Police Investigative Directorate 2016, p. 52). The 2015/2016 IPID Annual Report demonstrates that allegations of police torture and ill-treatment of criminal suspects remain high: there were 145 cases of torture and 3509 cases of assault (2016, p. 63). Further, rape by on and off duty police officers is high. Based only on incident reports submitted to the IPID, there were 112 rape cases reported in 2015/2016, of which 51 were committed by on-duty police officers (IPID 2016, p. 61), of which only 13 officers received disciplinary convictions (IPID 2016, p. 89).

Similar to the issues discussed in both the Canadian and Chilean cases in this book (Dupuis-Déri, Chapter 4; Bonner, Chapter 5), another indicator of police abuse is the excessive force frequently used against striking workers, civil society groups, and other protesters. Here, we see the central role of the police in upholding an extremely unequal social order. While international attention has focused on the Marikana massacre, police abuse frequently takes place in the form of "public order" policing during strikes or at political protests, both of which escalated in the late 1990s following the government's adoption of the Growth, Employment, and Redistribution Program (GEAR).

As many scholars have outlined (e.g., Bond 2000; Bassett and Clarke 2008), the ANC's replacement of the *Reconstruction and Development Programme* (RDP), a people-centered socioeconomic development plan that focused on state-led development and redistribution, with GEAR marked the formal acceptance of neoliberalism. Goals such as job creation, poverty reduction, and equitable economic growth present in the RDP were replaced with trade and market liberalization, debt reduction, and stringent fiscal deficit reduction targets. And, in contrast to the

ANC's previous commitment to improved and increased service provision and policies aimed at redistribution, GEAR called for the privatization of state assets and public utilities, wage restraint for public sector and other organized workers, and the relaxation of labor regulations, especially for unskilled workers. Thus, although the ANC government was relatively successful in extending services and infrastructure to millions during its first term in office, the widespread privatization of public utilities and services (e.g., water and electricity), and corresponding cost recovery in service delivery meant that households were forced to pay the cost of the provision of basic services. This has, in effect, "clawed back" many of the services newly extended to poor communities. Indeed, while water and electricity, for example, have been extended to new areas, even the poorest households are now expected to pay full market prices or they will be cut off.

High levels of unemployment and the continued segmentation of South Africa's labor market also reveal the limited nature of South Africa's transition, and help explain waves of strike action around the country and growing opposition to government policies. Unemployment—already high in the mid-1990s—has grown and is exceedingly high by international standards, as are the number of workers in precarious forms of employment. For example, according to the most recent labor force data, if discouraged job seekers are included, the country's unemployment rate is currently 36.3%—a 13 year high—with the youth unemployment rate a staggering 67.3%.

Alongside high levels of unemployment are high—and rising—levels of employment precariousness. Permanent employment has fallen and now accounts for less than 60% of the working population, with some sectors recording much higher levels of temporary or casual jobs. Similar to employment for black workers under apartheid, these jobs have high levels of insecurity, and limited—if any—benefits or protection (Clarke 2015). Segmentation and precariousness have increased, in part, as a result of more employers turning to temporary employment agencies (labor brokers) to staff their workplaces, thereby distancing themselves from most of the costs, risks, and responsibilities associated with employment. For example, by 2010 over one-third of the labor force in the mining sector was employed by a third party—generally a labor broker (Bezuidenhout and Buhlungu 2010). Overall, despite improvements to labor laws and social security provisions under the ANC, the labor market remains extremely segmented with black workers concentrated in the growing ranks of the systemically unemployed or in casual or temporary jobs with high levels of insecurity (Clarke 2015). Living and working conditions for farmworkers and for migrant mineworkers are especially dire.

The privatization of municipal services, inflation alongside low wages in many sectors, coupled with unemployment and precariousness, have contributed to exceptionally high rates of poverty and inequality. For example, national income inequality as measured by the Gini coefficient rose from 0.64 in 1995 to 0.69 in 2005 (du Toit and Neves 2008, p. 3), and then to 0.70 in 2008 (Narayan and Mahajan 2013, p. 1), making South Africa one of the most unequal countries in the world.[8] Colin Bundy's (2014, p. 49) succinct summary of the outcome of this "elite" transition and economically conservative post-apartheid settlement underscores this inequality: "the evidence is unequivocal. Wealth in South Africa has been partly deracialised. Poverty remains strongly racialised, visited with particular severity upon Africans, at the bottom of the economic pecking order now as they were under apartheid." Indeed, while South Africa has undergone a successful political transition to liberal democracy, there has been little radical redistribution in income, wealth, and other resources.

No surprise, then, that there has been a dramatic rise in the scale and intensity of social protests and strikes, such as the strike at the Lonmin Platinum mine in Marikana, over at least the last decade. Beginning in the early 2000s, new community-based organizations—what Ashwin Desai (2002) has called organizations of "the poors"—emerged and grew in response to the effects of the ANC's adoption of neoliberal policies, especially the privatization of public sector companies and cost recovery in service delivery. Groups such as the Anti-Privatization Forum (APF), Soweto Electricity Crisis Committee, and the Landless People's Movement emerged to oppose housing evictions, and water and electricity cut-offs resulting from "non-payment."

Police have frequently responded to protests and direct action organized by these groups with teargas, rubber bullets, and batons. Police also hire and work with the Red Ants Security and Eviction Services (known simply as the Red Ants due to the red uniforms they wear) to evict people and dismantle homes that have been informally constructed on the vacant land. Both the SAPS and the Red Ants are accused of being ruthless and using excessive force to carry out evictions (Iaccino 2016). Further, reminiscent of the private agencies that supported the police during the apartheid era, South Africa has a large and growing private security industry that increasingly performs many police functions, despite having few regulations to govern its activities and no public oversight. The industry is reported to be the largest in the world, with approximately 9000 companies and 400,000 registered active private security guards (Eastwood 2013), and frequently aids and supports the police, including carrying out arrests of suspected criminals.

Civil society and social movement protests at the 2002 World Summit on Sustainable Development (WSSD) in South Africa were especially confrontational. Activists gathered in Johannesburg in the days leading up to the WSSD, either to participate in the Global People's Forum—an NGO-led conference running parallel to the official WSSD—or to attend other civil society side events or the mass march. South Africans used the WSSD to challenge the neoliberal policies of the ANC and the growing subordination of sustainable development to free trade and other neoliberal policies by many delegates to the WSSD.

Similar to the "political profiling" discussed by Dupuis-Déri (Chapter 4), activists were monitored, questioned, and many arrested in the run-up to the summit—what Bond (2002) has called the "pre-WSSD intimidation raids"—and a march of people calling for the release of those arrested in pre-WSSD events was ambushed by police who fired "smoke and concussion grenades into the centre of the march without warning" (ENS 2002). Consistent with the overall "tough on crime approach" adopted by the government, the next day, South Africa's Safety and Security Minister, Charles Nqakula, warned that the "law would come down hard" on any persons or groups demonstrating at the WSSD without government approval. The government was forced to retreat from its position and reluctantly agreed to allow a protest march to the WSSD's heavily guarded site in the prosperous, white Sandton neighborhood after negative international media attention regarding the government's response to civil society protest.

State–civil society relations in the country have generally deteriorated since the WSSD, with police frequently accused of using unnecessary force against protesters. Strikes and workplace actions are high, with South Africa reported to have the highest rate of industrial action in the world with an average of 65 strikes per year between 2007 and 2012, 99 strikes in 2012 alone, and growing workplace action in the years following (Department of Labour 2013). While strikes are often a direct reaction to workplace problems such as low wages and poor working conditions, they are also an outlet for workers' frustration at continued poor service delivery, rising inequalities, poor living conditions, and various other community grievances. Such frustration is no surprise given the limited transformation that has taken place in the country and the persistence of exclusionary socioeconomic structures.

After a few years of declining civil society action following the 2009 national election, the last several years have seen an escalation of popular protest. Although beyond the scope of this chapter, critics have pointed out that tolerance for civil society opposition to government policies—indeed, even opposition to ANC leadership within the governing party—has steadily shrunk in the last decade. Nevertheless, protests have continued and are often described by critics of the government policies as "municipal revolts" or "rebellions of the poor"—as most protests involve those in informal settlements or poor urban areas in the country's largest cities, and are focused on poor and inadequate service delivery and slow land redistribution. The Community Law Centre's Civic Protest Barometer reported that in 2014 the number of protests reached an all-time high[9] (Powell, O'Donovan, and De Visser 2014), and have grown since. For instance, student protests that began in mid-2015 around the country as part of the "fees must fall" campaign in response to the government's proposed tuition hikes of between 10 and 12% were met by confrontations with the police.

Police have responded to these recent protests with increased force. As Bruce notes, beginning in about 2010, the SAPS began to utilize "brutal new methods" against protesters, methods that involve the use of live ammunition, the direct firing of rubber bullets at close range, and the targeting of leaders or other people playing a prominent role in the demonstrations (Bruce 2012a). Such brutal methods have continued to be used against protesters (Bruce 2012b). For example, the police tried to break up 2015 student protests on several campuses with teargas, stun grenades, and rubber bullets, but resisted using live ammunition, unlike in 2000 when police opened fire on students at the University of Durban-Westville (UDW), killing two and injuring three. And, police continue to be called to "deal with violent and unruly behavior" by striking workers, with the government supporting the violent suppression of protests as necessary to deal with violent strikes that "harm the economy" (Tenza 2015, p. 212).

As other scholars have argued (McMichael 2016, p. 11; von Holdt 2013), heavy-handed police action against strikers and demonstrators should not be seen in isolation from their role in protecting the economy, and the highly unequal social order. Indeed, as McMichael clearly outlines, the South African police have increasingly been called upon to ensure that a "safe" and "inviting" environment is created and maintained for big business and investors, as Dixon points out with reference to the mining industry (2015). This involves disciplining groups and individuals that are considered a threat to economic development and investment. For example, as he notes, the government justifies the removal—often quite ruthlessly—of informal settlements, street traders (even those with licences from the city) and shack dwellers using the language of economic and public security. Pre-dawn raids with armored vehicles and rubber bullets and the use of whips are not uncommon (Patel 2011, xiv as cited in McMichael 2016, p. 11). The government justifies such action with claims that informal settlements are sites of criminality, and that violent protest threatens the democracy the police are sworn to protect. According to Zuma:

> the right to protest, peacefully and unarmed, is enshrined in our Constitution. However, when protests threaten lives and property and destroy valuable infrastructure intended to serve the community, they undermine the very democracy that upholds the right to protest" [...] "the police are protectors and the buffer between a democratic society based on the rule of law and anarchy. As we hold the police to account, we should be careful not to end up delegitimising them and glorify anarchy in our society. (Zuma 2014)

CONCLUSION

During the apartheid period, South Africa had a worldwide reputation for systemic state violence and police brutality. Transforming the police force was one of many key challenges facing the new ANC government. As discussed in this chapter, emphasis was immediately placed on improving accountability, legitimacy, and improved community relations. Far-reaching reforms took place, including the introduction of a new curriculum and training procedures, and new policies to guide police action. In addition, reforms aimed at improving community relations, especially in the townships, and increasing crime prevention work in poor and marginalized communities were pursued. Such changes were important and had positive outcomes, especially with regard to community relations and trust in black communities.

Although initial reforms were certainly successful in many areas, statistics on lethal police abuse released by the Independent Complaints Directorate and media reports of heavy-handed police action against striking workers and civil society demonstrators reveal ongoing problems with police abuse. As is argued above, such actions should not be understood as the outcome of failed reform or evidence of the need for simply more training. Instead, the ongoing brutality of the police should be seen in the context of the country's stalled transition and related acceptance of neoliberal economic policies. Economic policies under the ANC have served to reinforce the deeply divided, unequal society inherited by the apartheid regime. Corresponding high levels of poverty, unemployment, and precarity—alongside deep social problems—have created an environment in which crime has grown. Public perception of "spiralling crime rates"—especially from white communities previously isolated from crime—and diminishing investor confidence in the country, resulted in the adoption of a "tough on crime" approach.

In addition to adopting harsh practices toward suspected criminals—such as "shoot to kill"—police brutality has also spilled over into the treatment of squatters, street vendors, striking workers, political protesters, and other groups characterized by the government as a threat to public order. Such targeted abuse parallels that found by Schneider in France (Chapter 2), Seri and Lokaneeta in Argentina, and India (Chapter 3) and Dupuis-Déri in Canada (Chapter 4). While in South Africa this approach might have increased public confidence in the police and given (some) citizens the impression that the government was taking action to deal with rising crime (Rauch 2000), it has also created an environment in which police abuse continues and in fact flourishes: It massively expands discretionary police action (and related actions of the burgeoning private security companies), and can justify the brutal crackdown on protesters and civil society groups. Thus, similar to the political role played by the police during the apartheid period, the SAPS in contemporary South Africa is playing a key role in upholding the highly unequal social order of the neoliberal democracy.

Echoing Bonner et al. (Chapter 1), and more specifically McMichael (2016) and others, police abuse in South Africa should not be seen as an aberration, or the result of failed police reform but rather part of wide, social conflict over the limited nature of South Africa's transition. Post-apartheid neoliberal reforms have reinforced, or in some cases exacerbated, socioeconomic inequality and related insecurities.

Rather than address these issues of political economy, South African political leaders have turned to "tough on crime" rhetoric and policies. The police abuse it has unleashed not only fails to reduce crime (e.g., Darley 2005; Waller 2006), but has been used to attempt to silence voices opposed to neoliberalism.

Thus, while some of the political science literature on democratization recognizes that a certain degree of socioeconomic equality is needed to maintain democracy, most of the literature would lead us to believe that strengthening institutions of liberal democracy is the best path to reducing police abuse (Bonner et al., Chapter 1). However, such remedies are insufficient. Police abuse is better seen as a symptom of political economy, and socioeconomic inequality in particular. The response, therefore, is not more resources to policing or greater police reforms but rather socioeconomic reforms aimed at the radical redistribution of income, wealth, and other resources.

NOTES

1. Apartheid sought to classify people by ethnicity and "race." Of course, the legacies of apartheid cannot be easily undone and ethnicity continues to shape citizens' socioeconomic positions in society. Given this, and that many South Africans continue to define themselves in this way, this chapter will use such terminology. In general, black is the preferred term in the new South Africa to describe the African, Asian, and Colored (as designated in the apartheid era by the state) communities and will be used throughout this chapter to refer to all three communities.
2. On March 21, 1960, at least 180 black Africans were injured (there are claims of as many as 300) and 69 were killed when police opened fire on approximately 300 demonstrators, who were protesting a new law, the Native Laws Amendment Act, in the township of Sharpeville. The new law required all black South Africans to carry a pass that restricted their movement in "white" urban areas. Political repression increased after the Sharpeville Massacre, with a number of harsh new laws introduced to crush political, trade union, and community-based resistance to apartheid.
3. Apartheid legislation segregated South Africans into ethnic groups and assigned each group a land area (a homeland) and some form of administration. Four of these homelands were given "independent," or "self-governing" arrangements.
4. For example, the National Key Points Act 1980 transferred the protection of sites of national strategic importance from the SAP to private security companies. The Act gave private security companies full powers of arrest.

5. South Africa had compulsory military service for all white men between 1967 and 1993.
6. The dismantling of apartheid and the creation of a democratic system of representation was a negotiated process in South Africa. Formal negotiations between the ANC and the de Klerk government began with the unbanning of the ANC, SACP, and other political organizations on February 2, 1990 and the release of Nelson Mandela and other political prisoners nine days later, and ended three years later when a formal political settlement was reached.
7. Formerly the Independent Complaints Directorate (ICD). The ICD was created in 1997 as part of police reforms. It was tasked with conducting independent and impartial investigations into deaths in police custody and other identified criminal offenses allegedly committed by members of the SAPS and Metro Police Services. Changes in the activities of the Directorate were made in 2012, along with the change in name. Similar to the ICD, the IPID, and the ICD before it investigates deaths in custody, deaths as a result of police action, and crimes allegedly committed by police officers, including rape, assault, and corruption.
8. A Gini coefficient of 0 represents total equality, while a coefficient of 1 would signal all income was earned by one person.
9. Now called the Dullah Omar Institute.

REFERENCES

Adam, Heribert, and Kogila Moodley. 1986. *South Africa Without Apartheid: Dismantling Racial Domination*. Berkeley: University of California Press.

Arias, Enrique Desmond, and Daniel Goldstein, eds. 2010. *Violent Democracies in Latin America*. Durham and London: Duke University Press.

Bassett, Carolyn, and Marlea Clarke. 2008. "The Zuma Affair: Labour and the Future of Democracy in South Africa." *Third World Quarterly* 29 (4): 787–803.

Berger, Sebastien. 2008. "'Kill the bastards' South African Police Advised." *The Telegraph*, April 10. http://www.telegraph.co.uk/news/worldnews/1584641/Kill-the-bastards-South-African-police-advised.html (last accessed November 22, 2017).

Bezuidenhout, Andries, and Sakhela Buhlungu. 2010. "From Compounded to Fragmented Labour: Mineworkers and the Demise of Compounds in South Africa." *Antipode* 43 (2): 237–63.

Bhana, B.D. 2003. "Custody-Related Deaths in Durban, South Africa 1998–2000." *American Journal of Forensic Medicine and Pathology* 24 (2): 202–7.

Bond, Patrick. 2000. *Elite Transition: From Apartheid to Neoliberalism in South Africa*. London and Sterling, VA: Pluto Press.

Bond, Patrick. 2002. *Geopolitics of Jo'burg Protests: Independent Left Beats Ruling Part* (Briefing Paper). Durban: Centre for Civil Society.

Bonner, Michelle. 2014. Policing Protest in Argentina and Chile. Boudler: First Forum (Lynn Rienner).

Brewer, John. 1989. "The Police in South African Politics." In *South Africa: No Turning Back*, edited by Shaun Johnson, 258–82. Bloomington: Indiana University Press.

Brewer, John, Adrian Guelke, Ian Hume, and Edward Moxon-Browne. 1988. "South Africa." In *The Police, Public Order and the State*. London: Macmillan Press.

Brogden, Mike, and Clifford Shearing. 1993. *Policing for a New South Africa*. London: Routledge.

Bruce, David. 2002. "New Wine from an Old Cask? The South African Police Service and the Process of Transformation." Paper presented at John Jay College of Criminal Justice, New York.

Bruce, David. 2005. "Interpreting the Body Count: South African Statistics on Lethal Police Violence." *South African Review of Sociology* 36 (2): 18.

Bruce, David. 2007. "Good Cops? Bad Cops? Assessing the South African Police Service." *South African Crime Quarterly* 21 (September): 15–20.

Bruce, David. 2012a. "The Road to Marikana: Abuses of Force during Public Order Operations." *The South African Civil Society Information Service*. http://sacsis.org.za/site/article/1455 (last accessed November 22, 2017).

Bruce, David. 2012b. *Marikana and the Doctrine of Maximum Force*. ebook: Mampoer Shorts.

Bruce, David, and Gareth Newham. 2007. *In Service of the People's Democracy: An Assessment of the South African Police Service* (Research Report). Johannesburg: Centre for the Study of Violence and Reconciliation.

Bundy, Colin. 2014. *Short-Changed? South Africa Since Apartheid*. Auckland Park: Jacana.

Calland, Richard. 2013. *The Zuma Years: South Africa's Changing Face of Power*. Cape Town: Zebra Press.

Cawthra, Gavin. 1993. *Policing South Africa: The SAP and the Transition from Apartheid*. London: Zed Books.

Cawthra, Gavin. 1997. *Securing South Africa's Democracy: Defence, Development and Security in Transition*. London: Palgrave Macmillan.

Chatterjee, Partha. 2004. *The Politics of the Governed: Reflections on Popular Politics in Most of the World*. New York: Columbia University Press.

Clarke, Marlea. 2015. "Social Policy in South Africa: Cushioning the Blow of the Recession?" In *The Global Crisis and Social Policy*, edited by Stephen McBride, Gerard Boychuk and Rianne Mahon. Vancouver: UBC Press.

Darley, John M. 2005. "On the Unlikely Prospect of Reducing Crime Rates by Increasing the Severity of Prison Sentences." *Journal of Law and Policy* 13 (1): 189–208.

de Kok, Annie and Elrena van der Spuy. 2015. "Inquiries into Policing 1910–2015." *South African Crime Quarterly* 53 (September): Online Supplement.

Department of Labour. 2013. *Annual Industrial Action Report, Department of Labour*. South Africa. http://www.labour.gov.za/DOL/documents/annual-reports/industrial-action-annual-report/2013/annual-industrial-action-report-2013 (last accessed November 22, 2017).

Desai, Ashwin. 2002. *We Are the Poors! Community Struggles in Post-apartheid South Africa*. New York: Monthly Review Press.

Diphoorn, Tessa G. 2016. *Twilight Policing*. Oakland: University of California Press.

Dippenaar, Marius de Witt 1988. *The History of the South African Police, 1913–1988*. Pretoria: Promedia.

Dixon, Bill. 2015. "A Violent Legacy: Policing Insurrection in South Africa from Sharpeville to Marikana." *The British Journal of Criminology* 6 (1): 1131–48.

du Toit, Andries, and David Neves. 2008. *Chronic and Structural Poverty in South Africa—An Overview* (Report for the Chronic Poverty Research Centre). Cape Town: Institute for Poverty, Land and Agrarian Studies.

Eastwood, Victoria. 2013. "Bigger than the Army: South Africa's Private Security Forces." CNN. http://www.cnn.com/2013/02/08/business/south-africa-private-security/index.html (last accessed November 22, 2017).

ENS. 2002. "Summit Protestors Face Police Brutality." *ENS-News*, August 26.

Gordon, Diana. 2009. *Transformation & Trouble*. Ann Arbor: University of Michigan Press.

Hart, Gillian. 2013. *Rethinking the South African Crisis: Nationalism, Populism, Hegemony*. Durban: University of KwaZulu-Natal Press.

Hornberger, Julia. 2013. "From General to Commissioner to General—On the Popular State of Policing in South Africa." *Law and Social Inquiry* 38 (3): 16.

Human Rights Watch. 2001. "World Report 2001: South Africa." *Human Rights Developments*. https://www.hrw.org/legacy/wr2k1/africa/southafrica.html (last accessed November 22, 2017).

Iaccino, Ludovica. 2016. "South Africa Forced Evictions: Who are the Red Ants?" *International Business Times*, May 24.

Independent Complaints Directorate. 2004. *Annual Report 2003–4 Independent Complaints Directorate*. Pretoria: Independent Complaints Directorate.

Independent Police Investigative Directorate. 2016. *Annual Report 2015/2016*. Pretoria: Independent Police Investigative Directorate.

Irish, Jenny. 1999. "Policing for Profit: The Future of South Africa's Private Security Industry." In *Monograph No. 39*, edited by Martin Schönteich. Pretoria, South Africa: Institute for Security Studies.

McMichael, Christopher. 2016. "Police Wars and State Repression in South Africa." *Journal of Asian and African Studies* 51 (1): 3–16.

Narayan, Ambar, and Sandeep Mahajan. 2013. *The State of Opportunities in South Africa: Inequality among Children and in the Labour Market*. Washington: World Bank, Poverty Reduction and Equity Department.

North, Douglass C., John Joseph Wallis, Steven B. Webb, and Barry R. Weingast. 2012. *In the Shadow of Violence: Politics, Economics and the Problems of Development.* Cambridge: Cambridge University Press.

Patel, Raj. 2011. Foreword. In *No Land! No House! No Vote!* edited by Symphony Way Pavement Dwellers. Cape Town: Pambazuka Press.

Philip, Kate. 1989. "The Private Sector and the Security Establishment." In *War and Society: The Militarisation of South Africa*, edited by Jacklyn Cock and Laurie Nathan. Cape Town: David Philip.

Powell, D.M., M. O'Donovan, and J. De Visser. 2014. *Civic Protests Barometer 2007–2014.* Cape Town: Dullah Omar Institute.

Rauch, Janine. 1996. *The 1996 National Crime Prevention Strategy.* Braamfontein, South Africa: Centre for the Study of Violence and Reconciliation, Institute for Security Studies.

Rauch, Janine. 2000. "Police Reform and South Africa's Transition." In *Crime and Policing in Transitional Societies: Conference Proceedings*, edited by Mark Shaw. Johannesburg, South Africa: University of Witswatersrand.

Shaw, Mark. 2002. *Crime and Policing in Post-apartheid South Africa.* Bloomington and Indianapolis: Indiana University Press.

Steinberg, Jonny, ed. 2001. *Crime Wave. The South African Underworld and Its Foes.* Johannesburg: Witwatersrand University Press.

Tenza, Mlungisi. 2015. "An Investigation into the Causes of Violent Strikes in South Africa: Some Lessons from Foreign Law and Possible Solutions." *Law, Democracy & Development* 19 (1): 211–31.

van der Spuy, Elrena. 2007. "Managerialist Pathways Toward 'Good Policing': Observations from South Africa." In *Crafting Transnational Policing*, edited by Andrew Goldsmith and James Sheptycki, 263–92. Oxford and Portland: Hart Publishing.

von Holdt, Karl. 2013. "South Africa: The Transition to Violent Democracy." *Review of African Political Economy* 40 (138): 589–604.

Waller, Irvin. 2006. *Less Law More Order: The Truth about Reducing Crime.* London: Praeger.

Zuma, Jacob. 2014. "State of the Nation Address." Speech, Cape Town, February 13, 2014. http://www.gov.za/node/632440 (last accessed November 22, 2017).

CHAPTER 9

Policing as Pacification: Postcolonial Legacies, Transnational Connections, and the Militarization of Urban Security in Democratic Brazil

Markus-Michael Müller

On December 19, 2008, Rio de Janeiro witnessed the inauguration of the first Pacification Police Unit (*Unidade de Polícia Pacificadora*, UPP) in the marginalized urban neighborhood, or *favela*, of Santa Marta.[1] This event signaled the start of the city's so-called "pacification strategy" (Koonings and Kruijt 2015, p. 49). According to Sérgio Cabral,

Research for this chapter was conducted within the context of the research project "Transnational Peacebuilding as South–South Cooperation: Brazil's MINUSTAH Experience," funded by the German Foundation for Peace Research. Portions of this chapter draw upon Markus-Michael Müller (2016) "Entangled Pacifications: Peacekeeping, Counterinsurgency and Policing in Port-au-Prince and Rio de Janeiro." In Jana Hönke and Markus-Michael Müller (eds.), *The Global Making of Policing: Post Colonial Perspectives.* Abingdon: Routledge, 2016, with permission of the publisher.

M.-M. Müller (✉)
ZI Lateinamerika-Institut, Freie Universität Berlin, Berlin, Germany

© The Author(s) 2018
M. D. Bonner et al. (eds.), *Police Abuse in Contemporary Democracies,*
https://doi.org/10.1007/978-3-319-72883-4_9

221

then-governor of the State of Rio de Janeiro, the UPP's purpose is "to fight criminal gangs and bring peace and security back to the people."[2] The main goal of the pacification effort consists of the suppression of violence related to drug trafficking and the "recovery of territories once dominated by the drug dealers."[3] To this end, the strategy first aims at expelling drug traffickers from targeted *favelas*. This is followed by the establishment of a permanent UPP presence and the provision of social as well as infrastructure projects (Koonings and Kruijt 2015, p. 49). As of early 2014, there were 38 UPPs with 9543 officers installed throughout Rio's *favelas*.[4] According to José Mariano Beltrame, Rio de Janeiro's former Secretary of Public Security, the creation of the UPPs is "not just a security project." Rather, it is "a public policy [*uma política de Estado*] for the improvement of life and the generation of hope."[5] Moreover, as stated on the UPP's website, "besides hope and citizenship, UPP symbolizes all the appreciation we have for human life."[6]

In a country that witnessed nearly two decades of military dictatorship (1964–1985) and where the "democratic Brazilian state has killed more people in its recent 'urban security operations' than any war in Latin America since the nineteenth century (except perhaps Colombia's conflicts)" (Amar 2009, p. 515), official commitments to "peace," "human life," "hope," and "citizenship" seem, indeed, revolutionary. Thus, for many observers, pacification is seen as a dramatic, and largely successful, change in the realm of democratic urban security governance in the country (Rodrigues 2014, p. 5; UN 2015, p. 2; Riccio et al. 2013; Suska 2015) and the emergence of "a new culture of more peaceful policing methods" in Brazil (da Silva 2012, p. 181), which has the potential of becoming a "model for the region and the world" (Muggah and Mulli 2012, p. 65).

This chapter offers a different, more critical, reading of the UPP experience by placing the notion of *pacification* at the center of analysis. Examining the UPP experience through the lens of pacification, as a practitioners' term as well as a theoretical concept, highlights two key issues: First, it enables us to locate a seemingly democratic policing effort within a broader global context of entangled histories and (post)colonial forms of rule and coercive order-making in the name of countering the insurgent "other." Second, as scholars working within the framework of "pacification theory" have stressed (e.g., Rigakos 2016; Wall et al. 2016a; Neocleous et al. 2013), pacification cannot be reduced to this colonial legacy. Rather, it is inherently embedded in the political economy of capitalist order-making as a "war for accumulation" that "involves the production of the multidimensional and multi-scale conditions for capital accumulation" (Wall et al. 2016b, p. 8).

Both perspectives are too often omitted in contemporary political science debates on police abuse in postauthoritarian and (post-)transitional postcolonies like Brazil. Related debates are overly concerned with the formal setup of a particular regime and questions of "authoritarian legacies" (Costa 2006; Denissen 2008). The political economy of policing, its implications for the perpetuation of socioeconomic inequality as well as its postcolonial legacies are ignored (see also Clarke, Chapter 8). Moreover, political science debates often tend to take the "domestic democratic peace" argument for granted. In other words, they assume "that democratic political institutions and activities decrease state repressive behavior" (Davenport 2007, p. 11). Therefore, police abuse—considered as "police actions that may or may not be 'illegal' but severely limit selective citizens' rights, receive minimal punishment (limited accountability), and may play a role in maintaining (or promoting) particular political and economic objectives" (Bonner et al., Chapter 1)—is seen as a deviation, or exception, from how things actually "should be," at least according to dominant political science perspectives on democracy and democratization.

As pointed out by recent research on Latin America's "violent democracies" (Arias and Goldstein 2010a; see also Denyer Willis 2015, p. 11; Müller 2016a, p. 11; Pansters 2012, pp. 7–8), political science, in particular what Arias and Goldstein (2010b, p. 10) have termed the "democratization school," is unable to account for the "messy realities of actually existing political systems as they are found in Latin America (and elsewhere) today." The "democratization school" promotes a minimalist conception of democracy as "polyarchy" by assuming that a democracy exists wherever formal institutions exist and social, political, and legal rights essential for these institutions to operate are granted to the local population (see also Bonner et al., Chapter 1). As Arias and Goldstein (2010b, p. 10) rightly stress: "Particularly problematic to these models is the existence of widespread violence, criminality, and insecurity in nations whose political systems might otherwise be characterized as democratic if not polyarchic."

This also holds true for the question of police abuse (as defined above). In fact, police abuse has largely been written out and made invisible by the "democratization school" that continues to "mirror a liberal ideology in depicting the state as an essentially benign institution: a sovereign entrusted with a monopoly over violence, legitimately exercised by its criminal justice system, in the name of protecting its citizenry from the threat of criminal disorder" (Comaroff and Comaroff 2016, p. 12). This has always been a myth. Even in "consolidated" democracies, the main function of the police has always been the (re)production of order—including its underlying divisions along class and ethnic lines—by "disciplining (some would say 'regulating' or 'sanitizing') the urban 'Other'" (Brogden and Ellison 2013, p. 11; see also Fassin 2013; Hills 2009; Müller 2012). Such efforts always include legal and extralegal means to discipline those at society's margins, "often characterized together as 'underclass,' often racialized, whose structural situation has made them most likely to violate existing property/or labor relations" (Comaroff and Comaroff 2016, p. 21). Stated otherwise, police abuse, mostly because of policing's intimate relationship to the protection of the "freedom of the market" and the underlying property/labor relations, is a defining feature of existing liberal democratic political systems, in Latin America and elsewhere. And in the former case, as this chapter elaborates with reference to Brazil, this has a lot to do with the region's (post)colonial context—which brings us back to the concept of pacification.

As the literature on (post)colonial policing and imperial rule—past and present—has shown, the term pacification looms large in the administrative, political, and policing vocabulary of colonial practices of violent order-making in general, and efforts at countering the "insurgent other" in particular (e.g., El Mechat 2014; Graham and Baker 2016; Kienscherf 2010; Moe and Müller 2017; McCoy 2016; Neocleous 2011). And as the Medal of Pacifier (*Medalha do Pacificador*) of the Brazilian Armed Forces indicates, the country has a long (post)colonial pacification experience (Müller and Müller 2016, pp. 78–79). This experience stretches from the submission of the Tupinambá tribe that represented a threat to the Portuguese conquest of Belém during the colonization of the Amazon (de Souza Pinheiro 1995) to the expansion and systematic pacification of Brazil's frontier regions in the eighteenth and nineteenth centuries during which pacification became the dominant administrative concept to describe the suppression of insurgent indigenous communities (Langfur 2006, p. 261). And in the twentieth century, it was most of all during the Cold War, and Brazil's military dictatorship, when pacification became the dominant concept for targeting so-called "subversives" through counterinsurgency policing (Huggins 1998, Chapter 7), in particular in cities like Rio de Janeiro:

> To deal with what were immediately dubbed terrorists, the dictators relied upon large-scale "urban pacification programs"—a tranquil sounding name for massive police and army dragnets. These sweeps resulted in hundreds and sometimes thousands of suspects being ensnarled in surprise road-blocks or neighborhood searches. (Rose 2005, p. 175)

The UPP experience, this chapter argues, has to be situated in this tradition of militarized pacification that dates back to the colonization of Brazil and stretches throughout many other moments of counterinsurgent order-making during the country's troubled history. It is telling in this regard that David Kilcullen, one of the world's leading contemporary counterinsurgency thinkers, in a passage of his book, *Out of the Mountains: The Coming Age of the Urban Guerrilla*, where he turns to the *favela* Rocinha, integrated into the UPP program in 2012, offers the following description of the UPP effort:

> Today it's occupied by the 28th Pacification Police Unit, which has deployed seven hundred paramilitary police in fortified patrol bases throughout La Rocinha, along with a hundred surveillance cameras that monitor every movement. Patrols roam the narrow streets on foot and by motorcycle, working the areas between outposts and checkpoints, *in an operational pattern that looks a lot like a police-led version of urban counterinsurgency, Baghdad style.* (Kilcullen 2013, p. 236, emphasis added)

The resemblance of the UPP experience to contemporary counterinsurgency practices—a resemblance that has not been of central concern for most authors working on the UPP (but see Muggah and Mulli 2012)—however, cannot be reduced to the historical legacy of Brazil's colonial past or earlier pacification efforts. While these historical experiences are central for understanding the UPP experience, the latter, as this chapter demonstrates, is inseparable from contemporary global power shifts that allow Brazil to experiment and refine previous domestic pacification experiences by adapting them to globally circulating pacification "best practices." The latter emerged in response to the setbacks of Western military interventions in the so-called Global War on Terror (GWOT), notably in Iraq and Afghanistan (Moe and Müller 2017). In turn, these challenges led to a reconsideration of the most adequate ways of suppressing insurgencies. They triggered a strategic shift away from an overemphasis on repression by force toward more nuanced "efforts to produce undisruptive and unthreatening forms of collective action through a combination of coercion and consent" (Kienscherf 2016, p. 1181), often articulated in the language of legality, development, peacebuilding, and human rights (Khalili 2013; Moe 2016; Turner 2014). This shift signaled the emergence of what has been termed the "new counterinsurgency era" (Ucko 2009). The latter is truly global in character with a growing number of non-Western countries experimenting with and adopting contemporary pacification "best practices" to better fight "home-turf counterinsurgency" (Kilcullen and Mills 2016, p. 15).

In locating democratic Brazil within these developments by assessing the question of police abuse in the country through the lens of pacification, this chapter seeks to move contemporary debates on policing in post-transitional contexts beyond the rather limiting normative straightjackets of polyarchic-reasoning by pointing toward: (a) the political economy of policing, (b) its colonial legacies and, in particular, (c) the transnational circulation of policing knowledge and practices—a point that even those scholars sensitive to the aforementioned aspects tend to forget.

To this end, in the remainder of this chapter I assess the recent return of pacification to the country and address the resulting implications for explaining ongoing police abuse and the militarization of domestic law enforcement in democratic Brazil. I will tease out the transnational connections behind the UPP experience by indicating how Brazil's own domestic pacification experience has been "upgraded" by incorporating contemporary counterinsurgency "lessons learned" from Colombia and Haiti. After that, I turn to the reimport of these lessons to contemporary Rio de Janeiro and illustrate how the UPP experience is not so much a move toward democratic policing but rather represents a growing militarization of urban security governance that deepens previous forms of pacification-centered violent order-making in the "marvelous city" in a neoliberal context. The concluding section summarizes the main findings of the chapter and highlights their implications for understanding the democracy-police abuse nexus.

COLOMBIA LESSONS

The fact that Rio de Janeiro's current pacification strategy is a deeply transnationalized affair, indicative of the ongoing global entanglements that shape contemporary policing in our postcolonial world (see Hönke and Müller 2016), is officially recognized. Local authorities admit that the "UPP program by the State of Rio de Janeiro administration was inspired by the successful experience in public security adopted in

Medellín, Colombia."[7] In fact, in 2007, one year before the inauguration of the first UPP, Sergio Cabral, then-governor of the state of Rio de Janeiro and José Mariano Beltrame, Rio de Janeiro's former Secretary of Public Security, visited Colombia. They traveled to Bogotá and Medellín in order to learn how these two cities, plagued by crime, violence and insurgency, dealt with their security problems in a seemingly successful way. The most important inspiration they found was Medellín's Operation Orion that eventually inspired the UPP program.[8]

That Medellín is an attractive reference point for Rio's political elite is understandable. By the mid-2000s, the city, which until the beginning of the new millennium was considered the world's "murder capital" with about 55,000 people having been killed between 1990 and 2002, turned into an economic boomtown. By 2002, Medellín's high-rise construction projects surpassed those of New York and Los Angeles combined, the city became the headquarters of Colombia's largest business conglomerates as well as over seventy major international companies. And its new convention center, opened in 2005, started to generate more than US$100 million investment annually. Moreover, by 2005 the city's homicide rate dropped to numbers below those of US cities like Detroit, Baltimore or Washington (Hylton 2010, pp. 338–39). Medellín, in this regard, reflects, in a paradigmatic way the success of the "Colombian model" or what others called "the Colombian Miracle" in dealing with pressing security issues framed in the language of insurgency. As David Kilcullen and Greg Mills (2015, p. 107) summed it up:

> Such progress has been made in Colombia that it is hard to remember that only 20 years ago, the country was renowned not for its practical people or its wonderful cities and rain-forests, but for its cocaine-fueled murder rate. At the height of the drug war in the 1990s, Colombians suffered ten kidnappings a day, 75 political assassinations a week, and 36,000 murders a year (fifteen times the rate in the United States). The military and police competed with an array of guerrillas, gangs, narcos and paramilitaries. Guerrillas had so isolated the largest cities that urban-dwellers traveling as little as five miles out of town risked kidnapping, or worse. Twenty-seven thousand two hundred thirteen people died in 1997–2001 alone. Colombia entered the 21st century at risk of becoming a failed state. Since then, national leaders have turned the situation around, applying a well-designed strategy with growing public and international support. Kidnappings, murders and cocaine cultivation are down, government control has expanded, and the economy is recovering.

The fact that a leading counterinsurgency expert, like David Kilcullen, pays attention to Colombia's "miracle" is indicative of a core feature of Colombia's success on the security front: the country's recent experience with counterinsurgent pacification efforts.

One of the main causes behind Colombia's security problems throughout most of the late twentieth century has been the ongoing insurgency waged by the Revolutionary Armed Forces of Colombia (*Fuerzas Armadas Revolucionarias de Colombia*, FARC) and the Army of National Liberation (*Ejército de Liberación Nacional*, ELN) against the Colombian state (on Colombia's conflict, see Davis et al. 2016; Leech 2011; Richani 2013; Roldán 2002). While the Colombian security forces, for a long time, seemed unable to deal with the insurgency threat posed by the FARC and ELN, this situation worsened during the presidency of Ernesto Samper (1994–1998). During these years, the guerrilla forces inflicted humiliating defeats on the military. They also managed to expand their territorial control and increase their military strength—in part by turning to the country's drug economy to finance their armed struggle—while paramilitary violence against guerrillas and their alleged supporters escalated.

As a consequence, Colombian and US military and government circles increasingly saw the country as threatened by a severe security crisis that could culminate in a FARC victory. In order to deal with this situation, a counterinsurgency program, with a strong counter-narcotics element, was designed within the so-called Plan Colombia, a multiyear multibillion-dollar US security assistance program that was implemented from 2000 onward "in order to build capacities for fighting the drug traffic and the guerrillas more effectively" (Tickner 2016, p. 99; on Plan Colombia, see also Rochlin 2011). With substantial support from the country's economic elites, who even accepted paying a "war tax" to contribute to the government's counterinsurgency effort, the governments of Andrés Pastrana (1998–2002) and, in particular, Álvaro Uribe (2002–2010), managed to turn the tide in the military campaign against the FARC, due to a "ruthless focus on taking the fight to the enemy" (Davis and Arnott 2016, p. 60).

Operation Orion in Medellín is indicative of what that meant in practice. It was here, or to be more precise, in the city's marginalized neighborhood *Comuna 13*, where after Uribe's election "the first major counterinsurgency crackdown and armed urban intervention by the state would take place" (Riaño-Alcalá 2006, p. 178).

The government offensive named "Operación Orion," was presented as a counter-insurgency campaign and an example of Uribe's democratic security's policy's goal of having "a greater presence in the areas where the state has been absent and armed groups control them." Terrorized residents witnessed the arrival in their narrow and steep streets of over 1,000 assault troops and police backed by helicopter gunships searching for the militias. After two days of battles, the militias were eradicated from the area, nine civilians killed, thirty-seven injured and several area houses damaged. The army took control of the zone and the government offered an ambitious program of social investment, which, more than a year later, had still not been implemented. Residents began to feel some respite and welcomed the presence of the State; soon after the offensive, however, selective assassinations began to be reported and recognized paramilitary fighters began circulating openly, controlling local activities and forcibly recruiting youth. (Riaño-Alcalá 2006, pp. 178–79)

While Operation Orion, effectively, turned *Comuna 13* "into a battlefield, with its 100,000 residents caught in the crossfire," it nonetheless "achieved its objective of clearing out the Leftist rebels."[9] In this regard, Operation Orion is a paradigmatic example of Uribe's "democratic security" agenda and the related counterinsurgency efforts implemented under Plan Colombia. It was a "success" in objectively reducing violence. However, it came at the price of severe human rights violations, substantial "collateral damage," and an overall "expense of democracy" (Tickner 2016, p. 100):

Between 2006 and 2008, three distinct political scandals, related to extensive ties between the Colombian political elite and paramilitary groups, widespread illegal wiretapping conducted by state authorities, and extrajudicial military executions of over 3,000 young men reported as guerrillas killed in combat, put into stark relief the waning of the rule of law in the country. (Tickner 2016, p. 100)

Irrespective of the human, legal, and democratic "collateral damage," it was the successful pacification of "insurgent" urban communities that "ultimately persuaded Beltrame and Cabral to introduce a similar system [of counterinsurgent pacification] for Rio de Janeiro."[10] However, in trying to replicate the "Colombian miracle," Rio's security forces—whose pacification practices were still informed by an "enemy-centric" logic that considered temporary raids of marginal communities with the aim of "killing the enemy" as the most effective means for pacifying the "urban other"—needed to be updated. And, as the next section will demonstrate, it was the United Nations' effort to stabilize Haiti, which offered a welcome opportunity for bringing Brazil's domestic pacification experience in line with "best practices" of the "new counterinsurgency era."

HAITIAN OPPORTUNITIES

As argued above, policing in Rio de Janeiro, ever since colonial times, was driven by a pacification logic, marked by a highly coercive racial and "underclass" bias (Holloway 1993) and supported by what, following Pereira (2000, pp. 220–22), can be termed as a form of "elite liberalism." The latter favors a selective application of the rule of law according to existing social hierarchies, leading to what Seri and Lokaneeta (Chapter 3) call "violent exclusion." In turn, police abuse targeting poor people, particularly Afro-Brazilians, is widely regarded as a legitimate means of protecting order and security for which the police will not be held accountable (Pereira 2000, pp. 220–22; on police accountability, see Bonner, Chapter 5; Squillacote and Feldman, Chapter 6; Davenport et al., Chapter 7). To a large extent, the resulting forms of police abuse in democratic Brazil are due to a particularly "kinetic" counterinsurgency/pacification-policing mindset by local police chiefs and politicians that presents *favelados* as the racialized and criminalized enemy in the guise of the "urban other" (on racialized policing in other contexts, see also Schneider, Chapter 2; Davenport et al., Chapter 7). For example, Rio's former secretary of public security, Anthony Garotinho, proudly claimed on a local radio program on *Radio Carioca* in 2003: "In my first twelve days in charge of the secretariat, one hundred criminals have already died in confrontations with police" (quoted in Amnesty International 2003, p. 7). Already in 1995, the local police had introduced so-called "bravery payments," which rewarded police officers with bonuses up to 150% of their monthly salary depending on their ability to meet "kill quotas" of "criminals" (Hendee 2013, p. 23). Recall that this happened in democratic Brazil.

In an increasingly mediatized world, such practices, however, are at odds with a city that since the 1990s started promoting itself as a vibrant urban democracy and a perfect location for global summits and mega-events—from the Rio de Janeiro Earth Summit in 2002 to the FIFA

Soccer Championship in 2014 and the Olympic Games in 2016, as well as a prime tourist destination and a "safe" investment location.

The opportunity for experimenting with less "kinetic" forms of pacification, more attuned to global sensitivities regarding human rights, democracy, and the rule of law, came on May 29, 2004. On this day, the United Nations Security Council Resolution 1542 was adopted. In light of ongoing political turmoil in Haiti, following the controversial ousting and forced exile of elected Haitian president Jean-Bertrand Aristide in February 2004, the United Nations Stabilization Mission in Haiti (MINUSTAH by its French acronym for *Mission des Nations Unies pour la stabilisation en Haïti*) was established. Its mission is to "foster principles and democratic governance and institutional development" and support "the Transitional Government as well as Haitian human rights institutions and groups in their efforts to promote and protect human rights, particularly of women and children, in order to ensure individual accountability for human rights abuses and redress for victims."[11] Since its creation, Brazil has been in charge of the military component of the UN mission, as of early 2017 about 2400 soldiers.[12]

This leading role of Brazil directly reflects the international recognition of Brazil's domestic pacification experience on the one hand, and the main threat for the stabilization of Haiti, on the other: *local gangs*. In fact, the main security problem Haiti was facing at the time MINUSTAH was created, was, in the words of David Becker, former director of the Haiti Stabilization Initiative (HSI), funded by the US Department of Defense (on HSI, see Moe and Müller 2015), a "criminal insurgency" (Becker 2011, p. 143) waged by street gangs—with clear parallels to contemporary GWOT theaters.

> The situation facing the United Nations at the end of 2006 was not unlike that facing any large hierarchical force that is targeting a loose coalition of independently financed urban guerrilla groups. The parallels with Sadr City or Fallujah are obvious: small, loosely organized groups able to swarm a target and hide among the population quickly have the advantage. (Becker 2011, p. 142)

To counter this problem, HSI implemented a "community counterinsurgency" program (Becker 2011, p. 145). Part and parcel of this was a "community building" strategy, which aimed at transforming community dynamics and in a way that the long-term sustainability of the gangs' self-organization and reproduction process was undermined. In practice, this effort basically consisted of the co-optation of community leaders through "development" funds, which were randomly made widely available for *any type* of community activity and offered the promise to "indirectly peel away the gang support base and leave gang leaders more exposed to possible police responses" (Becker 2011, p. 145).

Such perceptions regarding the insurgent threat posed by gangs, as well as the overall counterinsurgency-like character of the UN mission, were clearly shared by Brazilian UN troops. In fact, Brazilian troops and diplomats describe Brazil's MINUSTAH operations as "political counterinsurgency," or a form of "low-intensity warfare," where, in the words of Lt. Gen. Augusto Heleno Ribeiro Pereira Brazil's MINUSTAH commander (2004–2005), the task of his troops was to "kill the bandits […] but it will have to be the bandits only, not everybody" (quoted in Podur 2012, p. 78; see also Müller 2016b, p. 83).

In light of such perceptions of the Haitian "criminal insurgency" waged by street gangs, the decision to use Brazilian troops for these anti-gang operations was somehow "logical," as Sotomayor (2014, p. 139) argued. Most of all because "they had antigang training and knew how to 'clean' slums. […] In fact, most members of the Brazilian contingent were first recruited from units that were originally headquartered in Rio de Janeiro, where gang violence and drug trafficking were also common" (Sotomayor 2014, p. 139).

However, the traveling abroad of Rio de Janeiro's pacification experience substantially transformed the latter. Recall that previous pacification efforts in Rio de Janeiro were often marked by extremely violent, extralegal and frequently lethal, forms of police conduct. They were "kinetic," as contemporary counterinsurgency practitioners would say, by following an "enemy-centric" logic, clearly visible in Lt. Gen. Augusto Heleno Ribeiro Pereira's previously quoted statement regarding the need of "killing the bandits."

Such reasoning, however, is at odds with contemporary counterinsurgency discourses and practices. The latter portrays counterinsurgent pacification as "armed social work" aimed at "protecting the population," not at "killing the enemy," as the 2006 *United States Army/Marine Corps Counterinsurgency Field Manual FM 3-24*, the doctrinal manifestation of the "new counterinsurgency era" puts it (The US Army/ Marine Corps 2006, p. 179, 299). As shown elsewhere in greater detail

(Müller 2016b; Müller and Müller 2016), it was Brazil's participation in MINUSTAH's anti-gang operations that allowed the country to adapt its own domestic pacification experience to contemporary counterinsurgency "best practices," which are marked by a liberal embrace of the rule of law, legality, good governance, institution building, and humanitarianism. This allowed Brazil to learn the "gentle" way of pacifying insurgent urban communities through less kinetic, and more media-friendly, means; means that would attract less international press criticism than previous ways of pacifying *favelas* at home (see also Koonings and Kruijt 2015, p. 49). It also fitted nicely into the UN framework of liberal peace promotion that informed MINUSTAH's interest in enabling "Haitians to renounce violence, and recognizing, in this context, that rule of law and respect for human rights are vital components of democratic societies."[13]

The main targets of MINUSTAH's pacification campaign were the marginalized communities of Port-au-Prince, notably in Cité Soleil. Here, according to international observers, gangs "assumed responsibility for security in their neighborhoods, often extorting market sellers and other businesses in exchange for protection, and sometimes becoming involved in drug smuggling and other illicit activities" (Berg 2010, p. 3). Moreover, Cité Soleil is also a stronghold of militant supporters of former president Aristide (Hallward 2007, pp. 287–88). And, it has a unique strategic value. It is located in close proximity to many infrastructural arteries through which goods, persons, resources, and aid flow to support the UN presence (and the country's local post-Aristide political elite). As the gangs of Cité Soleil also "attacked vehicles of the adjunct airport road and threatened Haiti's principal port, petroleum storage facility, and industrial area, which were located nearby" (Dziedzic and Perito 2008, p. 2), the area was declared by MINUSTAH, as a "red zone" in need of military intervention and pacification (Higate and Henry 2009, p. 60).

In order to pacify Cité Soleil, MINUSTAH, under Brazilian leadership, intervened by launching a pacification campaign that was centered upon what has become popularized in contemporary counterinsurgency textbooks as the "clear-hold-build" (CHB) approach. CHB consists of three steps. First, local insurgents are killed, captured, or expelled ("clear"). Next, a permanent presence of host government security forces is expanded ("hold"), and finally, in the so-called "build" phase, "tasks that provide an overt and direct benefit for the community are key," including, for instance, the distribution of aid to local communities, trash collection, or infrastructure improvement (The US Army/Marine Corps 2006, pp. 174–188).

In Cité Soleil, the "clear" phase started on the January 24, 2007, with a MINUSTAH military offensive (Müller 2016b, p. 85). An initial invasion by UN troops was followed by a joint operation conducted by UN and local police forces. They conducted neighborhood sweeps during which some 800 gang members were arrested, including the apprehension or killing of "all but one gang leader" (Dziedzic and Perito 2008, p. 5). The "hold phase" consisted of the setting-up of so-called strong points, which allowed UN troops to establish a permanent military presence in Cité Soleil and to conduct patrols in critical areas: "Patrols took place roughly every three hours; the standard procedure was intended to reduce risk by assuming a 'ready to fight' position. [...] This procedure resembled an urban counterinsurgency operation more in tune with places like Afghanistan or Iraq, rather than a UN peacekeeping mission" (Sotomayor 2014, p. 250). That this was more than just a "resemblance," becomes obvious when considering that these operations were followed by a "build" phase in which social assistance and development aid were provided to the local population in order to win their "hearts and minds," often through the active incorporation of NGOs (The US Army/Marine Corps 2006, pp. 2-29–2-31). As one UN official stated in this regard, Brazilian soldiers "understood that they had to clear the area from gangs and then bring development projects, like Viva Rio" (quoted in Sotomayor 2014, p. 139)—a NGO with a decade-long experience in providing social assistance within community-centered policing programs in Rio de Janeiro (Harig 2015, p. 146).

Despite substantial "collateral damage," evidenced, for instance by a survey of the United States Institute for Peace, which documents that "52 per cent of Cité Soleil residents reported that family members, friends, or neighbors were killed or wounded in MINUSTAH's anti-gang operations" (Podur 2012, p. 131), it seems that "[t]he pacification had worked" (Podur 2012, p. 131). In the words of a secret cable from the US embassy in Port-au-Prince:

> Cite Soleil today is a changed environment. It is less a hair trigger population ready to riot on command or in reaction to any number of catalytic events – man-made or natural – and more of a community increasingly trying to work together. This represents a depoliticizing of conflict and a more pragmatic focus on grassroots self-interest. The stage is set for regular aid, training, health, education, and microenterprise programs to

begin operating, and they are. Elements of Haiti's private sector are coming around to the idea that there is value to be gained in promoting and supporting training and education opportunities and are beginning to consider the value of reinvesting in the larger neighborhood.[14]

It has been this image of the success of Brazil's first experiment with liberal counterinsurgency that contributed to the creation of the UPPs, one year after these pacification efforts in Cité Soleil.

Pacification Comes Home

In light of the above, the creation of the UPPs can mostly be seen as serving a symbolic purpose, demonstrating that the host city of the 2014 FIFA World Cup and the 2016 Olympic Games has the capacity of guaranteeing the security of these mega events and international visitors in a "progressive," community-oriented, democratic, and humanitarian way (Amar 2009; Swanson 2013; on the connection between these mega-events and pacification, see Saborio 2013) by applying the combined "lessons learned" from Colombia and Haiti.

It is telling, in this regard, that many Brazilian military commanders in charge of some of the most critical pacification efforts in Rio de Janeiro, like General Fernando José Lavaquiel, who was appointed by the Brazilian Defense Minister to be in charge of the pacification of one of the most "critical" *favela* complexes, the Complexo do Alemão, held leading command positions in and had combat experience with MINUSTAH (Sotomayor 2014, p. 88). This not only holds true for the upper levels of authority in charge of the implementation of the pacification strategy in Rio de Janeiro. Additionally, regular troops rotating back from Haiti to Brazil have actively participated in the pacification efforts, in what Harig termed a "reciprocal learning process among troops" (Harig 2015, pp. 142, 149–51). This can be seen, once again with regard to the pacification of the Complexo do Alemão, probably Rio de Janeiro's version of Cité Soleil. In this large-scale pacification operation, conducted in 2010, "many of the troops deployed this month [for the pacification of the Complexo do Alemão], were just back from peace-keeping in Haiti which prepared them for close work with civilians."[15]

The relevance of having had experience with "close work with civilians" is another clear reference to the "return" of the counterinsurgency/pacification component of Brazilian peacekeeping within the context of MINUSTAH to the *favelas* of Rio de Janeiro. This can be seen most clearly in the centrality that the CHB approach implemented during the pacification of Cité Soleil has for the UPP strategy, and which, in an albeit rudimentary way, was also central to Operation Orión in Medellín. Instead of a temporary occupation/raid, the success of the pacification effort in Medellín's *Comuna 13*, "stemmed from a decision on the part of the military and civilian authorities to maintain a permanent, physical presence of all parts of the government within the Comuna, often on the most conflictive pieces of terrain" (Demarest 2011, p. 4)—the decisive element of the CHB approach. While Operation Orion familiarized Brazil's authorities with the long-term benefits of applying an urban CHB approach, the country's participation in MINUSTAH allowed for the improvement of Brazil's own pacification experience.

In fact, the concrete implementation of the UPP operations perfectly follows the three phases of the CHB approach. First, in the "clear" phase, heavy armed special forces, frequently supported by military troops, invade and "clear" communities selected for "pacification" in order to capture, kill, or expel drug traffickers. Next, in the "hold" phase during which "firm government control of the populace and area" needs to be achieved, the permanent UPP presence is established through the creation of a permanent police presence, including mobile police compounds not too different from the "strong points" of Cité Soleil, clearly reflected in the slogan posted on the UPP's website: "A UPP VEIO PARA FICAR" (*THE UPP CAME TO STAY*).[16] According to official statements, once this presence, portrayed as the "recovery of territories once dominated by the drug dealers," is achieved, "the thugs no longer control the territory [and therefore] become weakened and they can be arrested more easily by the police."[17] In the final phase, the "build" phase, the UPP aims at gaining the support of the local population. According to their mission statement: "The community's engagement in this process is crucial because the local population usually knows who the drug dealers are and the location of their hideouts. The dwellers who tell on the criminals have also been of great value since they contribute to the arrest of thugs as well as the seizure of hidden firearms, drugs and other illegal products."[18]

The UPP's community outreach programs include social work projects, street building, and trash cleaning operations as well as health care, frequently in collaboration with NGOs, including *Viva Rio*—tellingly portrayed by the NGO as a "human security partnership."[19] The UPP's reliance upon the CHB approach has also been stressed in a confidential cable from the US embassy, leaked to WikiLeaks. The cable makes the following observation:

> While Rio's favelas have often been a target of police operations with a goal of disrupting narco-trafficking activities, the Favela Pacification Program marks the first time that state, municipal, or federal authorities are attempting a "clear and hold" approach, the success of which is predicated upon pushing criminal elements out of the community, establishing a permanent police and government presence, then providing basic services and civic privileges to favela residents. This approach closely resembles U.S. counter-insurgency doctrine in Afghanistan and Iraq, and highlights the extent to which favelas have been outside state authority.[20]

In 2010, the "local" version of this strategy has been refined with the creation of the so-called Social UPPs (*UPP Social*). The project's aim, with financial support from United Nations Human Settlements Program (UN HABITAT), is to contribute "to the consolidation of the pacifying process and promotion of local citizenship in the pacified territories; to promote urban, social and economic development in the territories; and to execute the full integration of these areas with the city as a whole."[21] To this end, it adopts the following strategy:

> Even before the implementation of the UPP, as of the occupation of the territory by security forces, the City Hall takes advantage of the new peaceful situation to start an intense effort of certifying the services of cleaning, urban preservation and collecting garbage and public illumination, mobilizing the various municipal agents and with the coordination of the Social UPP. In this phase prior to the UPP, the teams of the program also start speaking to the residents and leaders of the communities to map out the demands and priorities, study the public policies and services already available and produce information and indicators about the area. After having implemented the local pacifying police unit, the Social UPP makes its performance in the territory official by holding a forum which gathers together community leaders, NGOs and other local institutions, as well as representatives of the UPP and of bodies of several spheres of government for an open dialogue, in which the residents express their expectations and the public managers submit plans of immediate and future actions.[22]

While this seems to empower local residents, when put into practice, the implementation of liberal pacification efforts in Rio de Janeiro, as in Colombia and Haiti, produced substantial collateral damage in the guise of ongoing police abuse and human rights violations, including the reappearance of torture and extralegal killings by involved UPP forces (Alves and Evanson 2011; Gay 2012, pp. 92–95).[23]

The most relevant difference between previous and contemporary forms of counterinsurgent pacification in Rio de Janeiro, however, might be their spatial selectivity. They mostly target *favelas* "in the richest neighborhoods in the south and north zones of the city," which are also the most lucrative areas for real estate development and speculation (Reyes Novaes 2014, p. 218; Saborio 2013, p. 139).

As the UPP coordination proudly claims in this regard: "Decreasing crime rates and the increased sense of security have caused Rio to experience a wave of real estate valorization. The city has also seen an increase of products and services that are now being offered to the residents of pacified communities and surrounding neighborhoods, places that are beginning to follow the development seen in other areas of Rio."[24] In fact, in most pacified *favelas*, "land and real estate prices rocketed" (Koonings and Kruijt 2015, p. 50), with the consequence that many local residents are pushed out and make "space" for wealthier newcomers, often foreigners.[25]

Resonating with Medellín's successful urban pacification, and the related economic "miracle," Brazil's current pacification clearly entails a material component as well: the economic upgrading of the city through the policing and pacification of "undesired" urban populations that follow the logic of what John Gledhill recently termed the "new war on the poor" in Latin America. As he argues, *favela* residents

> are 'inconvenient' in a contemporary capitalist context for a number of reasons that are connected with the presence of criminals in these communities, reasons that boil down to the principle that capital accumulation can be enhanced through the removal of barriers to its penetration of the spaces that these inconvenient populations occupy, and barriers to its ability to extract the maximum profit from selling goods and services within them. (Gledhill 2015, p. 18)

This, Gledhill (2015, p. 18) adds, is the "hidden agenda behind the 'securitization' of *favelados* as a problem for the city as a whole and their pacification through a militaristic form of police occupation that often fails to deliver on its promise to respect the rights of these Brazilian citizens."

In this regard, it has to be recalled that policing the urban other in the name of pacification aims at the (re)production of a *particular* order. In democracies, this is also the order of the liberal market. Policing as pacification, in the words of Mark Neocleous (2011, p. 193) aims at "the fabrication of a social order organized around a constant revolutionizing of the instruments and relations of production and thus containing the everlasting uncertainty and agitation of all social relations." The pacification of the *favelas* of Rio de Janeiro promises exactly that. It allows for the containment of the potentially disruptive "urban other," while simultaneously "clearing" the communities from where the "urban other" emerges in order to better "integrate" the former into the city's neoliberalized urban economy. It might be precisely this material aspect of what Naomi Klein (2008, p. 508) in another context called "militarized gentrification," that also attracts Haitian police officials to join a cooperation with Viva Rio and the UPP project for reimporting the refined, post-2010 UPP (UPP + Social UPP) to "the more conflictive areas, such as Cité Soleil,"[26] thereby triggering a new round of transnational pacification entanglements.

CONCLUSION

Police abuse is often seen as a deviation from how public security should be provided in a democratic context. In countries undergoing, or having gone through, democratic transition periods, the existence of police abuse is in general attributed to institutional legacies of preceding authoritarian regimes. In analyzing the experience of the Police Pacification Units in democratic Rio de Janeiro, this chapter demonstrated that an exclusive focus on the immediate institutional legacies of authoritarian regimes as well as on decisively "domestic" factors misses the deeper historical, postcolonial, roots of contemporary forms of police abuse, its embeddedness in the political economy of capitalism, as well as its transnational dimension. In taking the term pacification as the analytical vantage point from which to assess the question of police abuse in the city, the chapter pointed toward the city's long history of violent and often extralegal policing in the name of pacifying the "urban other."

While the findings of the chapter thus situate the UPPs within this broader historical trajectory of policing as pacification, the analyses also illustrated that the UPP experience cannot be reduced to that. Rather, contemporary pacification efforts in Rio de Janeiro are directly inspired by new forms of South–South cooperation and "mutual learning," be it from the seemingly successful urban pacification efforts in Colombia or the participation of Brazil in MINUSTAH. These experiences, it was argued, enabled the Rio de Janeiro's security forces to improve and upgrade their domestic pacification practices in a way that they are more attuned to contemporary forms of "irregular warfare" and counterinsurgency. As the latter, in the words of Kahlili, are always marked by the unresolvable contradiction between "illiberal methods and liberal discourse, between bloody hands and honeyed tongues, between weapons of war and emancipatory hyperbole" (Khalili 2013, p. 5), the UPP experience, unsurprisingly, did not make an end to police abuse in democratic Rio but rather contributes to its perpetuation, in part because of the UPP's integration into a neoliberal project of "militarized gentrification." That these findings are not just a problem for (post-)transition contexts and democratic theory in and about the Global South has recently been evidenced, in a tragic way, by the events in Ferguson, Missouri. The killing of Michael Brown by a white police officer as well as the ensuring "policing crisis" and the formation of the Black Lives Matter movement (Camp and Heatherton 2016) point toward the difficulties of policing ethnically mixed postcolonial societies also within the Global North (also see Schneider, Chapter 2; Davenport et al., Chapter 7). And they raise the general question of how democratic policing can be in societies with long established and historically entrenched divisions along ethnic and socioeconomic lines. It is this conundrum that democratic theory and political science more broadly have not yet adequately addressed. The analysis presented in this chapter aims to provide insights that might spark further reflections regarding how to address this puzzle—not just "over there," but in all contemporary democracies.

NOTES

1. Governo Do Rio de Janeiro. Unidade de Polícia Pacificadora. "Historico." http://www.upprj.com/index.php/historico (last accessed February 22, 2014).
2. Governo Do Rio de Janeiro. Unidade de Polícia Pacificadora. http://www.upprj.com/index.php/as_upps (last accessed January 31, 2014).
3. Governo Do Rio de Janeiro. Unidade de Polícia Pacificadora. http://www.upprj.com/index.php/o_que_e_upp (last accessed February 22, 2014).

4. Ibid.
5. Governo Do Rio de Janeiro. Unidade de Polícia Pacificadora. http://www.upprj.com/index.php/as_upps (last accessed February 22, 2014).
6. Governo Do Rio de Janeiro. Unidade de Polícia Pacificadora. http://www.upprj.com/index.php/as_upps (last accessed February 22, 2014); http://www.upprj.com/index.php/as_upps_us (last accessed February 22, 2014).
7. Governo Do Rio de Janeiro. Unidade de Polícia Pacificadora. http://www.upprj.com/index.php/historico_us (last accessed February 22, 2014).
8. Halais, Flavie. "Pacifying Rio: What's behind Latin America's most talk about security operation." *Open Security*, March 21, 2013. https://www.opendemocracy.net/opensecurity/flavie-halais/pacifying-rio-whats-be-hind-latin-americas-most-talked-about-security-oper (last accessed January 15, 2017).
9. *The Telegraph.* "Colombia's biggest ever exhumation begins at Medellin rubbish dump." July 28, 2015. http://www.telegraph.co.uk/news/worldnews/southamerica/colombia/11769313/Colombias-biggest-ever-exhumation-begins-at-Medellin-rubbish-dump.html (last accessed October 13, 2017).
10. Lee, Tracey. 2013. "UPPs drive criminals from Rio's Favelas ahead of 2014 FIFA World Cup." *Díalogo-Digital Military Magazine*, June 17. https://dialogo-americas.com/en/articles/upps-drive-criminals-rios-favelas-ahead-2014-fifa-world-cup (last accessed November 20, 2017).
11. United Nations Security Council. "Security Council establishes UN stabilization mission in Haiti for initial six-month period." April 30, 2004. http://www.un.org/press/en/2004/sc8083.doc.htm (last accessed January 17, 2017).
12. United Nations Stabilization Mission in Haiti. MINUSTAH Facts and Figures. http://www.un.org/en/peacekeeping/missions/minustah/facts.shtml (last accessed January 4, 2017).
13. United Nations Security Council. "Security Council extends United Nations mission in Haiti until 15 February 2007, unanimously adoption resolution 1702 (2006)." August 15, 2006. http://www.un.org/News/Press/docs/2006/sc8811.doc.htm (last accessed January 22, 2014).
14. WikiLeaks. "Cite Soleil's door is open: Proving the concept and building credibility." April 13, 2009. http://www.wikileaks.org/plusd/cables/09PORTAUPRINCE398_a.html (last accessed January 17, 2014).
15. *The Economist.* "Conquering Complexo do Alemao. A big step towards reclaiming Rio de Janeiro from drug dealers." December 2, 2010.

http://www.economist.com/node/17627963 (last accessed November 20, 2017); See also *O Globo*. "Abuso de autoridade em favela com UPP preocupa pesquisadores." May 8, 2010. http://g1.globo.com/rio-de-janeiro/noticia/2010/05/abuso-de-autoridade-em-favela-com-upp-pre-ocupa-pesquisadores.html (last accessed November 20, 2017).

16. Governo do Rio de Janiero. http://www.upprj.com/index.php/as_upps (last accessed January 31, 2014).
17. Governo do Rio de Janiero. UPP Came to Stay. http://www.upprj.com/index.php/o_que_e_upp_us (last accessed February 22, 2014).
18. Ibid.
19. http://vivario.org.br/en/human-security/partnership-with-upp/ (last accessed February 19, 2014).
20. WikiLeaks. "Counter–insurgency doctrine comes to Rio's Favelas." September 30, 2009. https://www.wikileaks.org/plusd/cables/09RI-ODEJANEIRO329_a.html (last accessed March 2, 2014).
21. http://uppsocial.org/about/ (last accessed February 22, 2014).
22. Ibid.
23. *Folha de São Paulo*. "Comandante da UPP autorizou tortura de Amarildo, afirma delegado." February 20, 2014. http://www1.folha.uol.com.br/cotidiano/2014/02/1415487-comandante-da-upp-autorizou-tor-tura-de-amarildo-afirma-delegado.shtml; *Folha de São Paulo*. "PM infiltrado diz que UPP da Rocinha tinha tortura de traficantes." February 19, 2014. http://www1.folha.uol.com.br/cotidiano/2014/02/1414324-pm-infiltrado-diz-que-upp-da-rocinha-tinha-tortura-de-traficantes.shtml (last accessed November 20, 2017); *Folha de São Paulo*. "Moradores de Alemão divulgam video de confront com Exército." September 4, 2011. https://noticias.bol.uol.com.br/brasil/2011/09/06/moradores-divul-gam-imagens-de-balas-tracantes-no-alemao.jhtm (last accessed November 20, 2017); Gazet Do Povo. "Abuso de autoridade em favela com UPP preocupa pesquisadores." May 8, 2010. http://www.gazetadopovo.com.br/vida-e-cidadania/abuso-de-autoridade-em-favela-com-upp-preocu-pa-pesquisadores-0b01dzvg0r8wcgr2tfyp8wci6 (last accessed November 20, 2017); *O Globo*. "Imagem das UPPs for arranhada o caso Amarildo." October 8, 2013. http://g1.globo.com/globo-news/noticia/2013/10/imagem-das-upps-foi-arranhada-com-o-caso-amarildo.html (last accessed November 20, 2017).
24. Governo do Rio de Janiero. "O Gue E?" http://www.upprj.com/index.php/o_que_e_upp (last accessed February 22, 2014).
25. *The Guardian*. "Olympic exclusion zone: The gentrification of a Rio Favela." June 15, 2016. https://www.theguardian.com/cities/2016/jun/15/rio-olympics-exclusion-zone-gentrification-favela-babilonia (last accessed November 20, 2017).

26. http://vivario.org.br/en/upp-project-is-presented-to-haitian-police-officers/ (last accessed February 22, 2014).

References

Alves, Maria Helena Moreira, and Philip Evanson. 2011. *Living in the Crossfire. Favela Residents, Drug Dealers, and Police Violence in Rio de Janeiro.* Philadelphia, PA: Temple University Press.

Amar, Paul. 2009. "Operation Princess in Rio de Janeiro: Policing 'Sex Trafficking', Strengthening Worker Citizenship, and the Urban Geopolitics of Security in Brazil." *Security Dialogue* 40 (4–5): 513–41.

Amnesty International. 2003. *Brazil: Rio de Janeiro 2003: Candelaria and Vigario Geral 10 Years On.* http://www.refworld.org/docid/3f4dcda60.html.

Arias, Enrique Desmond, and Daniel M. Goldstein, eds. 2010a. *Violent Democracies in Latin America.* Durham, NC: Duke University Press.

Arias, Enrique Desmond, and Daniel M. Goldstein. 2010b. "Violent Pluralism. Understanding the New Democracies of Latin America." In *Violent Democracies in Latin America*, edited by Enrique Desmond Arias and Daniel M. Goldstein, 1–33. Durham, NC: Duke University Press.

Becker, David C. 2011. "Gangs, Netwar and 'Community Counterinsurgency' in Haiti." *PRISM* 2 (3): 137–54.

Berg, Luise-Alexandre. 2010. "Crime, Politics and Violence in Post-earthquake Haiti." *United States Institute of Peace Brief* 58: 1–4.

Brogden, Mike, and Graham Ellison. 2013. *Policing in an Age of Austerity: A Postcolonial Perspective.* London: Routledge.

Camp, Jordan, and Christina Heatherton, eds. 2016. *Policing the Planet: Why the Policing Crisis Led to Black Lives Matter.* London: Verso.

Comaroff, Jean, and John Comaroff. 2016. *The Truth about Crime. Sovereignty, Knowledge and Social Order.* Chicago, IL: University of Chicago Press.

Costa, Gino. 2006. "Two Steps Forward, One and a Half Step Back: Police Reform in Peru, 2001–2004. The Transformation of the Peruvian Police." *Civil Wars* 8 (2): 215–30.

da Silva, Robson R. 2012. "Rio de Janeiro: A Local Response to a Global Challenge." *Journal of International Affairs* 66 (1): 177–81.

Davenport, Christian. 2007. "State Repression and Political Order." *Annual Review of Political Science* 10: 1–23.

Davis, Dickie, and Anthony Arnott. 2016. "Building Tools for Military Success." In *A Great Perhaps? Colombia: Conflict and Convergence*, edited by Dickie Davis, David Kilcullen, Greg Mills, and David Spencer, 54–60. London: Hurst.

Davis, Dickie, David Kilcullen, Greg Mills, and David Spencer, eds. 2016. *A Great Perhaps? Colombia: Conflict and Convergence.* London: Hurst.

de Souza Pinheiro, Alvaro. 1995. "Guerrilla in The Brazilian Amazon." *Military Review*, Edicão Brasileira 1: 58–79.

Demarest, Geoffrey. 2011. *Urban Land Use by Illegal Armed Groups in Medellin.* Fort Leavenworth, KS: US Army Foreign Military Studies Office. http://www.dtic.mil/dtic/tr/fulltext/u2/a551055.pdf (last accessed November 20, 2017).

Denissen, Marieke. 2008. *Winning Small Battles, Losing the War. Police Violence, the Movimiento del Dolor and Democracy in Post-authoritarian Argentina.* Amsterdam: Rozenberg Publishers.

Denyer Willis, Graham. 2015. *The Killing Consensus. Police, Organized Crime, and the Regulation of Life and Death in Urban Brazil.* Oakland: University of California Press.

Dziedzic, Michael, and Robert M. Perito. 2008. *Haiti: Confronting the Gangs of Port-au Prince.* Washington: United States Institute of Peace Special Report. www.usip.org.

El Mechat, Samya, ed. 2014. *Coloniser, Pacifier, Administrer, XIX–XXI siècles.* Paris: CNRS.

Fassin, Didier. 2013. *Enforcing Order: An Ethnography of Urban Policing.* Cambridge: Polity Press.

Gay, Robert. 2012. "Clientelism, Democracy, and Violence in Rio de Janeiro." In *Clientelism in Everyday Latin American Politics*, edited by Tina Hilgers, 81–98. Basingstoke: Palgrave Macmillan.

Gledhill, John. 2015. *The New War on the Poor. The Production of Insecurity in Latin America.* London: Zed Books.

Graham, Stephen, and Alex Baker. 2016. "Laboratories of Pacification and Permanent War: Israeli–U.S. Collaboration in the Global Making of Policing." In *The Global Making of Policing. Postcolonial Perspectives*, edited by Jana Hönke and Markus-Michael Müller, 40–58. London: Routledge.

Hallward, Peter. 2007. *Damming the Flood: Haiti, Aristide, and the Politics of Containment.* London: Verso Books.

Harig, Christoph. 2015. "Synergy Effects between MINUSTAH and Public Security in Brazil." *Brasiliana—Journal for Brazilian Studies* 3 (2): 142–68.

Hendee, Thomas Alan. 2013. *The Health of Pacification: A Review of the Pacifying Police Unit Program in Rio de Janeiro, Brazil.* Stanford, CA: Center for Democracy, Development, and the Rule of Law Stanford University. http://iisdb.stanford.edu/docs/771/Thomas_Hendee.pdf.

Higate, Paul, and Marsha Henry. 2009. *Insecure Spaces: Peacekeeping, Power and Performance in Haiti, Kosovo and Liberia.* London: Zed Books.

Hills, Alice. 2009. *Policing Post-conflict Cities.* London: Zed Books.

Holloway, Thomas H. 1993. *Policing Rio de Janeiro: Repression and Resistance in a 19th-Century City.* Stanford: Stanford University Press.

Hönke, Jana, and Markus-Michael Müller, eds. 2016. *The Global Making of Policing. Postcolonial Perspectives.* London: Routledge.

Huggins, Martha K. 1998. *Political Policing: The United States and Latin America*. Durham, NC: Duke University Press.

Hylton, Forrest. 2010. "The Cold War That Didn't End: Paramilitary Modernization in Medellín, Colombia." In *A Century of Revolution: Insurgent and Counterinsurgent Violence During Latin America's Long Cold War*, edited by Greg Grandin and Gilbert M. Joseph, 338–69. Durham, NC: Duke University Press.

Khalili, Laleh. 2013. *Time in the Shadows. Confinement in Counterinsurgencies*. Palo Alto, CA: Stanford University Press.

Kienscherf, Markus. 2010. "Plugging Cultural Knowledge into the U.S. Military Machine: The Neo-orientalist Logic of Counterinsurgency." *Topia—Canadian Journal of Cultural Studies* 23 (24): 121–43.

Kienscherf, Markus. 2016. "Beyond Militarization and Repression: Liberal Social Control as Pacification." *Critical Sociology* 42 (1): 1179–94.

Kilcullen, David. 2013. *Out of the Mountains. The Coming Age of the Urban Guerilla*. Oxford: Oxford University Press.

Kilcullen, David, and Greg Mills. 2015. "Colombia—A Political Economy of War to an Inclusive Peace." *PRISM* 5 (3): 106–21.

Kilcullen, David, and Greg Mills. 2016. "Introduction: Colombia's Transition." In *A Great Perhaps? Colombia: Conflict and Convergence*, edited by Dickie Davis, David Kilcullen, Greg Mills, and David Spencer, 1–16. London: Hurst.

Klein, Naomi. 2008. *The Shock Doctrine: The Rise of Disaster Capitalism*. London: Penguin.

Koonings, Kees, and Dirk Kruijt. 2015. "Exclusion, Violence and Resilience in Five Latin American Megacities: A Comparison of Buenos Aires, Lima, Mexico City, Rio de Janeiro and São Paulo." In *Violence and Resilience in Latin American Cities*, edited by Kees Koonings and Dirk Kruijt, 30–52. London: Zed Books.

Langfur, Hal. 2006. *The Forbidden Lands Colonial Identity, Frontier Violence, and the Persistence of Brazil's Eastern Indians, 1750–1830*. Stanford, CA: Stanford University Press.

Leech, Garry. 2011. *FARC: The Longest Insurgency*. London: Zed Books.

McCoy, Alfred. 2016. "Capillaries of Empire: Colonial Pacification and the Origins of U.S. Global Surveillance." In *The Global Making of Policing. Postcolonial Perspectives*, edited by Jana Hönke and Markus-Michael Müller, 20–39. London: Routledge.

Moe, Louise Wiuff. 2016. "The Strange Wars of Liberal Peace: Hybridity, Complexity and the Governing Rationalities of Counterinsurgency in Somalia." *Peacebuilding* 4 (1): 99–117.

Moe, Louise Wiuff, and Markus-Michael Müller. 2015. "Resilience as Warfare: Interventions and the Militarization of the Social in Haiti and Somalia." *Kriminologisches Journal* 47: 279–96.

Moe, Louise Wiuff, and Markus-Michael Müller, eds. 2017. *Reconfiguring Intervention: Complexity, Resilience and the 'Local Turn' in Counterinsurgent Warfare*. Basingstoke: Palgrave Macmillan.

Muggah, Robert, and Albert Souza Mulli. 2012. "Rio Tries Counterinsurgency." *Current History* 111: 62–66.

Müller, Frank, and Markus-Michael Müller. 2016. "Im- und Export von Aufstandsbekämpfung. Von Rio de Janeiro nach Port-au-Prince und zurück." *Peripherie. Politik, Ökonomie, Kultur* 36 (141): 74–93.

Müller, Markus-Michael. 2012. *Public Security in the Negotiated State: Policing in Latin America and Beyond*. Basingstoke: Palgrave Macmillan.

Müller, Markus-Michael. 2016a. *The Punitive City: Privatised Protection and Policing in Neoliberal Mexico*. London: Zed Books.

Müller, Markus-Michael. 2016b. "Entangled Pacifications: Peacekeeping, Counterinsurgency and Policing in Port-au-Prince and Rio de Janeiro." In *The Global Making of Policing: Postcolonial Perspectives*, edited by Jana Hönke and Markus-Michael Müller, 77–95. Abingdon: Routledge.

Neocleous, Mark. 2011. "'A Brighter and Nicer New Life': Security as Pacification." *Social & Legal Studies* 20 (2):191–208.

Neocleous, Mark, George S. Rigakos, and Tyler Wall. 2013. "On Pacification: Introduction to the Special Issue." *Socialist Studies/Études socialistes* 9 (2): 1–6.

Pansters, Wil. 2012. "Zones of State-Making: Violence, Coercion, and Hegemony in Twentieth-Century Mexico." In *Violence, Coercion, and State-Making in Twentieth-Century Mexico. The Other Half of the Centaur*, edited by Wil Pansters, 3–42. Palo Alto, CA: Stanford University Press.

Pereira, Anthony W. 2000. "An Ugly Democracy? State Violence and the Rule of Law in Postauthoritarian Brazil." In *Democratic Brazil. Actors, Institutions and Processes*, edited by P.R. Kingstone and Timothy J. Power, 217–35. Pittsburgh, PA: University of Pittsburgh Press.

Podur, Justin. 2012. *Haiti's New Dictatorship. The Coup, the Earthquake and the UN Occupation*. London: Pluto Press.

Reyes Novaes, André. 2014. "Favelas and the Divided City: Mapping Silences and Calculations in Rio de Janeiro's Journalistic Cartography." *Social & Cultural Geography* 15 (2): 201–25.

Riaño-Alcalá, Pilar. 2006. *Dwellers of Memory. Youth and Violence in Medellín, Colombia*. New Brunswick, NJ: Transaction Publishers.

Riccio, Vicente, Marco Aurélio Ruediger, Steven Dutt Ross, and Wesley Skogan. 2013. "Community Policing in the Favelas of Rio de Janeiro." *Police Practice and Research* 14 (4): 308–18.

Richani, Chakib. 2013. *Systems of Violence. The Political Economy of War and Peace in Colombia* (2nd edition). Albany: State University of New York.

Rigakos, George S. 2016. *Security/Capital: A General Theory of Pacification*. Edinburgh: Edinburgh University Press.

Rochlin, Jim. 2011. "Plan Colombia and the Revolution in Military Affairs: The Demise of the FARC." *Review of International Studies* 37 (2): 715–40.

Rodrigues, Robson. 2014. "The Dilemmas of Pacification: News of War and Peace in the 'Marvelous City'." *Stability: International Journal of Security & Development* 3 (1): 1–16.

Roldán, Mary. 2002. *Blood and Fire. La Violencia in Antioquia, Colombia (1946–1953).* Durham, NC: Duke University Press.

Rose, R.S. 2005. *The Unpast: Elite Violence and Social Control in Brazil, 1954–2000.* Ohio: University of Ohio Press.

Saborio, Sebastian. 2013. "The Pacification of the Favelas: Mega Events, Global Competitiveness and the Neutralization of Marginality." *Socialist Studies/ Études Socialistes* 9 (2): 130–45.

Sotomayor Velázquez, Arturo C. 2014. *The Myth of the Democratic Peacekeeper. Civil-Military Relations and the United Nations.* Baltimore, MD: Johns Hopkins University Press.

Suska, Marta-Laura. 2015. *Recommendations for Two Violence-Reducing Policing Programs in Brazil: The Pacification Police Unit in Rio de Janeiro and the Pact for Life in Recife.* BPC Policy Brief 5/7. http://bricspolicycenter.org/homolog/uploads/trabalhos/6986/doc/2110268255.pdf (last accessed November 20, 2017).

Swanson, Kate. 2013. "Zero Tolerance in Latin America: Punitive Paradox in Urban Policy Mobilities." *Urban Geography* 34 (7): 972–98.

The US Army/Marine Corps. 2006. *Counterinsurgency Field Manual FM 3-24.* Chicago, IL: University of Chicago Press.

Tickner, Arlene. 2016. "Associated Dependent Security Cooperation: Colombia and the United States." In *The Global Making of Policing: Postcolonial Perspectives,* edited by Jana Hönke and Markus-Michael Müller, 96–113. London: Routledge.

Turner, Mandy. 2014. "Peacebuilding as Counterinsurgency in the Occupied Palestinian Territory." *Review of International Studies* 41 (1): 73–98.

Ucko, David. 2009. *The New Counterinsurgency Era: Transforming the U.S. Military for Modern Wars.* Baltimore, MD: Johns Hopkins University Press.

United Nations (UN). 2015. *13th United Nations Congress on Crime Prevention and Criminal Justice.* Meetings Coverage. http://www.un.org/en/events/crimecongress2015/pdf/pressrelease/dpimc7en.pdf.

Wall, Tyler, Parastou Saberi, and Will Jackson. 2016a. *Destroy, Build, Secure: Readings on Pacification.* Ottawa: Red Quill Books.

Wall, Tyler, Parastou Saberi, and Will Jackson. 2016b. "Introduction." In *Destroy, Build, Secure: Readings on Pacification,* edited by Tyler Wall, Parastou Saberi, and Will Jackson, 5–12. Ottawa: Red Quill Books.

PART IV

Conclusion

CHAPTER 10

Conclusion: Rethinking Police Abuse in Contemporary Democracies

Michelle D. Bonner

The police shooting of Michael Brown in Ferguson, Missouri in 2014 captured international media attention in part because the incident raises many questions about the definition of police abuse and its uncomfortable relationship with democracy. As we have seen throughout this book, Michael Brown's death is not an isolated event or a reflection of a stage of democratization. Police abuse exists in all democracies and it challenges scholars, including political scientists, to rethink how our concept of democracy is changed by its persistence. This book has aimed to initiate this discussion by focusing on the key concepts of citizenship, accountability, and socioeconomic (in)equality. The chapters have utilized different subfield approaches and methodologies, drawing on case studies from five continents, in order to reveal similarities and open up new questions in need of more research. In this final chapter, I summarize our findings and offer a few, but by no means exhaustive, ways to move forward.

M. D. Bonner (✉)
University of Victoria, Victoria, BC, Canada

© The Author(s) 2018
M. D. Bonner et al. (eds.), *Police Abuse in Contemporary Democracies*,
https://doi.org/10.1007/978-3-319-72883-4_10

251

CITIZENSHIP

We began the book with the concept of citizenship. Political scientists have long studied citizens' democratic rights through examinations of constitutions, laws, and international human rights agreements. Ideally, national and international courts enforce these rights, making the judiciary another important area of study in political science. Yet, as we have seen in this book the police define the experience of citizenship and its boundaries for many people. The chapters in this volume examined the impact of police abuse on select citizens' experience of belonging and rights in countries as diverse as France, Argentina, India, and Canada. The chapters reveal how police segregate citizens into those who belong and deserve rights, and those who do not belong and are a threat. Police often identify those who do not belong based on their ethnic background, race, class, sexual orientation, gender, political orientation, or other marginalized identity.

In Schneider's chapter, we saw how the complicated legacies and transformations of colonialism in France have shaped police abuse targeted at the Algerian or "immigrant" others. In contrast, the chapters by Seri and Lokaneeta and Dupuis-Déri draw our attention to how political economy (also discussed in the last section) and police abuse intersect in particular ways to shape citizenship. The cases of Argentina and India reveal that those marginalized from the economy (the poor, racialized, lower caste, migrants, etc.) are particularly targeted by police abuse, despite all the legal and constitutional gains these groups have made with democracy. Indeed, even in an established democracy such as Canada, Dupuis-Déri finds that police abuse is selectively used to silence certain political perspectives, particularly anarchist or anticapitalist perspectives. In all these cases, police actions are not necessarily illegal; they often fall within the realm of police discretion.

Thus together these chapters highlight that, for many people, police define their lived experience of citizenship, often more so than do laws or the courts. Police officers' selective abuse affects some citizens' experience of their rights to: mobility, security, freedom of association, protest, free speech, as well as their trust in the state and their sense of belonging to the larger political community and to a democracy. As Seri and Lokaneeta explain, police abuse can create pockets of authoritarianism within democracy where some citizens experience "violent exclusions." Schneider suggests that such violent exclusions could potentially contribute to violent responses from those excluded, as exemplified by riots or even terrorist attacks. Thus taking police abuse seriously is fundamental to democracy.

Certainly more research is needed on how best to integrate police abuse into our understanding of democratic citizenship. While police discretion may be needed to facilitate the ability of police to act in varying and potentially volatile situations, greater clarity is needed on the boundaries of this discretion that considers their implications for democratic inclusion and rights. There are many more marginalized people in democracies around the world who face persistent and disproportionate police abuse. We need to better understand its origins, the resulting practices, and consequences for citizenship for each type of identity to see how they may be similar or differ. Such studies would help provide the groundwork to develop a more robust concept of the place of policing in democracy, as well as what constitutes police abuse of citizenship rights and status and why.

Accountability

The first section of the book established one of the most fundamental challenges police abuse poses for democracy: its impact on selective people's experience of democratic citizenship. The second section of the book addresses the logical liberal democratic response to the problem of police abuse, accountability. That is, no democracy promises to end wrongdoing on the part of state actors. However, democracy does promise to place significant checks on state power. The chapters by Bonner, Squillacote and Feldman, and Davenport, McDermott and Armstrong explore the possibilities and limitations of dominant liberal democratic conceptualizations of accountability as they apply to the case of police abuse.

In all three chapters, we find that constitutional and judicial oversight is an important but insufficient check on police abuse. Bonner shows how, in the case of Chile, dominant narratives that define accountability as legal checks on police abuse aim to reinforce police legitimacy and officers' need for legal predictability. This definition of accountability, and its associated goals, marginalizes alternative narratives of accountability that prioritize its need to provide equality of the rule of law and ensure non-repetition. Thus, Bonner finds that clarifying the primary purpose of accountability in democracy is central to curbing police abuse.

Similarly, Squillacote and Feldman, drawing on political theory and examples from the United States, also find the judiciary to be an insufficient check on police abuse. Instead, they argue that the police need to be better understood as an administrative agent, which shapes the type of accountability that will most likely ensure non-repetition. This status then highlights the need for what they call "agonistic surveillance" by citizens and civil society organizations, such as Cop Watch. In this manner the perpetrators who "violently exclude" some people from citizenship (see Seri and Lokaneeta, Chapter 3), can be held accountable by those targeted (and others), allowing the victims to reclaim their inclusion in democracy.

Finally, Davenport, McDermott, and Armstrong, using an experimental method and a case study of the United States, show how citizens' perception of police actions as wrongdoing (or not) is influenced by the identities of the perpetrators and victims—in their case by the racial identities of both. Complicating both narratives of accountability and social movements as solutions, Davenport, McDermott, and Armstrong's chapter highlights the significant challenges to be overcome to reduce police abuse against members of the marginalized groups discussed in Chapters 1–3 (as well as other chapters). As Bonner and Davenport, McDermott, and Armstrong note in their chapters, wrongdoing needs to be recognized as such for accountability to be deemed necessary. How to overcome racial bias in the identification of wrongdoing is an important challenge that perhaps new ways of thinking about democratic accountability can address.

In this manner, introducing police abuse into political science discussions of democratic accountability opens up new questions. Beyond the issues raised in the chapters, more research is needed on the impact of other identity-based biases on observers' attribution of responsibility, as well as on the choices made by police and the institutions that hold them accountable. Given the limits of institutional accountability, we also need to better understand the role of the media in replicating observer bias or dominant narratives of accountability; or, alternatively, its potential role as an additional site of agonistic surveillance or advocate for broader definitions of accountability. We need to further explore how civil society organizations can be integrated into police reform projects without losing their strengths as agonistic and independent actors. Yet it is also possible that accountability is only a partial answer.

Socioeconomic (In)Equality

Certainly the liberal democratic solution of accountability is an important yet, as we have seen, very challenging means of reducing police abuse and defining its acceptable limits in democracy. These challenges are highlighted further when we shift our attention to questions of political economy. As discussed in the introduction, police abuse has always played an important economic function in democracy. Indeed, studies in political economy help us to better understand police abuse as intimately linked to particular political-economic goals. Different types of economic regimes require different types of policing and this, in turn, helps explain selective "violent exclusions" and some of the weaknesses of democratic institutions of accountability. From this perspective then, reducing police abuse in democracy requires rethinking the relationship between political economy and democracy.

This point is powerfully illustrated in Clarke's chapter on South Africa. By comparing pre- and post-apartheid policing, Clarke highlights the important continuities in police abuse. She reveals police abuse as less the result of institutional failures of police reform or accountability (although these are challenges), but rather the choice of political leaders to defend neoliberal reforms through police abuse. This is most visibly seen in police repression of strikes and other protests by those marginalized by and challenging neoliberalism. It is also seen in approaches to crime control. For example, rather than reduce crime through socioeconomic measures, as advocated by most criminologists, political leaders have actively advocated police abuse. Socioeconomic remedies run counter to neoliberal economic policies.

Whereas Clarke emphasizes the continuities in police abuse to defend socioeconomic inequality within apartheid and neoliberal post-apartheid South Africa, Müller draws our attention to transnational dynamics. In particular, he connects police abuse to broader global learning on how to make police abuse targeted at the (post)colonized "other" compatible with democracy. He does so by tracing the origins of the much lauded Pacification Police Units (UPP) in Brazil from (post)colonial practices of pacification, to learning from Colombia's counterinsurgency practices, to appropriating liberal counterinsurgency approaches from Brazil's participation in the UN's mission in Haiti. Müller finds that these newly refined techniques of police counterinsurgency have enabled Brazil to continue police abuse as a means to control certain segments of society, particularly those living in *favelas* (shantytowns) near the richer neighborhoods of Rio de Janeiro, while maintaining a democratic image consistent with a world-class city hosting the 2014 FIFA World Cup and 2016 Olympic Games. Moreover, the "democratic" UPP pacification efforts have contributed to increased land values and thus the pushing out of "undesirables," in favor of those better able to participate in the market. As Müller notes, policing is about maintaining a particular order. In the current international context, the order protected is one that maintains socioeconomic inequality in support of a neoliberal market.

Together, Clarke and Müller draw our attention to socioeconomic (in)equalities as not only a problem of citizenship (discussed in the first section of this book), but as a problem of political economy. By shifting the focus, we move police abuse from an independent variable (that erodes citizenship) to a dependent variable (affected by political economy). If certain political economies, notably neoliberalism, result in persistent or possibly even increased police abuse, then the solutions to reducing police abuse are no longer located exclusively in improving police accountability. In this case we need to look more closely at the compatibility of some political-economic models with democracy over others. Such a project challenges minimalist definitions of democracy but also forces us to take more seriously the place of police abuse in broader definitions of democracy.

Of course police abuse in democracy can be studied in political science from other angles than citizenship, accountability, and socioeconomic (in)equality. For example, it can be studied from the perspective of public policy, elections, or ideologies, to name only a few. What is important is that police abuse be included, not in terms of a technical fix, but in our very conceptualization of democracy. Such studies will help us work to mend the gap between formal democracy and its lived experience, as well as point to important avenues toward improving its quality.

APPENDIX A

Descriptive Statistics

Variable	Levels	n	%	Σ %
ppagecat	18–24	52	11.6	11.6
	25–34	52	11.6	23.3
	35–44	82	18.3	41.6
	45–54	93	20.8	62.4
	55–64	99	22.1	84.6
	65–74	47	10.5	95.1
	75+	22	4.9	100.0
	Under 18	0	0.0	100.0
ppagect4	18–29	79	17.7	17.7
	30–44	107	23.9	41.6
	45–59	147	32.9	74.5
	60+	114	25.5	100.0
	Under 18	0	0.0	100.0
PPEDUC	Not asked	0	0.0	0.0
	REFUSED	0	0.0	0.0
	No formal education	0	0.0	0.0
	1st, 2nd, 3rd, or 4th grade	0	0.0	0.0
	5th or 6th grade	0	0.0	0.0

(continued)

© The Editor(s) (if applicable) and The Author(s) 2018
M. D. Bonner et al. (eds.), *Police Abuse in Contemporary Democracies*,
https://doi.org/10.1007/978-3-319-72883-4

(continued)

Variable	Levels	*n*	%	Σ %
	7th or 8th grade	5	1.1	1.1
	9th grade	7	1.6	2.7
	10th grade	14	3.1	5.8
	11th grade	11	2.5	8.3
	12th grade NO DIPLOMA	10	2.2	10.5
	HIGH SCHOOL GRADUATE—high school DIPLOMA or the equivalent (GED)	135	30.2	40.7
	Some college, no degree	102	22.8	63.5
	Associate degree	35	7.8	71.4
	Bachelors degree	77	17.2	88.6
	Masters degree	42	9.4	98.0
	Professional or Doctorate degree	9	2.0	100.0
PPEDUCAT	<High School	47	10.5	10.5
	High school	135	30.2	40.7
	Some college	137	30.6	71.4
	Bachelor's degree+	128	28.6	100.0
PPETHM	White, non-Hispanic	240	53.7	53.7
	Black, non-Hispanic	207	46.3	100.0
	all	447	100.0	
PPGENDER	Male	210	47.0	47.0
	Female	237	53.0	100.0
PPHHHEAD	Not asked	0	0.0	0.0
	REFUSED	0	0.0	0.0
	No	98	21.9	21.9
	Yes	349	78.1	100.0
PPHOUSE	Not asked	0	0.0	0.0
	REFUSED	0	0.0	0.0
	A one-family house detached from any other house	300	67.1	67.1
	A one-family house attached to one or more houses	43	9.6	76.7
	A building with 2 or more apartments	82	18.3	95.1
	A mobile home	20	4.5	99.5
	Boat, RV, van, etc.	2	0.5	100.0
PPINCIMP	Not asked	0	0.0	0.0
	REFUSED	0	0.0	0.0
	Less than 5000	11	2.5	2.5
	5000–7499	7	1.6	4.0
	7500–9999	11	2.5	6.5
	10,000–12,499	18	4.0	10.5
	12,500–14,999	11	2.5	13.0

(continued)

(continued)

Variable	Levels	*n*	%	Σ %
	15,000–19,999	22	4.9	17.9
	20,000–24,999	20	4.5	22.4
	25,000–29,999	28	6.3	28.6
	30,000–34,999	17	3.8	32.4
	35,000–39,999	25	5.6	38.0
	40,000–49,999	33	7.4	45.4
	50,000–59,999	36	8.1	53.5
	60,000–74,999	45	10.1	63.5
	75,000–84,999	32	7.2	70.7
	85,000–99,999	27	6.0	76.7
	100,000–124,999	47	10.5	87.2
	125,000–149,999	30	6.7	93.9
	150,000–174,999	10	2.2	96.2
	175,000 or more	17	3.8	100.0
PPMARIT	Not asked	0	0.0	0.0
	REFUSED	0	0.0	0.0
	Married	219	49.0	49.0
	Widowed	17	3.8	52.8
	Divorced	54	12.1	64.9
	Separated	9	2.0	66.9
	Never married	117	26.2	93.0
	Living with partner	31	6.9	100.0
PPMSACAT	Not asked	0	0.0	0.0
	REFUSED	0	0.0	0.0
	Non-Metro	74	16.6	16.6
	Metro	373	83.5	100.0
PPNET	No	128	28.6	28.6
	Yes	319	71.4	100.0
PPREG4	Not asked	0	0.0	0.0
	Refused	0	0.0	0.0
	Northeast	68	15.2	15.2
	Midwest	106	23.7	38.9
	South	204	45.6	84.6
	West	69	15.4	100.0
ppreg9	New England	9	2.0	2.0
	Mid-Atlantic	59	13.2	15.2
	East-North Central	76	17.0	32.2
	West-North Central	30	6.7	38.9
	South Atlantic	119	26.6	65.5
	East-South Central	29	6.5	72.0
	West-South Central	56	12.5	84.6

(continued)

(continued)

Variable	Levels	*n*	%	Σ %
	Mountain	19	4.2	88.8
	Pacific	50	11.2	100.0
PPRENT	Not asked	0	0.0	0.0
	REFUSED	0	0.0	0.0
	Owned or being bought by you or someone in your household	300	67.1	67.1
	Rented for cash	134	30.0	97.1
	Occupied without payment of cash rent	13	2.9	100.0
PPSTATEN	Not asked	0	0.0	0.0
	REFUSED	0	0.0	0.0
	ME	2	0.5	0.5
	NH	2	0.5	0.9
	VT	0	0.0	0.9
	MA	4	0.9	1.8
	RI	0	0.0	1.8
	CT	1	0.2	2.0
	NY	26	5.8	7.8
	NJ	14	3.1	11.0
	PA	19	4.2	15.2
	OH	26	5.8	21.0
	IN	9	2.0	23.0
	IL	18	4.0	27.1
	MI	11	2.5	29.5
	WI	12	2.7	32.2
	MN	7	1.6	33.8
	IA	6	1.3	35.1
	MO	11	2.5	37.6
	ND	0	0.0	37.6
	SD	2	0.5	38.0
	NE	3	0.7	38.7
	KS	1	0.2	38.9
	DE	0	0.0	38.9
	MD	15	3.4	42.3
	DC	5	1.1	43.4
	VA	21	4.7	48.1
	WV	6	1.3	49.4
	NC	19	4.2	53.7
	SC	6	1.3	55.0
	GA	21	4.7	59.7
	FL	26	5.8	65.5
	KY	4	0.9	66.4
	TN	12	2.7	69.1

(continued)

(continued)

Variable	Levels	n	%	Σ %
	AL	7	1.6	70.7
	MS	6	1.3	72.0
	AR	5	1.1	73.2
	LA	7	1.6	74.7
	OK	7	1.6	76.3
	TX	37	8.3	84.6
	MT	1	0.2	84.8
	ID	1	0.2	85.0
	WY	1	0.2	85.2
	CO	5	1.1	86.4
	NM	2	0.5	86.8
	AZ	2	0.5	87.2
	UT	2	0.5	87.7
	NV	5	1.1	88.8
	WA	13	2.9	91.7
	OR	7	1.6	93.3
	CA	30	6.7	100.0
	AK	0	0.0	100.0
	HI	0	0.0	100.0
	AS	0	0.0	100.0
	GU	0	0.0	100.0
	PR	0	0.0	100.0
	VI	0	0.0	100.0
PPWORK	Not asked	0	0.0	0.0
	Refused	0	0.0	0.0
	Working—as a paid employee	215	48.1	48.1
	Working—self-employed	27	6.0	54.1
	Not working—on temporary layoff from a job	6	1.3	55.5
	Not working—looking for work	37	8.3	63.8
	Not working—retired	68	15.2	79.0
	Not working—disabled	53	11.9	90.8
	Not working—other	41	9.2	100.0
XPARTY7	Strong Republican	55	12.3	12.3
	Not Strong Republican	33	7.4	19.7
	Leans Republican	48	10.7	30.4
	Undecided/Independent/Other	16	3.6	34.0
	Leans Democrat	80	17.9	51.9
	Not Strong Democrat	77	17.2	69.1
	Strong Democrat	138	30.9	100.0
	Dummy	0	0.0	100.0
	Missing	0	0.0	100.0

(continued)

(continued)

Variable	Levels	n	%	Σ %
XIDEO	Extremely liberal	15	3.4	3.4
	Liberal	73	16.4	19.8
	Slightly liberal	53	11.9	31.8
	Moderate	153	34.5	66.2
	Slightly conservative	50	11.3	77.5
	Conservative	83	18.7	96.2
	Extremely conservative	17	3.8	100.0
XREL1	Baptist-any denomination	122	27.5	27.5
	Protestant (e.g., Methodist, Lutheran, Presbyterian, Episcopal)	93	20.9	48.4
	Catholic	62	14.0	62.4
	Mormon	1	0.2	62.6
	Jewish	12	2.7	65.3
	Muslim	1	0.2	65.5
	Hindu	0	0.0	65.5
	Buddhist	3	0.7	66.2
	Pentecostal	25	5.6	71.9
	Eastern Orthodox	2	0.5	72.3
	Other Christian	51	11.5	83.8
	Other non-Christian, please specify	12	2.7	86.5
	None	60	13.5	100.0
	Missing	0	0.0	100.0
XTESS068	1	102	22.8	22.8
	2	121	27.1	49.9
	3	112	25.1	75.0
	4	112	25.1	100.0
Q1	1—Protesters	119	27.1	27.1
	2	55	12.5	39.5
	3	61	13.9	53.4
	4	150	34.1	87.5
	5	29	6.6	94.1
	6	14	3.2	97.3
	7—Police	12	2.7	100.0
Q2	1—Very strongly	241	54.9	54.9
	2	85	19.4	74.3
	3	27	6.2	80.4
	4	44	10.0	90.4
	5	20	4.6	95.0
	6	10	2.3	97.3
	7—Not strongly	12	2.7	100.0

(continued)

(continued)

Variable	Levels	n	%	$\sum$ %
Q3	1—Yes	77	17.5	17.5
	2	54	12.3	29.8
	3	60	13.6	43.4
	4	162	36.8	80.2
	5	42	9.6	89.8
	6	23	5.2	95.0
	7—No	22	5.0	100.0
Q4	Strong Republican	53	12.1	12.1
	Weak Republican	12	2.8	14.9
	Independent Republican	47	10.8	25.6
	Pure Independent	82	18.8	44.4
	Independent Democrat	103	23.6	68.0
	Weak Democrat	39	8.9	76.9
	Strong Democrat	101	23.1	100.0
Q5	Strongly favor	77	17.5	17.5
	Favor	74	16.8	34.2
	Neither favor nor oppose	172	39.0	73.2
	Oppose	69	15.7	88.9
	Strongly oppose	49	11.1	100.0
Q3b	Positive	191	43.4	43.4
	Neutral	162	36.8	80.2
	Negative	87	19.8	100.0

Appendix B

Scenario

Over the weekend in New Rochelle, Connecticut, several hundred individuals gathered for the commemoration of the death of Laura Polson—a local school teacher turned New York Times best selling author—who died in a car accident 2 years before. The group had convened to protest the lack of initiative in developing stricter laws regarding drivers not having car insurance. The situation had become a sore point as Polson's two daughters, who were in the car with their mother during the accident, had not been able to receive compensation from the driver despite their right under state and federal law.

At the event, an altercation broke out between protesters and the police:

Manipulation A: *The confrontation took on a racial overtone when primarily black protesters at the intersection of Vine and Lasoule began throwing bottles at a line of mostly white officers standing nearby*

Manipulation B: *The confrontation took on a racial overtone when primarily white protesters at the intersection of Vine and Lasoule began throwing bottles at a line of mostly black officers standing nearby*

Manipulation C: *Primarily white protesters at the intersection of Vine and Lasoule began throwing bottles at a line of mostly white officers standing nearby*

© The Editor(s) (if applicable) and The Author(s) 2018   265
M. D. Bonner et al. (eds.), *Police Abuse in Contemporary Democracies*,
https://doi.org/10.1007/978-3-319-72883-4

Manipulation D: *Primarily black protesters at the intersection of Vine and Lasoule began throwing bottles at a line of mostly black officers standing nearby.*

All were spared further damage and bloodshed because everyone was forced to disburse suddenly when an unexpected rainstorm began to plummet the entire area with a torrential downpour. Two inches of rain came down within 4 hours, precipitating dramatic mudslides in the region recently devastated by major fires last summer.

APPENDIX C

Response Questions

1. Which group do you find most responsible for escalating the conflict in this scenario?

    1_____2_____3_____4_____5____6____7
    Protesters   Police

2. How strongly do you support stricter laws to enforce drivers to carry car insurance?

    1_____2_____3_____4____5____6____7
    Very strongly   Not strongly

3. Do you think the police took the proper action in trying to stop the protesters?

    1_____2_____3_____4____5____6____7
    Yes   No

4. Generally speaking, do you usually think of yourself as a:

Strong Republican	Weak Republican	Independent Republican	Pure Independent	Independent Democrat	Weak Democrat	Strong Democrat

5. Do you oppose or support providing special college scholarships for blacks?

Strongly favor	Favor	Neither Favor nor oppose	Oppose	Strongly oppose

© The Editor(s) (if applicable) and The Author(s) 2018   267
M. D. Bonner et al. (eds.), *Police Abuse in Contemporary Democracies*,
https://doi.org/10.1007/978-3-319-72883-4

INDEX

A

accountability, 2–5, 9, 13, 16–19, 22, 23, 32, 45, 55, 66, 68, 71, 73, 74, 84, 114–129, 136, 138, 139, 141, 142, 144, 146, 147, 150–155, 157, 166, 167, 169, 175, 180, 187, 188, 197, 200, 203, 205, 206, 208, 214, 223, 230, 231, 251, 253–256
  discursive, 17, 117, 124, 167
  judicial, 17, 119, 125, 136, 169
  perceived, 165, 179
  political, 120, 125, 166
African Americans, 1, 22, 166, 168, 175, 176, 183, 186
African National Congress (ANC), 197, 204–206, 209–215, 217
Afrikaans/Afrikanerisation, 203
agonistic surveillance, 19, 135, 136, 149, 150, 152, 254
Algeria, 32–35, 37–39, 42, 47, 48, 51
Algerians, 3, 15, 20, 32–39, 47
Algerian War, 34, 37, 40, 45, 49

Amnesty International, 50, 123, 127, 230
anarchists/anarchism, 83, 86–89, 101
apartheid, 20, 195–206, 208, 210–212, 214–217, 255
Arabs, 20, 32, 41, 42, 45, 48
Argentina, 3, 14, 56–58, 60, 62–66, 68–72, 74–77, 215, 252
Aubervilliers, 44, 47
authoritarianism, competitive, 16

B

Balibar, Etienne, 56
banlieue (suburb), 49
Bardeche, Maurice, 40
Barthélomy, Victor, 40
Bataclan Theater, 49
Baylot, Jean, 34
La Belle Epoque, 49
Benhabib, Seyla, 15, 59
Bentounsi, Amal, 50
Beurs, 48

© The Editor(s) (if applicable) and The Author(s) 2018
M. D. Bonner et al. (eds.), *Police Abuse in Contemporary Democracies*,
https://doi.org/10.1007/978-3-319-72883-4

bidonvilles, 43, 44
Black Lives Matter, 143, 144, 153, 158, 240
Bompard, Jacques, 40
Bonelli, Laurent, 45
Bousquet, Pierre, 40
Boutih, Malek, 49
Bratton, William, 145
Brazil, 21, 221–226, 230–233, 235, 236, 238, 240, 255
Brigade des aggressions et violences (BAV), 34, 39
Broken Windows, 144–146, 150
Brown, Michael, 1, 3, 23, 135, 153, 240, 251
Bulacio, Walter, 69

C
Canada, 21, 82, 83, 85, 86, 89–93, 97, 99, 100, 215, 252
Carabineros, 113, 119–122, 124–127, 129–133
Le Carillon bar, 49
La Cas Nostra Pizzeria, 49
Casspir, 199
Charonne, 36
Chicago, 143
Cingranelli-Richards Index, 11
citizenship, 5, 6, 9, 13–16, 19, 20, 22, 23, 32, 48, 51, 56–63, 66, 67, 69, 70, 75, 76, 81, 84, 89, 91, 115, 149, 153, 154, 156, 157, 222, 237, 251–254, 256
    participation, 13, 14, 156
    rights, 6, 15, 32, 56–58, 60, 61, 75, 76, 81, 84, 91, 154, 253
civilian review boards, 148
civil rights movement, 165, 169
Coalition contre la répression et les abus policiers (CRAP), 96, 100
Colombia, 21, 222, 226–229, 235, 237, 240, 241, 255

colonialism, 20, 61, 252
    neo, 20–22
    post, 20–22, 65, 66, 84, 221–224, 226, 239, 240, 255
Communism/communist/Communist Party, 34, 36, 46, 83, 124
community policing, 19, 143–145, 151
Convergence des luttes anticapitalistes (CLAC), 88, 96
Coppedge, Michael, 6, 74
Cop Watch, 19, 136, 149, 150, 152–154, 156–158, 254
Correpi, 55, 69–71
corruption, 4, 45, 66, 72, 148, 200, 205, 208, 217
Coubali, Amedy, 50
counterinsurgency, 21, 33, 35, 221, 224–226, 228–235, 240, 255
Crime, 4, 7, 20, 22, 41, 42, 45, 46, 49, 63, 70, 84, 86, 90, 91, 95, 120, 123, 128, 143–146, 150, 155, 196–200, 202–208, 215–217, 227, 238, 255
    criminalization, 15, 56, 62, 94
    tough on, 20, 49, 196, 197, 204, 206–208, 212, 215, 216
    violent, 196, 197
    white-collar, 4
criminology, 255

D
Dahl, Robert, 6, 140
Déat, Marcel, 40
De Gaulle, Charles, 37, 39
democracy, 1–23, 31, 51, 56, 58, 61, 62, 64–66, 69, 74, 76, 81, 82, 100, 102, 114–119, 128, 129, 136–139, 142, 143, 151, 157, 166, 167, 188, 196, 203, 204, 208, 211, 214–216, 223, 226, 229–231, 251–256

electoral, 5, 9, 10
liberal, 5, 6, 9, 10, 13, 16, 19, 61,
    102, 115, 211, 216
procedural, 6, 21
radical, 211
ratings, 11
violent, 21, 195, 196, 214, 223
democratic policing, 5, 7, 12, 20, 21,
    222, 226, 240
democratization school, 223
Doriat, Jacques, 40
Dubber, Markus, 62, 137
Dufraisse, André, 40
Duprat, François, 40

F
Fassin, Didier, 45
favelas, 222, 233, 235, 237–239, 241,
    242, 256
foreigners/immigrants/migrants, 15,
    20, 37–48, 63–65, 67, 91, 198,
    207, 211, 238, 252
Foucault, Michel, 2, 57
France, 3, 15, 20, 32, 33, 37–39,
    41, 42, 45, 47, 48, 50, 56, 215,
    252
Freedom House, 10, 11

G
Gang(s), 120, 222, 227, 231–234
garde à vue, 48
Garges-lés-Gonesse, 47
Gaucher, Roland, 40
General Salan, 39
Giscard d'Estaing, Valéry, 41
Green Party, 48
Growth, Employment and
    Redistribution Program (GEAR),
    209, 210

Guet des activités et des mouve-
    ments marginaux et anarchistes
    (GAMMA), 95–97

H
Habitations à Loyer Modéré (HLMs),
    35, 44
Haiti, 21, 82, 226, 230, 231, 233,
    235, 237, 241, 255
Hinzpeter, Rodrigo (law), 122, 126
Holeindre, Roger, 40
homelands, 200, 216
human rights, 3, 6, 7, 10, 11, 50, 56,
    58, 64–71, 73, 74, 77, 83, 92,
    115, 118, 123, 125–128, 132,
    197, 204, 205, 207, 208, 226,
    229, 231, 233, 238, 252

I
India, 14, 55–58, 60, 62–68, 70–78,
    215, 252
inequality, socioeconomic, 19, 20,
    215, 216, 223, 256
insecurity, 15, 42, 46, 210, 211, 223

J
judiciary, 16, 17, 50, 72, 75, 78, 113,
    115, 123, 124, 128, 142, 252, 254
juvenile offenders, 42

K
Khosokravar, Farhad, 50
King, Rodney, 179

L
legitimacy, police, 18, 117, 123, 128,
    205, 253

Le Pen, Jean-Marie, 41
Lévy, René, 44

M
Macron, Emmanuel, 51
Marcellin-Fontanet, 41
Marikana, 195, 196, 198, 209, 211
Marshall, T.H., 59
Media, 3, 10, 17, 18, 36, 56–58,
    67–69, 71, 83, 85, 88, 96–98,
    102, 117–119, 121, 123, 124,
    128, 144, 150, 152, 168, 178,
    212, 215, 233, 251, 254
  internet, 10
  journalism, 150
  newspapers, 119, 178
  television, 144
Militarization, 21, 195, 226
Les Minguettes, 45, 46
MINUSTAH, 21, 221, 231–236, 240,
    241
Mitterrand, François, 45
Montreal, 84, 87, 88, 90, 91, 93–100,
    103
Mouvement des travailleurs Arabes
    (MTA), 42

N
National Front, 40, 41, 46, 49
National Party, 198, 202, 203
National Popular Rally (RNP), 40
Nazi Occupation, 32, 33
Nazis, 32
Neocleous, Mark, 2, 8, 239
Neoliberalism/neoliberal, 20, 22, 56,
    59, 196, 197, 199, 208, 209,
    211, 212, 215, 216, 226, 240,
    255, 256
New York, 93, 135, 144–146, 148,
    150, 152, 155, 157, 188, 227

O
October 17, 1961, 35, 37
Operation Orion, 227–229, 236
Order Nouveau, 40, 41
Organisation Armée Secrete (OAS),
    36, 37, 39, 40

P
Pacification, 21, 221, 222, 224–226,
    228–240, 255, 256
Pacification Police Unit/Unidade de
    Polícia Pacificadora (UPP), 221,
    222, 225, 226, 236–240, 255,
    256
Papon, Maurice, 33, 34
Parti Popular Français, 40
Penal Code and Code of Criminal
    Procedure, 45
Le Petite Cambodge Restaurant, 49
Peyrefitte Commission, 42
Piñera, Sebastián, 122
población, 118
police, 102
  abuse, 1–5, 7, 9, 12–23, 32, 56–58,
    64, 70–72, 76, 83, 84, 89,
    91, 100, 102, 114, 117, 118,
    124, 127, 129, 135, 136, 141,
    144, 147, 149, 153, 156, 166,
    187, 196–198, 209, 215, 216,
    223, 224, 226, 230, 238–240,
    251–256
  body cameras, 19, 136, 154–157
  brutality, 2, 42, 96, 99, 152, 173,
    199, 214, 215
  excesses, 4, 73
  killings, 18, 22, 57, 58, 64, 66, 68,
    71, 125, 136, 153, 209
  knowledge, 18, 102
  misconduct, 135, 143, 146–148,
    150, 152, 154
  reform, 7, 19, 45, 73, 74, 135–137,
    139, 144–150, 152, 155, 156,

196, 197, 199, 204, 206, 208, 215–217, 254, 255
repression, 3, 15, 21, 22, 47, 70, 82, 83, 87–89, 96, 100, 166, 255
science, 23
trust in, 19, 64
violence, 3, 4, 7, 32, 47, 50, 63, 118, 136, 141, 144, 147, 150, 153, 154, 158, 169, 198
political science, 2, 5, 8, 9, 12–14, 16, 17, 20, 23, 31, 81, 114, 115, 129, 136, 166, 170, 187, 196, 216, 223, 240, 252, 254, 256
Political Terror Scale, 11
Polity IV, 11
polyarchy, 6, 21, 223
Postel-Viney, André, 41
privatization, 200, 210, 211
profiling, 95
    criminal, 90–92, 97
    geographic, 90
    political, 14, 82–84, 89, 91, 93–97, 100–102, 212
    prospective, 90, 91
    racial, 50, 83, 89, 91–96, 101
    social, 83, 93, 94, 100–102
protest, 17, 18, 21, 36, 45, 71, 82, 83, 86, 88, 89, 94, 96, 98, 100, 103, 113, 118, 122, 127, 128, 147, 165–169, 171, 172, 178, 179, 186–188, 196, 197, 201, 212–214, 252
    demonstration, 88, 98
    mobilization, 82
    public, 21, 22, 36
    social, 89, 211

Q
Quebec, 83–89, 91, 92, 94–97, 100–103

R
Race/blacks/racialization/racial bias. See profiling
Reconstruction and Development Programme (RDP), 209
riots, 31, 49, 253
rodeo, 46
Royal Canadian Mounted Police (RCMP), 90
rule of law, 6, 7, 14, 16, 17, 42, 56, 65, 66, 73, 114–116, 124, 140, 214, 229–231, 233, 253

S
Sartre, Jean-Paul, 37
Sayad, Abdelmalek, 38
security, 10, 21, 22, 35, 45, 46, 50, 60, 64, 65, 77, 83, 91, 92, 95, 97, 99, 101, 102, 140, 170, 187, 197, 199–204, 206–208, 210–212, 214–216, 222, 226–231, 233, 235–241, 252
Service de police de la Ville de Montréal (SPVM), 90, 92–96, 98, 103
shantytown, 44, 118
Silverstein, Paul, 44
Socialist/Socialist Party, 45, 49, 51, 125
Someveille, Pierre, 39
Sompal, 55, 56, 66, 67, 71, 75
SOS Racism, 49
South Africa, 3, 20, 21, 195–198, 205, 206, 210–212, 214–217, 255
South African Defense Force (SADF), 201
South African Police (SAP)/South African Police Services (SAPS), 198
Stoléru, Lionel, 41
Stop-and-frisk, 136, 145, 146, 188

strikes, 42, 86, 89, 172, 196, 199, 209, 211–213, 255
Students, 2, 14, 42, 45, 65, 86, 98, 125, 199, 213
  in Chile, 113, 118, 125
  in Quebec, 100
Sûreté du Québec, 85, 90
surveillance, agonistic, 19, 135, 136, 149, 150, 152, 254

T
Tabert, Abdelkrim, 43
Taser, 156
terrorist/terrorism, 15, 36, 37, 48–50, 68, 90, 100, 101, 152, 170, 172, 201, 253
Thiry, Jean-Marie Bastien, 39
Tixier-Vignacour, Jean-Louis, 39
Toronto, 83, 87, 95, 101, 103
torture, 2, 4, 14, 15, 35, 57, 60, 62, 64, 66–68, 70–75, 78, 118, 171, 199, 205, 209, 238
Townships, 34, 199–203, 206, 214
transformation, 139, 196, 205, 206, 213

U
United Democratic Front (UDF), 199, 203
United Nations, 82, 230, 231, 237, 241
United States, 2, 3, 9, 19, 21, 44, 49, 56, 76, 89, 91, 92, 100, 156, 157, 167, 170, 172, 173, 186, 227, 232, 234

V
Vancouver, 87, 103
Varieties of Democracy, (V-Dem), 6, 74

violence, 3, 4, 7, 14, 17, 32, 39, 42, 46, 47, 50, 58, 60–67, 69–71, 73–76, 84, 86–88, 116, 118, 120, 122–124, 135, 136, 138, 141, 143, 144, 147, 149, 150, 153, 154, 158, 167, 169, 196, 198, 199, 202, 205–207, 214, 222–224, 227–229, 232, 233
  gender-based, 4
  police, 4, 7, 32, 47, 50, 63, 118, 136, 141, 144, 147, 150, 153, 154, 158, 169, 198
violent exclusion, 57, 58, 66, 230

W
Waffen SS, 40
War on Terror, terrorism, 10, 89, 171, 225
Weil, Patrick, 51
World Summit on Sustainable Development (WSSD), 212

X
X, Malcom, 48

Z
Zauberman, Renee, 44
Zero Tolerance, 144
Zones à urbaniser en priorité (ZUPS), 41
Zuma, Jacob, 214

CPSIA information can be obtained
at www.ICGtesting.com
Printed in the USA
LVHW07*0931220418
574435LV00016B/798/P